Cities and Citizenship

A Public Culture Book

James Holston, editor **CITIES AND CITIZENSHIP**

Duke University Press   Durham and London 1999

© 1999 Duke University Press
All rights reserved
Printed in the United States of America on acid-free paper ∞
Typeset in Quadrat by Keystone Typesetting, Inc.
Library of Congress Cataloging-in-Publication Data appear
on the last printed page of this book.
The text of this book was originally published without the
preface, index, and essays by Thomas Bender and James
Holston as Public Culture 8, no. 2 (winter 1996).
James Holston, "Spaces of Insurgent Citizenship," was
originally published in Planning Theory 13 (1995): 35–51;
© University of California Press.

Contents

Preface

The essays in this volume engage a vital if neglected subject: the importance of cities in the making of modern citizens. For most of the modern era, the nation and not the city has been the principal domain of citizenship. Moreover, the triumph of the nation-state over the city in defining this domain was fundamental to the project of modern nation building itself. Nevertheless, these essays demonstrate the need to reconsider the city as the arena of citizenship. They suggest that relations between nations and their cities are changing, as are relations between nations themselves, in the present phase of global capitalism. They propose that cities are especially salient sites for analyzing the current renegotiations of citizenship, democracy, and national belonging. Through case studies from Africa, Europe, Latin America, and North America, the essays show how cities make manifest these national and transnational realignments, how cities inscribe the consequences of these changes in the spaces and relations of urban daily life, how cities generate new possibilities for democracy that transform people as citizens, and how cities are both a strategic arena for the reformulations of citizenship and a stage on which these processes find expression in collective violence. Taken together, the essays demonstrate that the city remains a vital site for the development of citizenship as the lived space not only of its uncertainties but also of its emergent forms.

Cities and Citizenship makes available to a much wider public essays previously published as a special issue of the journal *Public Culture*. This issue won the 1996 Best Single Issue of a Journal Award from the Professional/Scholarly Publishing Division of the Association of American Publishers. Several new chapters have now been added to the original set for inclusion in this book. Although it is impossible in an edited volume to address every issue of importance directly, this new collection makes its point about cities and citizenship with a vast array of examples from the perspectives of many disciplines.

I am especially grateful to Arjun Appadurai for first suggesting that we undertake the project that resulted in this book and for our many stimulating conversations about it. Carol Breckenridge, editor of *Public Culture*, gave indispensable support and shape to the undertaking. I had the good fortune of always being able to count on her critical suggestions and editorial wisdom. I would also like to thank Lise McKean, former managing editor of *Public Culture*, for her assistance in producing the first version and Ken Wissoker of Duke University Press for taking on the second with enthusiasm. I owe special thanks to the contributors, without whose sustained commitment the volume would not have been possible. It has been my privilege to work with them.

Cities and Citizenship

Cities and Citizenship

James Holston and Arjun Appadurai

Why cities? Why citizenship? Since the eighteenth century, one of the defining marks of modernity has been the use of two linked concepts of association—citizenship and nationality—to establish the meaning of full membership in society. Citizenship rather than subjectship or kinship or cultship has defined the prerogatives and encumbrances of that membership, and the nation-state rather than the neighborhood or the city or the region established its scope. What it means to be a member of society in many areas of the world came to be understood, to a significant degree, in terms of what it means to be a rights-bearing citizen of a territorial nation-state. Undeniably, this historical development has been both revolutionary and democratic, even as it has also been conservative and exclusionary. On the one hand, for persons deemed eligible, nation-states have sought to establish citizenship as that identity which subordinates and coordinates all other identities—of religion, estate, family, gender, ethnicity, region, and the like—to its framework of a uniform body of law. Overwhelming other titles with its universal *citoyen*, citizenship thus erodes local hierarchies, statuses, and privileges in favor of national jurisdictions and contractual relations based in principle on an equality of rights. On the other hand, the mobilizations of those excluded from the circle of citizens, their rallies against the hypocrisies of its ideology of universal equality and respect, have expanded democracies everywhere: they generate new kinds of citizens, new sources of law, and new participation in the decisions that bind. As much as anything else, these conflicting and disjunctive processes of change constitute the core meaning of modern citizenship, constantly unsettling its assumptions.

Although one of the essential projects of nation building has been to dismantle the historic primacy of urban citizenship and to replace it with the national, cities remain the strategic arena for the development of citizenship. They are not the only arena. And not all cities are strategic. But with their concentrations of the nonlocal, the strange, the mixed, and the public, cities engage most palpably the tumult of citizenship. Their crowds catalyze processes that decisively expand and erode the rules, meanings, and practices of citizenship. Their streets conflate identities of territory and contract with those of race, religion, class, culture, and gender to produce the reactive ingredients of both progressive and reactionary political movements. Like nothing else, the modern urban public signifies both the defamiliarizing enormity of national citizenship and the exhilaration of its liberties.

But if cities have historically been the locus of such tumult, they experience today an unsettling of national citizenship that promises unprecedented change. In some places, the nation itself is no longer a successful arbiter of citizenship. As a result, the project of a national society of citizens, especially liberalism's twentieth-century version, appears increasingly exhausted and discredited. In other places, the nation may maintain the envelope of citizenship, but the substance has been so changed or at least challenged that the emerging social morphologies are radically unfamiliar and force a reconsideration of the basic principles of membership. Such transformations have generated profound uncertainties about many aspects of citizenship that only recently seemed secure: uncertainty about the community of allegiance, its form of organization, manner of election and repudiation, inclusiveness, ethical foundations, and signifying performances; uncertainty about the location of sovereign power; uncertainty about the priorities of the right and the good; uncertainty about the role of cultural identities increasingly viewed as defining natural memberships.

It has become common in the literature on national identity to consider such transformations in terms of a dichotomy between the national and the global. Cities usually drop out of the analysis because this dichotomy tends to present globalization, especially of labor, capital, and communication, as neutralizing the importance of place, indeed of rendering it irrelevant. This volume proposes that such dematerialization is mistaken, that place remains fundamental to the problems of membership in society, and that cities (understood here to include their regional suburbs) are especially privileged sites for considering the current renegotiations of citizenship. It regards cities as the place where the business of modern society gets done, including that of transnationalization. Some essays in this volume suggest that cities may be reemerging as more salient sites for citizenship; other essays suggest that citizens are producing new (in some cases expansive, in some restrictive) notions of membership and solidarity. As a whole, moreover, they suggest that in many postcolonial societies, a new generation has arisen to create urban cultures severed from the colonial memories and nationalist fictions on which independence and subsequent rule were founded. These cultures are especially detached from the paradigm of nation building that celebrates the rural as the fundamental expression of the indigenous and the authentic and that despises the city as responsible for the loss of both, for detribalization, corruption, and social death. This rural paradigm has often dominated the representation of postcolonial society in the arts and social sciences, especially anthropology. Insofar as that is the case, this volume speaks as well to the urgent need to develop a framework of investigation that considers cities challenging, diverging from, and even replacing nations as the important space of citizenship—as the lived space not only of its uncertainties but also of its emergent forms.

Our point is not to argue that the transnational flow of ideas, goods, images, and persons—intensified by recent developments in the globalization of capital—is obliterating the salience of the nation-state. Rather, it is to suggest that this flow tends to drive a deeper wedge between national space and its urban centers. There are a growing number of societies in which cities have a different relationship to global processes than the visions and policies of their nation-states may admit or endorse. London today is a global city in many ways that do not fit with the politics of the United Kingdom, just as Shanghai may be oriented to a global traffic beyond the control of the government of the People's Republic of China, as Mogadishu may represent a civil war only tangentially tied to a wider Somali politics, and as Los Angeles may sustain many aspects of a multicultural society and economy at odds with mainstream ideologies of American identity. Cities have always been stages for politics of a different sort than their hinterlands. But in the era of mass migration, globalization of the economy, and rapid circulation of rights discourse, cities represent the localization of global forces as much as they do the dense articulation of national resources, persons, and projects. Michael Watt's essay in this volume shows, for example, the extent to which the transnational political economy of oil and Islam impinges on the urban life of Nigeria. In some cases, at any rate, cities may be sites of entropy for the energies that might have sustained a national politics of democracy.

The conventional distinction between formal and substantive aspects of citizenship is helpful in sorting out various dimensions of these proposals. In particular, it suggests why cities may be especially salient sites for the constitution of different citizens, or at least for considering the exhaustion of national modes. If the formal refers to membership in the nation-state and the substantive to the array of civil, political, socioeconomic, and cultural rights people possess and exercise, much of the turmoil of citizenship derives from the following problem: although in theory full access to rights depends on membership, in practice that which constitutes citizenship substantively is often independent of its formal status. In other words, formal membership in the nation-state is increasingly neither a necessary nor a sufficient condition for substantive citizenship. That it is not sufficient is obvious for many poor citizens who have formal membership in the state but who are excluded in fact or law from enjoying the rights of citizenship and participating effectively in its organization. This condition also applies to citizens of all classes who find that their preferences for a desirable or proper form of life—for example, with regard to sexual or religious practices—are not adequately embodied in the national-public sphere of rights even though the communities in which they live may overwhelmingly approve them. Moreover, it is now evident that a condition of formal membership without much substantive citizenship characterizes many of the societies that have experienced recent transitions to democracy and market capitalism in Latin America, Asia, and Eastern Europe.

That formal citizenship is less necessary for access to substantive rights is also clear: although it is required for a few rights (like voting in national elections), it is not for most. Indeed, legally resident noncitizens often possess virtually identical socioeconomic and civil rights as citizens. Moreover, the exclusive rights of citizens are often onerous, like jury duty, military service, and certain tax requirements. Thus people tend to perceive them more as burdens than as rights. It is not surprising, therefore, that recent surveys indicate that many immigrants are not as anxious as they once might have been to embrace the citizenship of their new countries, thereby compromising their right of return.[1]

---

1. See Schuck 1989 for a discussion of the problematic relation between the form and substance of citizenship in the United States, with specific reference to (and a disputable conclusion about) the reluctance of more recent immigrants to assume U.S. citizenship.

Such disjunctions between the form and substance of citizenship have made defining it in terms of membership in the nation-state less convincing and have thus devalued this form of association for both members and nonmembers alike. As a result, there have been two general responses. One tries to make citizenship more exclusive. Hence we witness a host of reactionary movements: some aim to deny social services to various categories of noncitizens or to legislate the exclusive use of one language or another. Others employ urban incorporation to gain the powers of local government. Their objective is to privatize or dismantle public spaces and services and to implant zoning regulations that in effect keep the undesired out. Around the world, it is all too common to find homeowner associations using these powers and privileges of democratic organization to exclude, discriminate, and segregate. For example, in the Los Angeles metropolitan region alone there are over twenty-five such exclusive urban incorporations, and in São Paulo there are hundreds of so-called closed condominiums using somewhat different legal mechanisms to achieve similar ends. Other exclusionary movements (some militia-backed) attack federalism and the idea of national government itself, advancing the priority of local, small-scale communities.[2] All these movements tend to emphasize private security and vigilantism as acceptable forms of self-determination. Most are tinged with racism if not outright violence.

The other kind of response has gone in the opposite direction. It tries to make citizenship more inclusive. It aims to reconceive citizenship in supranational and nonlocal terms in which rights are available to individuals regardless of national origins, residence, or place of work. Examples include movements for human rights, transnational citizenship, and continental associations (e.g., EEC, NAFTA, and Mercosur). But if both types of response aim to reinvigorate citizenship, they both typically have their perverse outcomes: in the one case, localism can generate xenophobic violence; in the other, the elimination of local community as the ground of citizenship tends to preclude active participation in the business of rule. Instead, it leads to the replacement of that civic ideal with a more passive sense of entitlement to benefits that seem to derive from remote sources. Far from renewing citizenship, violence and passivity further erode its foundations.

2. Examples of these exclusionary movements include California's Proposition 187, which passed overwhelmingly in 1994; French-only legislation in Quebec; urban incorporations in Los Angeles (Davis 1990) and closed condominiums in São Paulo (Caldeira forthcoming, and in this volume); the bombing of the Murrah Federal Building in Oklahoma City; and recent opinions by Supreme Court Justice Thomas.

As such erosion spreads, it threatens the very notion of a shared community and culture as the basis of citizenship. The extension of the shared beyond the local and the homogeneous is, of course, an essential part of citizenship's revolutionary and democratic promise. This extension of citizenship corrodes other notions of the shared precisely because its concept of allegiance is, ultimately, volitional and consensual rather than natural. Yet, one would be hard-pressed to find a major urban population today that felt compelled, except in extraordinary moments like war, by "a direct sense of community membership based on loyalty to a civilization which is a common possession," to use a phrase from T. H. Marshall's classic study of citizenship ([1950] 1977: 94). The exhaustion of this sense over the half century forces us to reconsider not only the national basis of citizenship but also its democratic ideals of commonwealth, participation, and equality.

The project of national citizenship depends less on the idea of the nation as a neutral framework for competing interests than on that of the nation as a community of shared purposes and commensurable citizens. Its working assumption is that this national community is committed to constituting a common good and to shaping a common life well suited to the conditions of modernity. This notion requires a set of self-understandings on the part of citizens that lies at the core of the liberal compact of citizenship: it requires that people perceive, through a kind of leap of faith, that they are sufficiently similar to form common purpose. This perception is sustained in the long run through performances of citizenship. These determine, first, that there are meaningful common goods; second, that active participation rather than mere reception or inheritance establishes the fundamental claim to goods; and, third, that those who participate have equal—or at least fairly adjusted—rights regardless of other differences. This liberal compact is now under tremendous strain. With the unprecedented growth of economic and social inequalities during the last few decades in so many nations, the differences between residents have become too gross and the areas of commonality too few to sustain this compact. As a result, the social imaginary of a nation of commensurable citizens disintegrates. And the performances that sustain it fail. In the breach, the idea of a shared culture seems implausible.

One could argue that where liberalism encounters this failure—at different times in different places—its response has been to replace the teleological notion of common good and measure with the priority of right over good. In this more modern version, the nation of citizens is based not on constitutive ends but on procedural means of justice that ensure that no particular end (a vision of the good life) "trumps" any other, to use

Dworkin's famous image.[3] Deriving from Kant, this liberal ethic asserts principles of justice that do not presuppose or promote any substantive conception of the good. Rather, they are supposed to enable citizens to pursue their own ends consistent with a similar liberty for all. In elevating the priority of right to a supreme value, it opposes the regulation of society in terms of utilitarian ends or communist needs that ultimately may sacrifice individual rights for the sake of the general welfare.

If this version of liberalism has triumphed globally in twentieth-century models of democracy and citizenship, it has also come under powerful attack. Critics across many spectrums—from Left to Right, from Islamic to American Fundamentalism, from Aztlan to Common Cause—argue that it relies in theory and practice on a notion of shared allegiance that it officially rejects. This notion derives from the argument that without prior formative attachments and commitments to family, culture, ethnicity, religion, and the like, people cannot achieve the very sense of moral depth and personhood that the liberal compact requires. However, it is precisely these kinds of prior affiliations that liberal citizenship refuses. Hence, liberalism in reality gives lie to its official values; and yet, in insisting on them, it undermines the sense of community on which it actually depends. In effect, procedural liberalism leaves citizens more entangled in obligations they do not choose and less attached to common identifications that would render these obligations not just bearable but even virtuous. Thus, it produces citizens who are predominately passive in their citizenship. They are, for the most part, spectators who vote. Yet, without active participation in the business of rule, they are citizens whose citizenship is managed, for better or worse, by an unelected bureaucracy.

Among the most vocal critics of liberal citizenship in this sense are groups organized around specific identities—the kind of prior differences liberalism relegates to the private sphere—which affirm the importance of these identities in the public calculus of citizenship. That is, they affirm the right to difference as an integral part of the foundation of citizenship. Feminism launched this critique by arguing that liberalism depends in fact on an ideology of difference because its supposedly universal citizen is, historically, of a particular type, namely, a white, European, propertied, male.[4] The ideology of universal equality arises because members of this referent group have never had to assert their difference, but only their equality, to claim citizenship. From the perspective of the rest who are

3. On this version of liberalism, several of the important discussions are Berlin 1969, Dworkin 1977, Sandel 1982, Rawls 1988, and Walzer 1983.
4. Feminist studies of citizenship include Pateman 1989, Dietz 1992, and Okin 1992.

excluded, this assertion looks like one of difference, not equality. In any case, it will not work for those not already equal in these terms. Hence, for the excluded, the political question is to change the terms. Therefore, the politics of difference becomes more important and potentially incompatible with that of universal equality as the real basis for citizenship.[5]

For example, this politics argues that although different treatment (e.g., with regard to gender) can produce inequality, equal treatment, when it means sameness, can discriminate against just the kinds of values and identities people find most meaningful. Thus, it asks whether citizenship rights should be difference-specific or difference-neutral. Do the former constitute a more just basis for the integration of citizens into market and polity, especially for those who have been traditionally excluded? Does it make sense, for instance, to secure equal treatment for women in the workplace by conceiving of pregnancy as just another kind of disability for which employers grant leave? The current U.S. Pregnancy Disability Act is based on exactly this difference-neutral conception of rights. Or does that violate our moral sense of the unique importance of pregnancy? Should pregnancy leave rather be a specific right of women, who, occasionally in their lives, give birth? Many argue that only the latter gives due recognition to the unique contribution of women to society and that citizenship must therefore include difference-specific rights.[6]

As in the case of gender, many other distinguishing identities have given focus to organized groups who challenge established, difference-neutral conceptions of citizenship. These include national and cultural minorities, sexual-orientation groups, and racial, religious, and ethnic organizations.[7] They demand different treatment on the basis of their inalienable right to retain and realize their unique qualities, contributions, and histories. Their core argument usually entails the claim they have been denied respect and opportunity because they are different. That difference in fact constitutes their authentic and original character, which they have every right to develop to full capacity. Thus, they demand citizenship rights as persons who have authentic needs and interests that must be met if they are to live fully human lives. As Taylor demonstrates, the argument from authenticity leads to a politics of difference rather than to a politics of universalism or equalization of rights (1992: 3–73). It results in a claim on others to recognize special qualities and to accord them rights on that account that will ensure their survival and well-being. Although this kind of demand would seem

5. For opposing views on this question of difference and equality, see Schlesinger 1992 and Scott 1992.
6. Eisenstein (1988: 79–116) and Pateman (1989: 179–209) analyze the problem of difference-specific rights in relation to gender. The former discusses the question of maternity leave.
7. For examples, see Anzaldúa 1987, Kallen 1924, Ferguson et al. 1990, and Warner 1993.

contradictory and incompatible with citizenship as an ideology of equality, there is nevertheless a growing sense that it is changing the meaning of equality itself. What it objects to is the equation that equality means sameness. It rejects citizenship as a homogenizing identity with the charge that homogenization reduces and impoverishes. Rather, it would take equality to mean equal opportunity. Thus, it would define citizenship on the basis of rights to different treatment with equal opportunity.

Identity politics of this sort is having a major impact because the identities of difference are competing more successfully for people's time and passion than the tired identity of formal, national citizenship. Without doubt, this impact is divisive. Identity politics tends to disrupt established ideologies of civic unity and moral solidarity in ways that often make people angry and anxious. For example, the politics of difference challenges the basic premise of liberal citizenship that the principles of justice impose negative restrictions on the kinds of goods individuals can pursue. Hence, when Muslim women in France demand the right to use the veil in public schools, or American fundamentalists to include creationism in the curriculum, they contest that priority and the plural public sphere it supposedly creates. By demanding the right to pursue their definitions of the good and proper life in the public sphere, they challenge the liberal democratic conviction that the res publica should articulate all interests according to conditions that subscribe to none in particular. Precisely because their demands are opposed, they show that Western liberal republics neither achieve nor in fact subscribe to such a procedurally neutral articulation. Thus, they debunk a fundamental premise of liberal ideology. The politics of difference has become so intense precisely because it suggests a basic change in the historical role of citizenship: it indicates the increasing disarticulation of formal citizenship as the principal norm for coordinating and managing the simultaneity of modern social identities in highly differentiated societies. In that suggestion, it ignites deep anxieties about what form such coordination might take, both juridically and symbolically, if citizenship no longer has that primary role.

As nowhere else, the world's major cities make manifest these reconstitutions of citizenship. The compaction and reterritorialization of so many different kinds of groups within them grind away at citizenship's assumptions. They compel it to bend to the recognition that contemporary urban life comprises multiple and diverse cultural identities, modes of life, and forms of appropriating urban space (Hannerz 1992; Holston, this volume). Immigration is a central link between classical issues of citizenship—imaged as a rights-bearing form of membership in the territorial nation-state—and the city as this dense and heterogeneous lived space. Immigrants typically congregate and work in cities because the demands for their labor tend to be generated by urban commerce, infrastructure, and wage-differentiation. Moreover, immigrants tend to rely on previous networks of knowledge and affiliation for jobs and basic amenities. Thus, the politics of immigration is closely tied to the politics of cities, and the violence surrounding immigration is intimately connected with urban youth, gangs, slums, and politics. In the recent hunt for Islamic terrorists in the subways of Paris, or the recent expulsion of Bangladeshi immigrants from Bombay (which also involved the deportation of many Indian Muslims by "accident"), we see that in cities the politics of quality (in particular of difference) meets the politics of quantity (and of the anxieties of density). Immigration politics cannot be abstractly conducted evenly across all national space. It tends to be implosive (Appadurai 1996), and its most intense points of implosion are cities.

Because of this volatile complexity, cities are especially sensitive to the peregrinations of capital and labor. When these produce sharp increases in socioeconomic inequality, they affect citizenship profoundly because they provoke new notions of membership, solidarity, and alienage. That is, they generate new morphologies of social category and class that interact not only to shift sociabilities and cultures but also to transform the legal regimes of state and local community in keeping with these displacements. The politics of immigration largely concerns these shifting interactions between culture and law. Especially in the developing world, this dynamic of change seems extraordinary today because many cities are undergoing two kinds of localizations of capital and labor simultaneously. First, most cities are still in the grip of nationally oriented processes of industrialization, with corresponding commercial, financial, and bureaucratic consequences. Second, some cities have become, often at the same time, strategic and specialized sites for the operations of more globally oriented capital and labor.

In the first case, the great turmoil of citizenship in cities derives in large measure from new concentrations of wealth and misery among nationals related to industrialization. Where the shanties of migrants sprout next to the mansions, factories, and skyscrapers of industrial-state capitalism, new kinds of citizens engage each other in struggles over the nature of belonging to the national society. Such struggles are particularly evident in the social movements of the urban poor for rights to the city. They are especially associated with the emergence of democracy because they empower poor citizens to mobilize around the redistributive right-claims of citizenship.[8] These movements are new not only because they force the

8. For examples from Brazil, see Alvarez 1993, Caldeira 1986, and Holston 1989.

state to respond to new social conditions of the working poor—in which sense they are, indeed, one of the significant consequences of massive urban poverty for citizenship. They are also unprecedented in many cases because they create new kinds of rights outside the normative and institutional definitions of the state and its legal codes. These rights generally address the new collective and personal spaces of the modern metropolis, especially its impoverished residential neighborhoods. They affirm access to housing, property, sanitation, health services, education, child care, and so forth on the basis of citizenship. In this assertion, they expand the scope and understanding of entitlement. Is adequate housing a right? Is employment? In this sense, the development of the economy itself fuels the growth of citizenship as new areas of social and economic life are brought under the calculus of rights.

This expansion amounts to more than multiplying the number and beneficiaries of socioeconomic rights, itself no small achievement. In addition, it changes the very conception of rights and citizenship. Rights become more of a claim on than possessions held against the world. They become claims on society for the resources necessary to meet the basic needs and interests of members rather than a kind of property some possess and others do not. It is probably the case that this change applies mostly to socioeconomic and political rights rather than to civil rights. In the emerging democracies of the developing world, the latter tends to remain decidedly underdeveloped. But in terms of rights to the city and rights to political participation, rights become conceived as aspects of social relatedness rather than as inherent and natural properties of individuals. This sort of claim is often based on the deeply felt capacity of new urban workers to contribute morally and politically to the public sphere because they do so economically. That is, even though poor, even if illegal squatters, they have rights because they are consumers and taxpayers. Moreover, in the development of this mode of reasoning, it is also possible to discern the beginnings of a more radical argument: people have rights to a minimum standard of living that does not depend on their relative economic or market worth but on their absolute rights as citizens to a measure of economic well being and dignity. Potentially, this argument is radically redistributive of a society's wealth because it breaks down entrenched, elite-based explanations for relative worth and inequality.

Furthermore, as mobilizations for these rights are organized in relation to new conditions of work and residence, and concern people for the most part previously excluded from the resources of the state, they come to be based on specific claims that are generally not defined in existing constitutions or legal codes. Where there are urban housing problems on a massive scale, for example, movements arise that claim that property must fulfill a social function or risk expropriation and redistribution. This claim relativizes the traditionally positivist and absolute right to property. In many cases, such unprecedented claims are so strong that they succeed in producing new legal regimes in the form of new constitutional principles, and new legal codes in the form of new constitutions, as well as revising legal codes, and reforming judiciaries. In terms of the last, they force isolated judiciaries to confront social and legal contradictions. They create new services that permit broader access to justice, especially in civil law.[9] Moreover, although such changes may be legislated from the top down, they often result from popular participation in constitutional congresses. In turn, they mobilize people into helping frame legislation and government reform at the local level. In sum, as the social movements of the urban poor create unprecedented claims on and to the city, they expand citizenship to new social bases. In so doing, they create new sources of citizenship rights and corresponding forms of self-rule.

Many of these same cities around the world are now also sites of a second and more encompassing localization of capital and labor. Even as they undergo national industrialization, they have become strategic arenas in which global capital structures its operations, for these too require place (Appadurai 1990; Sassen 1991). The accompanying transnationalization of labor includes both highly skilled and unskilled immigrants: it produces a new set of class fractions in the city of high-income capital managers and the low-income manual and service workers who attend them. Increasingly, managers see the workers as marginal "others." Although this transnationalization generates its own forms of politics, these fractions are less likely to engage in struggles over the form and substance of national citizenship. Rather, they are more likely to produce new forms of overlapping citizenships and multiple jurisdictions for several reasons.

First, transnationalization initiates a new dynamic of inequality that significantly reduces the possibility of common allegiances and civilities, even of a mythological sort, between capital managers and others. Although they may both work in the transnational economy, their life-worlds are too different. Each world tends to its own promotion, delegitimizing if not criminalizing the other. Second, as mostly non- or postnationals (Appadurai 1993), neither feels much loyalty to the place in which they are perhaps only temporary transplants. They need state government for their economic activity. But they have reduced moral and personal commitments

9. See Holston (1991) for an example of such legal change concerning property and residence among the urban poor.

to it. Instead, they are likely to retain primary loyalty—at least in cultural terms—to diasporic identities. Third, transnationalization generates a new global network of cities through which capital and labor pass. The fluidity of this network causes nation-states to modify their organizational, and especially legal, structure to attract global resources. In particular, they change the legal regulation of borders and modes of association because it is through these that global capital and labor must flow. Also vulnerable are laws of monopoly over national resources. In addition, labor codes frequently suffer rewriting to meet the exigencies of international capital and its local partners. Thus, to mediate between national sovereignty and global economic interests, nation-states tend not only to produce new legal regimes but also to accept the legal authority of transnational regulatory bodies (e.g., of trade and banking) within their borders.

This new legal cocktail tends to give special privileges to the managers of global capital, in the sense that it absolves them from local duties and makes them immune to local legal powers. However, it tends to disempower labor. In part this is because it renders significant segments of the transnational low-income labor force illegal by using the system of national boundaries to criminalize the immigrants it attracts for low-wage work. Even though immigrant manual and service workers contribute substantially to the local community—and thereby should earn at least partial standing according to the modern calculus of citizenship—the local does not reciprocate by offering membership.[10] Rather, it tends to exploit the illegal status of workers, using the threat of deportation to keep wages low and workers from organizing. But since what brings these new class fractions together, the international market, has its own rules and networks that contradict national boundaries, both rich and poor immigrants also successfully evade state control to a significant degree. Therefore, even as their translocation to the city generates new legal regimes, it also propagates new and diverse forms of illegality. This unstable mix of the legal and the illegal, and of various forms of each, turns the city into a honeycomb of jurisdictions in which there are in effect as many kinds of citizens as there are kinds of law. Such multiplicity delegitimates the national justice system and its framework of uniform law, both hallmarks of national citizenship. Although, as we have seen, this urban multiplicity can spawn new and more democratic forms of citizenship, it also suggests the emergence of an almost medieval body of overlapping, heterogeneous, nonuniform, and increasingly private memberships.

To the extent that we have theories of citizenship that link these factors

10. On immigration and the politics of citizenship, see Brubaker 1989.

of globalization, economic change, immigration, and cities, they tend to focus either on the labor/immigration nexus or on the narrative of the erosion of Fordist ideas about industrial production. Yet, to deal with the range of cities in which dramas of citizenship are today played out, we need a broader image of urban processes that breaks out of the constraints of the Fordist (and post-Fordist) narrative. The histories of many cities in Africa, Asia, and Latin America have little to do with industry, manufacture, or production. Some of these cities are fundamentally commercial and financial, others are military and bureaucratic, and yet others are monumental and re-creative of nationalist historiographies. This variety of cities generates a variety of dramas of citizenship, and in each of them the relationship between production, finance, labor, and service is somewhat different. We need more images and narratives of urban economies so that we can better identify the various ways in which such cities spawn class fragments, ethnic enclaves, gang territories, and varied maps of work, crime, and kinship. Among the following essays, those by Diouf, Caldeira, and Sassen point to the variety of ways in which the economic lives of cities differentially put pressure on the idea of the national citizen.

If the city is a special site for such formations and re-formations of citizens, it can also be a special war zone, a space in which these processes find expression in collective violence. The city has always been a site of violent social and cultural confrontation. But in the contemporary world, the density of new social formations and the superimposition of diverse cultural identifications produce a corresponding complexity of violence: urban terrorism from the extreme right and left, racist attacks, Islamic bombings, gang shootings, death squads, riots, vandalism, human rights abuses, vigilante lynchings, political assassinations, kidnappings, police shootings, high-tech security harassments, private justice making, civil disobedience, shantytown eradication, and soccer hooliganism suggest the enormous range of contemporary forms of collective violence. How are these related to conflicts of citizenship and in what way is the violence of citizenship city-specific?

As we have suggested throughout this introductory chapter, citizenship concerns more than rights to participate in politics. It also includes other kinds of rights in the public sphere, namely, civil, socioeconomic, and cultural. Moreover, in addition to the legal, it concerns the moral and performative dimensions of membership that define the meanings and practices of belonging in society. Undeniably, people use violence to make claims about all of these dimensions of belonging. In this sense, violence is a specific type of social action. Moreover, different social processes have their stock expressions of violence. This is not to say that industrialization features one repertoire of violence and globalization another. It is rather to suggest, as Wieviorka argues in his essay, that social processes instigate their own forms of violence in a given social and historical context, the meanings of which consolidate around specific problems, for example, of cultural identity, labor, or residence.

Thus, it is possible to observe that in many countries today democratization brings its own forms of violence. Moreover, as democratization is always a disjunctive process, in which citizenship rights expand and erode in complex arhythmic ways (Holston and Caldeira, forthcoming), it is possible to discern the effects of disjunction on the forms of violence. As discussed earlier, many transitions to democracy included a sustained expansion of political and socioeconomic rights for the urban poor. Strikes that are violently repressed and turn into riots, land invasions and expulsions, destruction of public transportation, and political assassinations typically express the conflicts of this expansion. But even where the political and socioeconomic components of citizenship are relatively consolidated in these transitions to democracy, the civil component that guarantees liberty, security, and above all justice is often inchoate and ineffectual. This disjunction is common to many countries undergoing democratization today. Where it happens, the majority cannot expect the institutions of state—the courts and the police especially—to respect or guarantee their individual rights, arbitrate their conflicts justly, or control violence legally. In this situation, violence takes a well-known course (Holston and Caldeira, forthcoming). There is a broad criminalization of the poor at the same time that social groups at all levels come to support the privatization of security and the extralegalization of justice as the only effective means to deal with "marginals." In other words, there is massive support for market forms of justice on the one hand (private security, vigilantes, enforcers) and, on the other, for extralegal and even illegal measures of control by state institutions, particularly the police (and related death squads) who kill large numbers of "marginals." This kind of violence further discredits the justice system and with it the entire project of democracy and its citizenship.

If there are, therefore, certain forms and meanings of violence associated with citizenship conflicts, how might they be specific to the city? To suggest such specificity is not to reduce violence to an overdetermining urban pathology. Nor is it to consider the city as a mere spatial metaphor of social relations. The city is more important to the conflicts of belonging than these options indicate. Rather, we might say that the city both provides a map of violence and establishes its features. In this geography of violence, the city can be pretext and context, form and substance, stage and script. Of course, a great deal of collective violence has always been identity-based in ways that do not coincide with the administrative areas of city or nation—think of religious wars, anti-Semitism, the European witch-hunts. Surely, violence is not city-bound. But coincidence does not have to be absolute or exclusive to establish correspondence. The point is that people use violence to make claims on the city and use the city to make violent claims. They appropriate a space to which they then declare they belong; they violate a space that others claim. Such acts generate a city-specific violence of citizenship. Its geography is too legible, too visible to be missed in the abandoned public spaces of the modern city, in its fortified residential enclaves, its division into corporate luxury zones and quarantined war zones, its forbidden sectors of gangs and "armed response" security, its bunkers of fundamentalists, its illegally constructed shanties, its endless neighborhoods of unemployed youth.

With the breakdown of civility and nationality thus evident, many are seeking alternatives in the post-, trans-, de-, re- (and plain con) of current speculations about the future of the nation-state. It is a heady moment, full of great creativity and uncertainty. Many proposals are circulating for new kinds of public spheres, third spaces, virtual communities, transnations, and diasporic networks. The results are surely contradictory. It may be that cybercitizenship draws some into a more tolerant and accessible public realm. But it also seems to drive others further into the recesses of the private and the market. The failure of nation-states to produce convincing fantasies of the commensurability of its citizens ("The People") compels some to imagine recombinant forms of nonterritorial, life-world sovereignties while it forces others into even more primordial and violent affiliations of territory, religion, and race. The grand theories that were once used to explain pushes and pulls of such magnitude have themselves splintered, in keeping with the nations that gave them sustenance. Contemporary theory seems as displaced and dislocated, as hybrid and diasporic, as so many of the world's populations.

In all of this commotion, it is perhaps understandable to treat the city, that old form of human society, as irrelevant. But until transnations attain more flesh and bone, cities may still be the important sites in which we experience the crises of national membership and through which we may rethink citizenship. It may even be, after all, that there is something irreducible and nontransferable, necessary but not quite sufficient, about the city's public street and square for the realization of a meaningfully democratic citizenship. If we support the latter, we may have to do much more to defend the former.

References

Alvarez, S. E. 1993. " 'Deepening' Democracy: Popular Movement Networks, Constitutional Reform, and Radical Urban Regimes in Contemporary Brazil." In *Mobilizing the Community: Local Politics in the Era of the Global City*, Robert Fisher and Joseph Kling, eds. Newbury Park: Sage, 191–219.

Anzaldúa, Gloria. 1987. *Borderlands-La Frontera: The New Mestiza*. San Francisco: Spinsters/Aunt Lute Foundation.

Appadurai, Arjun. 1990. "Disjuncture and Difference in the Global Cultural Economy." *Public Culture* 2(2): 1–24.

——. 1993. "Patriotism and Its Futures." *Public Culture* 5(3): 411–29.

——. 1996. *Modernity at Large: Cultural Dimensions of Globalization*. Minneapolis: University of Minnesota Press.

Berlin, Isaiah. 1969. *Four Essays on Liberty*. Oxford: Oxford University Press.

Brubaker, William Rogers, ed. 1989. *Immigration and the Politics of Citizenship in Europe and North America*. Lanham, Md.: University Press of America.

Caldeira, Teresa Pires do Rio. 1986. "Electoral Struggles in a Neighborhood on the Periphery of São Paulo." *Politics and Society* 15(1): 43–66.

——. *City of Walls: Crime, Segregation, and Citizenship in São Paulo*. Berkeley: University of California Press, forthcoming.

Davis, Mike. 1990. *City of Quartz: Excavating the Future in Los Angeles*. New York: Vintage.

Dietz, Mary. 1992. "Context Is All: Feminism and Theories of Citizenship." In *Dimensions of Radical Democracy: Pluralism, Citizenship, Community*. Chantal Mouffe, ed. London: Verso, 63–85.

Dworkin, Ronald. 1977. *Taking Rights Seriously*. Cambridge: Harvard University Press.

Eisenstein, Zillah R. 1988. *The Female Body and the Law*. Berkeley: University of California Press.

Ferguson, Russell, Martha Gever, Trinh T. Minh-ha, and Cornel West, eds. 1990. *Out There: Marginalization and Contemporary Cultures*. Cambridge: MIT Press.

Hannerz, Ulf. 1992. *Cultural Complexity: Studies in the Social Organization of Meaning*. New York: Columbia University Press.

Holston, James. 1989. *The Modernist City: An Anthropological Critique of Brasília*. Chicago: University of Chicago Press.

——. 1991. "The Misrule of Law: Land and Usurpation in Brazil." *Comparative Studies in Society and History* 33(4): 695–725.

Holston, James, and Teresa P. R. Caldeira. "Democracy, Law, and Violence: Disjunctions of Brazilian Citizenship." In *Fault Lines of Democratic Governance in the Americas*. Felipe Agüero and Jeffrey Stark, eds. Boulder, Colo.: Lynne Rienner Press, forthcoming.

Kallen, Horace M. 1924. *Culture and Democracy in the United States*. New York: Boni and Liveright.

Marshall, T. H. [1950] 1977. "Citizenship and Social Class." In *Class, Citizenship, and Social Development*. Chicago: University of Chicago Press, 71–134.

Okin, Susan Moller. 1992. "Women, Equality, and Citizenship." *Queens's Quarterly* 99(1): 56–71.

Pateman, Carole. 1989. *The Disorder of Women*. Stanford: Stanford University Press.

Rawls, John. 1988. "The Priority of Right and the Ideas of the Good." *Philosophy and Public Affairs* 17: 151–76.

Sandel, Michael. 1982. *Liberalism and the Limits of Justice*. Cambridge: Cambridge University Press.

Sassen, Saskia. 1991. *The Global City: New York, London, Tokyo*. Princeton: Princeton University Press.

Schlesinger, Arthur. 1992. *The Disuniting of America*. New York: Norton.

Schuck, Peter H. 1989. "Membership in the Liberal Polity: The Devaluation of American Citizenship." In *Immigration and the Politics of Citizenship in North America*, William Brubaker, ed. Lanham, Md.: University Press of America, 51–65.

Scott, Joan W. 1992. "Multiculturalism and the Politics of Identity." *October* 61: 12–19.

Taylor, Charles. 1992. "Multiculturalism and the Politics of Recognition." In *Multiculturalism and the Politics of Recognition*, Charles Taylor, edited with commentary by Amy Gutmann. Princeton: Princeton University Press, 3–73.

Walzer, Michael. 1983. *Spheres of Justice: A Defence of Pluralism and Equality*. New York: Basic Books.

Warner, Michael, ed. 1993. *Fear of a Queer Planet*. Minneapolis: University of Minnesota Press.

Part One · Cities and the Making of Citizens

Intellectuals, Cities, and Citizenship in the United States: The 1890s and 1990s

Thomas Bender

Through most of the twentieth century, the nation has been the domain of citizenship, and social politics has been associated with the national welfare state. But such was not always the case. A century ago in the United States, the city provided a vital platform for men and women to think themselves into politics, to make themselves into citizens, to initiate a social politics. In the decade of the 1890s, reformers, journalists, and academic intellectuals (a cluster not so differentiated then as now) thought urban democracy possible, even necessary. They were able to imagine the city, in the words of Frederick C. Howe (1905), a leader of the movement, as "the hope of democracy."[1]

A slightly different version of this essay was prepared for a conference on "The Rights to the City: Cities, Citizenship, and Democracy in the Global Era," Toronto, 1998. It will appear in *Citizenship Studies*, along with other papers for that conference. I wish to acknowledge the research assistance of John Baick, a graduate student in history at New York University. He skillfully located the literature on home rule for me, and in addition counted urban articles in the *Political Science Quarterly* (1986–95) and the *American Political Science Review* (1906–95).

1. See the positive reference to Howe's aspiration in the more hard-headed pioneering textbook on municipal government by Charles A. Beard (1912a: 38). However, Beard's position, as will be seen, was in fact more nation-centered than Howe's.

Though my intention is to recall that moment and movement, I do not want to associate myself with those who speak loosely about the dissolution of the nation-state in the contemporary world. It would be a mistake to underestimate the continuing capacity of the national state to sustain citizenship and to nurture social welfare. Yet there has been a realignment of the relations and powers of cities and nations, and that circumstance invites a reconsideration of the city as a site for a politics that addresses the social consequences of the present phase of global capitalism, manifestations of social change dramatically inscribed in the physical form and daily life of cities. How might the city, then, be a site that opens up political possibilities and empowers men and women as citizens?

A century ago such inquiry was the work of the fledgling social science disciplines, particularly political science. Today, political science and the social sciences generally are less attentive to the particularity of time and place or, to be more specific, to the city. Looking backward, however, we discover a generation of academic intellectuals who were engaged with urban questions. That engagement proved fruitful to their professional agenda of disciplinary development, infusing a formal and abstract discipline with both vitality and realism, while it sustained a sense of civic participation that enriched the political culture of the city and extended urban democracy. I am not proposing that the city is permanently available for such political work; my point is simply that a certain mobility of such political sites exists and that historical circumstances may in any given instance favor cities. Such was the case in the 1890s in the United States, and in the 1990s cities may again have a special role in defining a social politics.

After some account of the relation of academic social science, particularly political science, to late-nineteenth-century social reform, I turn to the specific history of the reform movement for urban "home rule," which was a campaign to win political as well as administrative powers for the city. That quest forged an alliance between political scientists and urban reformers. I try to specify the circumstances and chronology of this moment in American political history, ending with some observations on the relevance of that history to our own historical moment.

The emerging social sciences provided a new language for reform, one stressing social connection and interdependence. After experiencing new levels of interdependence during the Civil War and in growing cities, Americans found in the language of the social, on which the new social sciences were being built, a better way to describe and explain the world around them. The idea of social causation weakened the hold of those notions of individual agency that were articles of faith for Americans in the middle third of the nineteenth century.[2] In Europe and America, the social sciences developed in a dialectical relationship to the massive social transformations driven by industrial capitalism: social explanation was both a product of new experience and a way of understanding that new experience. Indeed, to explain and manage that society was the raison d'être of these new disciplines.[3]

Although one can speak of the social sciences as a single movement of thought in the nineteenth century, there were important distinctions among them, and they approached the task of explanation and management in different ways, with different dialects. Economics was the first of these new social sciences to professionalize in the United States, and in the 1880s economists supplied a method of historical economics that enabled reformers to enter the troubling question of the political economy of labor and capital in a new way. By playing down ideology and shifting the ground from the formal and deductive approach favored by theorists of laissez-faire, the historical economists, relying on empirical and historicist claims, intervened with significant effect, arguing for historically specific and strategic interventions in the economy.[4]

Gradually, however, the focus and language of reform changed. The new society increasingly became identified with the city rather than with the conflict between labor and capital, which generally did not have a geographical referent. Sociologists claimed the city, a novel "social aggregation," as their subject. Sociology and social reform were nearly assimilated the one to the other, especially at Chicago, where Albion Small created the first sociology department in the United States. But with their focus on civil society and voluntary action, the sociologists in the end offered little access to politics, a matter of significance because the social concerns of the era were increasingly being understood in terms of a politics, a new social politics.[5]

During the 1890s and 1900s, in the first years of the intellectual and political movement that assumed the name Progressivim, political scientists, following the lead of Columbia's Frank Goodnow, achieved primacy for the language of politics as a means of addressing the social implications of industrial capitalism as they revealed themselves in the city. In the phrasing of Goodnow ([1904] 1910: 21), "the city must be studied not merely from the sociological point of view, but also from the political point

2. See Haskell 1977.
3. See Glazer 1959; Bender 1993, esp. chap. 3; and Haskell 1977.
4. See Furner 1975 and Bender 1993: chap. 4.
5. See Rodgers 1998 on the history of social politics in the United States, particularly chapter 4.

of view: the city is not merely an urban community, a social fact; it is also a political organization."[6]

The challenge for a generation of ambitious political scientists was to bring the city into a general theory of democratic politics.[7] To Frederick C. Howe, "The city [had] grown more rapidly than social science," and it "is what it is because political thought has not kept pace with changing conditions" (1915: 6). The problems of industrial society—standard of living, equality of opportunity, uplifting life—not only presented themselves in the city, but were, according to Howe (1905: 302), "almost all municipal matters." By 1933, as we shall see, these problems would be understood as national problems. This mobility of political perception is part of my subject here, but first we must establish the movement from the nation to the city at the turn of the century.

"While our attention has been fixed upon the national state," observed Delos F. Wilcox, "the theory and practice of local government have been partially neglected" (1897: 3). Wilcox, a recent Ph.D. in political science, urged younger students to follow him into the study of cities. "The student who aspires to be a scholar can devote himself to no richer or inspiring field than the modern city, its government, its institutions, and its tendencies" (ibid.: vii). At this period in American history, he assured his readers, no other area of specialization was of so great importance, for "it is here that the reconstruction of political practice and of social institutions goes on most rapidly" (ibid.: 235). A writer in *The Nation* had recognized this shift in attention two years earlier: "Perhaps there never was time when a deeper interest was felt in the government of cities."[8]

At the heart of a new, activist political science was an aspiration to revitalize a democratic public that had been diminished, especially in cities, by monopoly and privilege.[9] Such a public, reformers believed, would detach power from wealth and empower the people.[10] Cities and the essential character of city life seemed to constitute a challenge to the premises of the laissez-faire market celebrated by the regnant political economy of the Gilded Age. Cities were collective in spirit and in experience. Thus they might be the staging ground for mounting a collectivist challenge to exces-

6. See also Goodnow and Bates [1909] 1919: 3.

7. See Wilcox 1897: 12.

8. Review of Frank J. Goodnow's *Home Rule*, in *The Nation* 61 (31 October 1895), 316.

9. See Wiebe 1995: pt. 2.

10. A generation of sensitivity to elite strategies of social control has made historians insensitive to the intensity of Progressive faith in a revitalized and empowered public. Some worried about empowering immigrants, but in the end there was remarkable faith in an empowered urban citizenry. The strongest arguments are in Howe, but see also Mattson 1997.

sive individualism. The "formless" capitalist development of the city, argues Daniel Rodgers, encouraged the development of a countervailing urban political consciousness. The practical work of municipal administration in fact had an ideological dimension. When cities assumed the tasks of providing the modern array of municipal services, it represented a "recognition of the *de facto* collectivity of city life." The municipalization of transportation or utilities, for example, meant a diminution of the exclusive domain of the market, replacing private supply with public provision.[11]

It was a commonplace among reformers that "if socialism ever comes, it will come by way of the city" (Wilcox 1897: 238). Charles Beard (1912a: 28–29) in the first college-level textbook on urban politics, argued that "collectivist" responses to the implications of the industrial revolution were being developed first and mainly in the cities. In cities, he pointed out, one could observe a cross-class confluence of political interests pointing to collectivist approaches: working-class organization was taking form in trade unions while there was mounting bourgeois support for municipal services.[12] In *The Modern City*, Frederick C. Howe (1915: 367) claimed that in the city Americans were overcoming "the laissez faire and are acquiring a belief in democracy." The city, he insisted, reveals this "new point of view even more markedly than does the nation."

This new generation of political scientists challenged the philosophic idealism and formalism of the discipline's founding generation.[13] In the city these political scientists and other social scientists found a locale of engagement where theory and practice would be brought closer together in new ways. The city provided a means of rethinking the political in a nonformalist, more pragmatic way, moving from the formal and abstract concept of the state to political experience.[14] Both the language of the state and the language of class were partially displaced by a language of place or, more precisely, relations in space. It was in the particularity of place that the various interests of society converged, and the task of modern political life was to imagine and construct a cooperative relation among these interests.[15]

However, this strategy for reform and professional development posed for political scientists a particular and quite difficult theoretical problem. The object of inquiry that defined the discipline was the state, the supreme

11. See the forthcoming study by Rodgers, chap. 4.

12. See also Wilcox 1906: 13–14.

13. See Rodgers 1987: chaps. 5–6, and Kloppenberg 1986.

14. Charles Beard was a leader in theorizing and practicing this new political science. See his *Politics*, and the introduction to his classic, *An Economic Interpretation of the Constitution*. For a broader discussion of Beard and the city, see Bender 1993: chap. 6.

15. See Wilcox 1906: 7–14.

political entity, not the city. There was no category of urban politics in American political theory nor, consequently, any concept of urban citizenship. Law was no more helpful. The city has no constitutional standing in the American state. The word *city* does not appear in the Constitution, and American municipal law in the late nineteenth century was controlled by the authoritative Dillon Rule, enunciated by Justice John F. Dillon of the Iowa Supreme Court in *City of Clinton v. The Cedar Rapids and Missouri River Railroad* (1868).[16] His long-standing and universally endorsed interpretation insisted that the city was not a political entity. Rather it was merely an administrative agency with strictly enumerated powers. The timing of this formulation and of the general embrace of it by legal and political elites is explained by a profound fear of urban political mobilization. Under the Dillon Rule, cities, which had always been objects of suspicion in the American political tradition, were to be denied political standing, even disenfranchised.[17] But the target in fact was more specific: it was the specter of the voting power of the urban masses. Political and economic elites, having witnessed the depredations of the Tweed ring, blurred the mob and the increasingly organized working classes of cities. They feared that these irresponsible classes might initiate a regime of excessive sending and redistributive taxation of the rich.[18] By denying the political character of the city, the Dillon Rule delegitimated urban political movements and limited the power of cities to do damage—and good.

Thus the first order of business for political scientists was to redefine the status of the city, giving it a political character. They did this by associating themselves with a contemporary urban political movement for "home rule," a demand that state legislatures stop passing special legislation interfering with the cities and that state constitutions give cities the powers necessary to make policy in those areas that are distinctively local and characteristic of such concentrated settlement. There is, therefore, an interesting confluence of the theoretical, the professional, and the political, all pointing toward an expansion of the possibilities of urban citizenship. For political scientists and for urban activists, some of whom were the same individuals, achieving home rule created a domain of the political that was essential both for their own work and to make city dwellers into citizens. Intellectuals and cities thus needed each other at this moment.

American historiography has been too complacent about the question of

16. *Iowa Law Review* 455 (1868). The "rule" became part of standard American jurisprudence largely through Dillon's *Municipal Corporations* (many editions, cite one).
17. For cities in American political culture, see Bender 1992.
18. For a good account of the Dillon rule, see Grumm and Murphy 1974: 120–32.

citizenship. Historians have assumed that the state-by-state enactment of white male suffrage in the 1820s settled the question of citizenship and set the terms for future American politics.[19] Alan Dawley (1976) goes so far as to lament that the ballot box was the coffin for American socialism. But, as David Quigley (1997) has recently demonstrated, the issue of suffrage and citizenship, even for white males, remained highly contested in northern cities in the third quarter of the nineteenth century, especially in New York City.

At midcentury, before the crisis of union, as Mary Ryan (1997: 128) has so ably demonstrated, there was an inclusive and robust democracy in the cities. Not only was participation widespread and active, Ryan's point, but urban leaders were also developing a strong sense of the capacity of government to undertake projects of urban development and social improvement, the most notable being the Croton Water System and Central Park in New York City. In fact, it was this confidence in positive government among urban elites that had initially helped define the ambitious program of postwar Reconstruction in the South.[20]

The Civil War and the postwar issue of suffrage for freedmen opened a wide-ranging public debate on suffrage and citizenship. Other exclusions were noted, most importantly women.[21] The former slaves were granted the vote, but almost immediately the North weakened in its resolve to provide national support for these rights newly won by the freedmen. Within a dozen years their suffrage and thus citizenship were severely compromised. This retreat from Reconstruction in the South had a complex relation to a fear of political mobilization in northern cities. Developments in the North, by producing fear of a state that might empower the lower classes, contributed to the federal abandonment of the freedmen with the ending of Reconstruction in 1877. The controversy over the political rights of the former slaves in the South in turn contributed to the worries about urban democracy in the north.[22]

As early as 1868, however, these urban elites were becoming uneasy about positive government. Conflict in the South over suffrage and work for the freedmen as well as political controversy in the North, including working-class agitation for the eight-hour day, the demands by women for the vote, and the activities of the Tweed ring in New York, made the metropolitan gentry increasingly uncomfortable about an expansive urban democracy. Many agreed with Francis Parkman (1878), the great historian,

19. On this development, see Williamson 1960.
20. See Bender 1987: 184.
21. Besides Quigley 1997, see Foner 1988, Shklar 1991, and Smith 1997.
22. See Bender 1987: 184–91.

who wrote in the *North American Review* that universal suffrage had been a failure.[23] Samuel Bowles (1878), editor of the *Springfield Republican* and perhaps the nation's most influential newspaper editor among the educated elite, openly worried that the Civil War and the growth of cities had seriously weakened the power of the state governments. That development was worrisome for Bowles and his readers because state, as opposed to city governments, were understood to be supportive of the Victorian values and political agenda of the middle classes. He proposed limiting suffrage in cities to those with a "responsible interest," by which he meant taxpayers. In addition, he strongly supported the creation of state commissions, such as had been developed in New York at the end of the war, to establish state control of certain municipal functions, including police and health.

The attack on urban citizenship in the 1870s pursued two related lines. The first was to challenge universal suffrage, arguing that democracy did not necessarily imply the vote. It was also argued that the city was a corporation, and only those with an interest (stockholder or taxpayer) ought to have a vote. In New York in 1876, the Tilden Commission actually proposed a state constitutional revision that would have disenfranchised the working classes in New York City. Constitutional revision in New York required a vote by two consecutive legislatures, which allowed for a legislative campaign focused on urban citizenship. In an intensely fought campaign, voters elected a legislature that would not re-pass the measure, and it failed. But in proposing to empower only taxpayers and property owners it was a powerful challenge to the idea of urban citizenship.[24]

The second approach to disempowering democracy involved a rejection of the idea of positive government. Even if the masses retained the vote, they should know that government was limited. Such was the context for elite celebration of the idea of laissez-faire. There is a fit between the dominance of laissez-faire principles at the national level and the Dillon Rule on the local level.

With the political character and autonomy of cities denied, legislatures routinely passed special legislation affecting cities, often motivated by partisan politics at the state level. More often than not, state legislation imposed obligations on cities for which no state funding was supplied. Furthermore, state commissions were created to administer vital city services. All of this undermined any notion of urban citizenship.

In the minds of the elites who created this regime, such denial of politi-

---

23. Note also that Thomas Carlyle, in an essay that had prompted Walt Whitman to write his "Democratic Vistas" (1871), had earlier pronounced universal suffrage in America a failure.
24. See Quigley 1997.

cal standing to the city and its citizens was a means of limiting damage. By the 1890s, however, it was recognized as limiting in another way. It prevented cities from undertaking the development and effective management of vital municipal functions. Home rule became a rallying cry that united urban populations; the need for political authority was great enough to produce a cross-class collaboration.[25] The state legislatures had become so irresponsible in their treatment of cities that the bourgeoisie no longer found security in the disempowerment of cities. More important yet: the city, where the impact of industrial capitalism was most graphically evident, was increasingly understood to be the proper point of political response or intervention. The manifest needs of urban populations prompted the invention of a social politics.

Life in cities, Howe argued, "is creating a new moral sense, a new conception of the obligations of political life, obligations which, in earlier conditions of society did not and could not exist" (1905: 27–28). The social needs of cities has forced the democratic polity "into activities which have heretofore lain outside of the sphere of government" (ibid.: 30). Here in the city, he prophesized "the industrial issues" that are "becoming dominant in political life will first be worked out" (ibid.: 7). The city, reformers believed, was the place to face and address modern industrial conditions, not the national state, where the laissez-faire ideology seemed unassailable.

When Frederick C. Howe entered graduate school at Johns Hopkins in 1890, the lectures of Albert Shaw—the political scientist, journalist, and social activist—captured his imagination. Unlike so much of the subject matter of the political science he was being taught, which was formal and abstract, Shaw made cities concrete, material, a part of daily experience. One could grasp the relations of society and politics in the city.[26] Here he could think himself into politics, his original intention in going to Hopkins. The city, he concluded, "was the place we had to begin" (1925: 236).

He was not alone. In the 1890s Frank Goodnow, professor of political science and administrative law at Columbia University, turned to the problem of home rule, and he brought some of his best graduate students with him into the field, including Delos F. Wilcox and Charles A. Beard, whose dissertation was on medieval English municipal law. Woodrow Wilson, whose lectures on state administration Howe attended at Johns Hopkins, was already beginning to rethink the topic from the point of view of cities, and in 1896 he delivered a series of lectures at Johns Hopkins on municipal

25. There was still some middle-class fear of fiscal irresponsibility by nontaxpaying voters, but they felt that various mechanisms of review at the state level could prevent such abuse.
26. See Howe 1925: 5–6.

politics that were open to the public and were widely reported in the local press.[27] For this generation, the city, as Howe put it, was to be "the arena where the social and political forces that are coming to the fore will play" (1905: 23).

By the 1890s the new position and role of the city in American political theory had changed so much that E. L. Godkin, a member of the Tilden Commission in 1876 and spokesman for taxpayer suffrage, became an advocate of home rule and urban democracy. The founding editor of *The Nation* magazine and editor of the staid *Evening Post*, Godkin was a powerful political voice for the educated classes of America. He decided that hostility to the city—and a futile hope that somehow the city would simply go away—had produced undue fear of urban democracy and a distorted urban politics. The modern city, he now recognized, was unlike any previous cities. Cities would be central to society, not peripheral, and in this new era in the history of cities there were no natural limits to their growth. The modern city was global in its reach. "The introduction of steam and electricity," he reflected, enabled them to draw people and resources from "the uttermost ends of the earth" (1894: 877, 878–79). What can one do? "Make the government of cities as good as possible, to meet it as the most solemn, the most difficult, but also the most imperative of all the political duties which our age imposes on modern man." For the conservative Godkin (1897: 633), as well as for the radical Howe, the challenge of modern democracy had become the transformation of the urban dweller into the citizen and the acceptance of the authority of urban majorities to address the "many wants peculiar to such large collections [of people]."[28]

The theoretical work of creating an urban polity fell mainly to Frank Goodnow. In a series of influential books and articles, he proposed "delimiting a sphere" for municipal politics. In this sphere, there would be local autonomy and freedom from legislative interference. This approach, he argued, recognized the undeniable presence of local political facts, and it empowered urban citizens to act politically for the "satisfaction of local needs."[29]

It was a theoretical claim of significant public importance. "The determination of the proper position of the city," he explained, "is of much more than mere academic interest" (1911: 24). It made a difference whether the city is understood as only a "business corporation, as so many have said that it is," for if it is, then "it should be governed in accordance with

27. For Wilson's notes of 1890, see Link 1969: 484–521.
28. See Howe 1905: 47.
29. Among his many works, those dealing with the question of an urban polity are Goodnow 1895a, 1895b, 1897, 1906, [1904] 1910, and [1897] 1911, and Goodnow and Bates [1909] 1919.

the principle of business. If, on the other hand, it is a governmental organ, it should be governed in accordance with the principles of government." He acknowledged that cities were in some sense both "politic and corporate," but he insisted that they are "more politic than they are corporate" ([1897] 1911: 25). Historically, the city, even after its subordination to the state, had been more than a mere agent. It "became as well an organ for the satisfaction of local needs, needs which while quite distinct from the general governmental needs of the country were still of a social and governmental, and not of a mere business character." He thus rejected the major theoretical argument offered by propertied elites against urban citizenship. By the 1920s Goodnow's definition of municipal government had established space for a degree of home rule for American cities, without completely displacing the Dillon Rule.[30] Citizens formed an urban polity, even if it was limited in its sphere of operation.

Goodnow proposed following the European model of municipal government, where cities were recognized as "political corporations" (1897: 699), subject to supervision by a central state administration. This approach, he believed, would end the evil of legislative interference with municipalities. In his theoretical framework, central administrative supervision implied that the work of cities was local administration on the basis of local interests and conditions. It is easy to miss the political empowerment embedded in this formulation. Some commentators, with a later understanding of administration as a form of bureaucratic authority guided by expertise rather than by the incorporation of political interests, have misread Goodnow. From their point of view, the word *administrative* suggests a depoliticizing of the city and turning cities over to bureaucratic experts.[31] Such a view, as Michael Frisch (1982) explained long ago, seriously distorts Goodnow's theory, even though it does predict later developments.[32] In his own time, however, he legitimated the city as a political entity.

Goodnow's ([1904] 1910: 35–36) perspective was historical. Much like the historical economists who stressed particular historical conditions rather than relying on the a priori and formal argumentative style of the

---

30. See Teaford 1981.

31. Contemporary with Goodnow, there were early proposals for such expertise in cities, and this became the dominant pattern in American cities after World War I. For an early proposal of this sort, see Eliot 1891. For a later one, see Merriam 1925.

32. Frisch (1982) argues persuasively that it was not his intention to depoliticize the administration of cities. Admitting that point, it remains likely that theory he developed may well have enabled developments that reduced political authority and increased the authority of functional state bureaucracies over cities. On later developments, see Grumm and Murphy 1974: 130–31 and Teaford 1981.

proponents of laissez-faire, Goodnow rejected general rules or any a priori specification of the place of the city in American jurisprudence. He insisted that each city must be understood in its historical circumstance. What local needs to be satisfied can be identified? What political authority is required? Over time, and from place to place, answers may differ. The historical approach, again following the economists, had two advantages: first, it lowered the ideological temperature, and, second, it provided a permanent need for political scientists able to make such determinations. Here, again, we see how new, antiformalist methods in the social sciences invited an urban focus. A new intellectual agenda and professional ambition were both served by the idea of continuous engagement and of the play between theory and practice. Professional interests and the interests of urban citizenship met in this historical conjuncture.

Goodnow, often following the arguments of his colleague, the sociologist Franklin Giddings, held a dim view of the capacity of ethnic and racial minorities. He was skeptical of their capacities as citizens, and this was one reason he strongly supported the notion of a limited sphere of municipal power. "Municipal home rule without limitations," he wrote, "has no place in correct theory" (Goodnow and Bates [1909] 1919: 109). Yet in the end, he declined to challenge universal suffrage in cities. And he observed that more "local autonomy" will prompt "a healthy sense of responsibility" (1895a: 9).

Woodrow Wilson, who was more democratic than Goodnow, had an even stronger sense of how the city provided a way for political scientists and American citizens to think themselves into politics and to act politically. In extensive "Notes on Administration," written in 1890, Wilson explored the relation of administration to democracy. He had previously studied and written about this theme from the perspective of the national state, but now he assumed a municipal point of view.[33]

"The modern industrial city," Wilson (Link 1969: 487–88) believed, posed new problems for government and administration, yet it also presented new possibilities for political theory. The "industrial city," in its "recent and rapid growth," had "outstripped . . . the hitherto possible speed of political development." The theorist of modern democracy must turn, therefore, to the city, and Wilson did, addressing the problem of urban politics with a strong commitment to redistributing political power. The "leading classes," as Wilson called them, ruled in their own interest. They would provide police, but they would not support needed sanitary services and education, and they would routinely corrupt the process of

33. These extensive notes are found in Link 1969: 484–521.

urban development. Only if the whole citizenry were empowered would justice and democracy be realized under modern, industrial conditions. Social justice was to be achieved through politics, and home rule was the means of making that politics possible.

Wilson took as his task the legitimation of a participatory urban democracy. "The selfish interests of the wealthy city classes cannot be relied upon to promote the delicate and difficult tasks which come from the masses of men economically dependent. The only wholesome power," Wilson argued, "is the general interest" (Link 1969: 490). How might all classes be involved? By creating a sense of urban citizenship. The political scientist must establish that a city is a "body politic" with important functions. Like Goodnow, Wilson insisted that while the city is an organ of the state, it has local political responsibilities and powers.

The Tilden Commission was sharply criticized by Wilson; its proposals made sense, he said, only if "real estate administration is admitted as the basis of municipal function" (Link 1969: 499–501). But in fact the city is a polity, not a public works corporation. Its political structure must, therefore, represent the totality of the population. "A city is not a group of localities, nor an aggregation of interests, nor an improving (public works) corporation, but an organism, whole and vital only when whole and conscious of its wholeness and identity" (ibid.: 492).

He had great ambition for the city. In time, the work of supplying municipal services, which he construed rather widely to include most of what later would be called the work of the welfare state, would, he thought, yield a modern theory of political administration. In contrast to the medieval city, which he defined as a "locality of trades," granting to "liberty" to conduct trade there, the modern city demanded civic responsibility. The spirit of its constitution would be the political determination of collective "duties" (Link 1969: 499). If the city were responsible for "more important, far-reaching and conspicuous functions" under a regime of home rule, a more vital and responsible public would be formed. Such, for Wilson, was the value of home rule and of the municipalization of gas, transit, and charity. How "they are managed affects the whole community" and might nourish a collectivist ethic (ibid.: 450).[34]

Clearly pointing toward the development of a social politics—or in our more recent terminology a welfare state—Wilson argued that the modern city ought to make itself "a humane economic society." The municipality, in Wilson's view, was an "ordinance-making body," meaning an admin-

---

34. Howe makes the same point: "Municipal ownership will create a public sense, a social conscience, a belief in the city and an interest in it" (1905: 123).

istrative body dealing with all classes of the city, ensuring health, safety, education, and aid to those in distress. This vision of democratic administration wedded local need and pragmatic social science. Such municipal administration as Wilson proposed was antiformal and empirical, giving it a pragmatic quality that was for Wilson, as it would later be for Dewey, inherently democratic.[35] "An ordinance lies closer to facts, to practical conditions and details than does law. Its test is its feasibility as shown by direct-experiment." And these policies should "be determined by the representative general voice" (Link 1970: 450, 470). The city thus becomes a laboratory for modern democracy. Wilson, like F. C. Howe, and unlike Goodnow and Beard, had no hesitation about empowering urban immigrants and the lower classes. In a public lecture in Baltimore, he offered the case of Princeton, where, he said, the "management of affairs" by the "poorer classes—mostly Irish and Negroes—has resulted in a better condition of things than if it had been left to the educated classes" (Link 1970: 471).[36]

My point, however, is not specifically the democratic qualities of Goodnow or Wilson. It is rather the way in which they gave political legitimacy to the city, and the way Wilson, Howe, and Wilcox, especially, used the city as a point of political engagement as intellectuals and activists seeking to deal with the social implications of industrial capitalism.

Here two points need to be emphasized. The first is how the political scientists establish the primacy of the language of politics (as opposed to economics or sociology) as the means of addressing the challenge of modernity. The second is their faith that societal problems are best addressed in the city, that, as Wilcox put it, the city "is the center of the complex web of national life" (1906: 14). Contrary to the way American liberals have thought about social politics for most of this century, these early liberals are not asking the nation to rescue the city. They are in fact proposing just the opposite: the city can save the nation. That is the argument of Howe's *The City: The Hope of Democracy*, and it is the point Wilcox made in *The American City*, when he wrote: "The city must face and solve its own problem for its own sake and *for the nation*" (1906: 22; emphasis mine).

Goodnow ([1904] 1910: 106–7), historicist that he was, cautioned that the political standing he proposed for cities at the end of the nineteenth century may not be justified at other times. States eclipsed cities and subor-

---

35. For Dewey's most concise theorization of the relation of pragmatism to democracy, see his "Philosophy and Democracy," in Boydston 1982, 11: 41–53. See more broadly, Westbrook 1991.

36. Howe (1905: 2–3) is at least as strong in his affirmation of the political capacity of the poor and the immigrant.

dinated them in the eighteenth century. Citizenship became attached exclusively to the nation-state. At that time there was little social need for urban autonomy, according to Goodnow. Moreover, he argued that urban autonomy had tended historically to produce rule by oligarchies. The introduction of state power, Goodnow insisted, was welcomed by cities for advancing the democratic cause. In the nineteenth century, however, with the development of a new kind of society and economy, cities needed limited but real political authority. Goodnow devoted himself to theorizing and justifying that authority. But, he speculated, in time—and perhaps sooner than one might realize—the urbanization of society would no doubt make those issues presently identified with the city into national issues. When that happened, home rule would not be necessary, for there would be no distinctive political work for cities. At that point, should it come, the city would no longer be the focal point for democratic reform of industrial society, nor would it be a place and a concept for thinking oneself into politics and acting politically.

Though Charles Beard was the author of the first college textbook in the field of urban politics, he never granted the city the elevated position that Wilson had given it in the 1890s and that Wilcox and Howe continued to give it at least through World War I. One striking quality of Beard's career as a scholar and activist was his continual shift between the nation and the city as the locale for political inquiry and action. Indeed, he felt compelled to note his different "point of view" in the preface to *American City Government* (1912a: ix). "The position is here taken that, strictly speaking, there can be no such thing as 'municipal science,' because the most fundamental concerns of the cities, the underlying economic foundations, are primarily matters of state and national, not local, control." It is fitting, I suppose, that Beard's (1912b and 1913) next two books addressed the national government, particularly the Constitution, conservative readings of which had allowed the courts to strike down so much progressive legislation. Although Beard continued his urban activism—working three afternoons a week at the Bureau of Municipal Research in New York—by the time of World War I, Beard was convinced that the future of social politics was to be at the national level.

By the 1930s the city had dropped out of the center of social politics. It no longer provided a way to grasp the politics of modern industrial society. The New Deal did not recognize the city as focal point for policy, even if its various policies directed toward labor, families with dependent children, housing, unemployment, occupational safety, and social security, among others, were vastly and intentionally helpful to urban dwellers.

The shift from an urban perspective for social politics had been announced as early as 1909, with Herbert Croly's publication of his immensely influential book, *The Promise of American Life*. Interestingly, like Beard, Croly's reputation before 1909 was that of an insightful commentator on cities and editor of *Architectural Record*.[37] One enters a different world of reform thought with Croly's *The Promise of American Life*. He explicitly rejected Howe's vision of the city as the hope of democracy. He instead assumed as his task to be the articulation or rearticulation of the connection between democracy and nationalism. The issue to be addressed, as Croly (1909) phrased it in the title of the final chapter, was "the individual and the national purpose." Not the city but the nation was now to be the focus of political identity and engagement for Croly and for the *New Republic*, of which he was the founding editor in 1914.[38]

The *Promise of American Life* pointed to and inspired the "New Nationalism" of Theodore Roosevelt. In this context it pointed to Wilson as well. Wilson had returned to his earlier nationalism. He never published his work on cities, and he himself moved from municipal concerns, to the governorship of New Jersey, to the presidency. More generally, as Allan Davis (1967) has shown, Jane Addams and other social progressives addressing the implications of industrial society shifted their political focus from the city to the nation after World War I.[39] And as Nancy Weiss (1974) has shown, the National Urban League, which had been urban-based and urban-focused, reorganized itself in 1918 as a national organization with a national program for advancing the interests of African Americans. Another index of this shift reveals itself in the pages of *The Political Science Quarterly*. From 1887 to 1910, rarely was there an issue without at least one article on the city. Over the next twenty years few articles appeared, and there were even fewer in the decade of the 1930s.[40] The address of citizenship in modern, industrial society, whether one refers to disciplinary agenda of political scientists or the location of political action, had shifted from the city to the nation. Of course, urban thinking continued in the social sciences, but politics was reduced to city planning and administration, largely under the aegis of Charles Merriam at Chicago. Even the sociologists at Chicago, noted as they have been for the remarkable school of urban studies they created, largely avoided the political, especially after World War I, when, following Robert Park, they turned to ecological mod-

37. See especially Croly 1905.

38. For the specific reference to Howe's phrase, see Croly 1909: 349.

39. The nationalizing impact of World War I has been noted by historians, but its role in this shift seems likely to have been quite important and worth exploration. See the interesting essay of Leuchtenburg 1964.

40. This is based on a survey of the journal by John Baick.

els and local ethnographies, mapping neighborhoods and real estate markets or describing urban types. Such social science was not a site for democratic discourse or for thinking oneself into politics.

Today one looks in vain in the *Political Science Quarterly* or *The American Political Science Review* for an article dealing with the city.[41] Yet there may now be reasons for a revival of the city as a focal point for a discourse on citizenship and democracy. There is much that is reminiscent of the conditions that prompted such a discussion a century ago.

Both economics and political science then and now were and are trapped in a formalistic mode of analysis that discourages interest in and in fact offers little capacity to address the circumstantial facts of time, place, or culture. Both have been focused on the national unit—whether in gathering economic statistics or in examining the state and its constituents—at a time when the hold of the state on the political imagination and as the primary structure of social, economic, and cultural processes is being questioned and even doubted. Most important of all, a laissez-faire political economy is producing a dramatic transformation of metropolitan areas—a massive influx of immigrants from a variety of global diasporas, both very rich and, more numerously, very poor; serious levels of inequality; unprecedented (and utterly unplanned and formless) physical extension of the urban areas; a dissolution of public culture; and evident municipal incapacity.

There is a strong awareness, by academics and the public, that the economic structure of modern society is being transformed—*and* that the spatial relations of everyday life are being radically altered. The implications for the nation-state are not clear, but it is generally anticipated that they will be significant. Likewise, the future of cities is difficult to predict. At first it seemed that the importance of place would be diminished to the vanishing point by cyberspace and a placeless global economy and culture. Such expectations do not, however, seem to be borne out. The persistence of place in our global age has been striking. Cities may even be advancing at the expense of nations. Most striking—and like the circumstance in the 1890s—the social impact of global change is most evident in metropolitan areas. Here one witnesses the manifestations of contemporary modernity. Might the city—in its metropolitan form, acknowledging its embeddedness in structures larger than itself—again be the place and means for

41. John Baick, a graduate student at New York University's history department, examined both journals from their founding to the present, and this statement is based on that survey. The city is especially invisible in recent issues of the APSR, with only six articles on American cities and seven on any city since 1986, representing 1 percent of the articles over that period.

thinking oneself into politics and acting politically in the social circumstances of our time?

The centrality of metropolitan/regional areas in contemporary economic development has been brilliantly proposed by Jane Jacobs (1984), in her fascinating book, *Cities and the Wealth of Nations*, and more recently the widely read economist Paul Krugman (1993a, 1993b, 1995, and 1991) has begun to argue from a geographical perspective the importance of cities and regions. This new thinking about cities and economies has gotten wide distribution and elaboration in a supplement on cities in the *Economist*.[42]

Is political consciousness moving in the same direction? Might it be expected to do so? There is some evidence pointing in this direction. Geographer Peter J. Taylor has argued that "cities are replacing states in the construction of social identities" (1995: 58). This development, if accurately identified, alters a pattern of more than two centuries. The great deflation of the political character of cities in the eighteenth century was linked to the creation of a modern, national citizenship. Since then citizens have had primary, even exclusive loyalty to the state, not the city. Social identity and political identity are not exactly the same thing, but the former is the foundation for the latter, and Taylor points out that immigrants to London today do not understand themselves to be English or even British, but rather to be "Londoners" (ibid.). The same pattern of identity formation may be occurring in other global cities—and more and more cities are becoming aware of their having a global dimension.

Understanding globalism as an aspect and not the totality of contemporary metropolitan life brings me to my last point. Our situation is not so different than it had been in 1890, and that recognition suggests to me the continuing vitality of turning to the city as a way of thinking oneself into the politics of contemporary social life. Those who lived through the 1890s described their era's transformation much as we describe ours. They had not coined the term *globalization*, but it seemed much like globalization to the writers I have discussed. They were intensely aware of a dramatic revolution in technologies of communication. The movement of capital was global, as was the movement of peoples. And anyone who could travel would witness the internationalization of Western urban culture, from principles of urban design to architecture to the manifestations of commercial culture—the same domains in which cultural globalization reveals itself most powerfully today.

Aware of these developments, Delos F. Wilcox in 1906 asked some of the questions we are asking ourselves, and I think we would do well to listen

---

42. "Cities," *Economist* (29 July 1995): survey supplement, 1–18.

closely to him. "The vast expansion of the facilities for transmitting intelligence and goods," he observed, "has seemed of late to be breaking down the barriers of space and diminishing its significance. . . . We think that, space being annihilated, we need no rooms and so will live all in one place" (1906: 201). Wilcox challenged that logic. "Locality," he insisted, "persistently reasserts itself, and the faster distance is abolished the more rapidly the price of standing room rises." This observation, based on the remarkable burst of skyscraper development in lower Manhattan between 1895 and 1905, resonates with the Manhattan experience in the 1980s.

Wilcox would not deny, nor would we, that "for industrial society, in considerable degree, distance has been annihilated and space overcome" (1906: 200, 206, 226–27). But his special insight—and one worthy of our consideration today—is that "industrial society and political society are organized on radically different principles. . . . For political society . . . place and territorial limits are fundamental." Citizens experience industrial society in a particular place, and, more important, people become citizens in a place. "It is in this primitive relation to land and locality that citizenship largely consists." The city, therefore, remains, even in an era of the global movement of goods, capital, people, and ideas, a place, perhaps the place, for thinking oneself into politics. The urban polity, Wilcox declared, "is the most emphatic protest of local interests against the organization of society without reference to place," and as he and the other urban Progressives always insisted, the interest of the city is a democratic social politics. For that reason, according to Wilcox, it is "upon the effectiveness of this protest [that] the life of democracy depends."

Metropolitan dwellers may well have to develop a new political language that "fits" the new social and spatial arrangement of their lives. That work will require an adequate language of metropolitan representation as well as a fuller sense of metropolitan political obligation. Social scientists have an opportunity, as did their predecessors, to contribute to the creation of these new understandings. Such work might again revitalize the disciplines by contact with the texture of local life and at the same time provide the basis for a political definition of the metropolitan citizenship that will, in turn, enable a political mobilization to address the most serious social and economic challenges of our time.

References

Beard, Charles A. 1912a. *American City Government*. New York: Century.
——. 1912b. *The Supreme Court and the Constitution*. New York: Macmillan.
——. 1913. *An Economic Interpretation of the Constitution*. New York: Macmillan.

Bender, Thomas. 1987. *New York Intellect*. New York: Knopf.

——. 1993. *Intellect and Public Life*. Baltimore: Johns Hopkins University Press.

Bowles, Samuel. 1878. "The Relation of City and State Governments." *Journal of Social Science* 9: 140–46.

Boydston, Jo Ann, ed. 1976–83. *The Middle Works of John Dewey, 1899–1914*, 14 vols. Carbondale: Southern Illinois University Press.

Croly, Herbert. 1905. "New York as the American Metropolis." *Architectural Record* 17: 137–39.

——. 1909. *The Promise of American Life*. New York: Macmillan.

Davis, Allan. 1967. *Spearheads for Reform: The Social Settlements and the Progressive Movement, 1890–1914*. New York: Oxford University Press.

Dawley, Alan. 1976. *Class and Community: The Industrial Revolution in Lynn*. Cambridge: Harvard University Press.

Eliot, C. W. 1891. "One Remedy for Municipal Mismanagement." *The Forum* 12 (October): 153–58.

Foner, Eric. 1988. *Reconstruction*. New York: Harper.

Frisch, Michael H. 1982. "Urban Theorists, Urban Reform, and American Political Culture in the Progressive Period." *Political Science Quarterly* 97: 295–316.

Furner, Mary O. 1975. *Advocacy and Objectivity: A Crisis in the Professionalization of American Social Science, 1865–1905*. Lexington: University Press of Kentucky.

Glazer, Nathan. 1959. "The Rise of Social Research in Europe." In *The Human Meaning of the Social Sciences*, Daniel Lerner, ed. New York: Meridian.

Godkin, E. L. 1894. "The Problem of Municipal Government." *Annals of the American Academy of Political and Social Science* 4: 877.

——. 1897. "Peculiarities of American Municipal Government." *Atlantic Monthly* 80: 633.

Goodnow, Frank J. 1895a. "Municipal Home Rule." *Political Science Quarterly* 10: 1–21.

——. 1895b. *Municipal Home Rule: A Study in Administration*. New York: Macmillan.

——. 1897. "The Relation of City and State." *Municipal Affairs* 1: 689–704.

——. 1906. "Municipal Home Rule." *Political Science Quarterly* 21: 77–90.

——. [1904] 1910. *City Government in the United States*. New York: Century.

——. [1897] 1911. *Municipal Problems*. New York: Columbia University Press.

Goodnow, Frank J., and Frank G. Bates. [1909] 1919. *Municipal Government*. New York: Century.

Grumm, John G., and Russell D. Murphy. 1974. "Dillon's Rule Reconsidered." *Annals of the American Academy of Political and Social Science* 416: 120–32.

Haskell, Thomas L. 1977. *The Emergence of Professional Social Science*. Urbana: University of Illinois.

Howe, Frederick C. 1905. *The City: The Hope of Democracy*. New York: Scribners.

——. 1907. *The British City*. New York: Scribners.

——. 1915. *The Modern City and Its Problems*. New York: Scribners.

——. 1925. *The Confessions of a Reformer*. New York: Scribners.

Jacobs, Jane. 1984. *Cities and the Wealth of Nations*. New York: Random House.

Kloppenberg, James T. 1986. *Uncertain Victory: Social Democracy and Progressivism in European and American Thought, 1870–1920*. New York: Oxford University Press.

Krugman, Paul. 1991. *Geography and Trade*. Cambridge: MIT Press.

——. 1993a. "First Nature, Second Nature, and Metropolitan Location." *Journal of Regional Science* 33: 129–44.

——. 1993b. "On the Number and Location of Cities." *European Economic Review* 37: 293–98.

——. 1995. *Development, Geography, and Economic Theory*. Cambridge: MIT Press.

Leuchtenburg, William E. 1964. "The New Deal and the Analogue of War." In *Change and*

Continuity in Twentieth-Century America: The 1920s. John Braeman, Robert Bremner, and David Brody, eds. Columbus: Ohio State University Press.

Link, Arthur, ed. 1969. The Papers of Woodrow Wilson, vol. 6. Princeton: Princeton University Press.

——. 1970. The Papers of Woodrow Wilson, vol. 9. Princeton: Princeton University Press.

Mattson, Kevin. 1997. Creating a Democratic Public: The Struggle for Urban Participatory Democracy during the Progressive Era. University Park: Pennsylvania State University Press.

Merriam, Charles. 1925. "The Place of Politics, Civic Education, and Science in City Government." American City Magazine 32: 192–93.

Parkman, Francis. 1878. "The Failure of Universal Suffrage." North American Review 127.

Quigley, David. 1997. "Reconstructing Democracy: Politics and Ideas in New York City, 1865–1880." Ph.D. diss., New York University, New York.

Rodgers, Daniel. 1987. Contested Truths. New York: Basic Books.

——. 1998. Atlantic Crossings: Social Politics in a Progressive Age. Cambridge: Harvard University Press.

Ryan, Mary P. 1997. Civic Wars: Democracy and Public Life in the American City during the Nineteenth Century. Berkeley: University of California Press.

Shklar, Judith. 1991. American Citizenship. Cambridge: Harvard University Press.

Smith, Rogers M. 1997. Civic Ideals: Conflicting Visions of Citizenship in U.S. History. New Haven: Yale University Press.

Taylor, Peter J. 1995. "World Cities and Territorial State: The Rise and Fall of Their Mutuality." In World Cities in a World-System. Paul L. Knox and Peter J. Taylor, eds. Cambridge: Cambridge University Press.

Teaford, John C. 1981. "State Administrative Agencies and the Cities, 1890–1920." American Journal of Legal History 25: 225–48.

Weiss, Nancy. 1974. The National Urban League, 1910–1940. New York: Oxford University Press.

Westbrook, Robert. 1991. John Dewey and American Democracy. Ithaca: Cornell University Press.

Wiebe, Robert. 1995. Self-Rule: A Cultural History of American Democracy. Chicago: University of Chicago Press.

Wilcox, Delos F. 1897. The Study of City Government. New York: Macmillan.

——. 1906. The American City: A Problem in Democracy. New York: Macmillan.

Williamson, Chilton. 1960. American Suffrage: From Property to Democracy, 1760–1860. Princeton: Princeton University Press.

Urban Youth and Senegalese Politics: Dakar 1988–1994

Mamadou Diouf

The extraordinary vitality of African youth in the political arena—the high visibility achieved by their spectacular demonstrations—is perceived as signifying that African societies have broken with the authoritarian enterprises inaugurated by the nationalist ruling classes. Youth has played a crucial role in the configuration of nationalist coalitions,[1] even if it has subsequently been swept aside through the invocation of African traditions that uphold rules of deference and submission between both social and generational juniors and seniors. The young have also been the first group in society to have manifested, in practical and often violent ways, hostility toward the reconstituted nationalist movement.

The young have produced a precocious reading of the nationalist movement's evolution, identifying the authoritarian drift of the postcolonial powers whose neocolonial economic and political orientations they denounce. This awareness seems to have been the basis for youth's resistance to the repression, *encadrement*,[2] and co-optation through which the state

The author is grateful to Molly Roth for translating this essay from French.

1. On the nationalist coalitions, see Anyang'Nyong'o 1992.
2. Deriving from *cadre* (frame), *encadrement* combines implications of state control and sub-

handles social movements.[3] Logics of exclusion based on tradition, like those of the postcolony's treatment of the young, render public space as an adult territory off limits to youth at the same time that it denies them a private space. As Claude Lefort remarks apropos of totalitarianism—defined as a regime in which power is not the object of open contestation, that is, a regime in which public space is devoid of exchange[4]—"the effect of the identification of power with society is that society enjoys no autonomy by 'right,' it is contained within power as 'private space' " (Habib and Mouchard 1993).

The correspondence underlined here is accentuated in the African contexts where the subordination of the young is conceived as a traditional imperative. In this essay, I analyze the social movements, in particular those led by young people (high school and university students, unemployed youth, members of political parties) that violently shook the Senegalese political scene at the end of the 1980s and the beginning of the 1990s. During this period youth marked their territory, painting the city walls throughout Dakar and its suburbs with representations that fashioned, in however hesitant a manner, a new way of being, of living—and a new rhythm. Their practices expressed a will to break with the historic memory that accompanied the nationalist generation's rise to power at the end of World War II.[5] It is this memory whose expressions, however rhetorical, still furnish the guidelines for the political discourse of consensus and unanimity and for public displays like commemorations as the convocations of memory and independence parades as institutional celebrations of the army and youth.

The sudden appearance of youth in politics is not exclusive to Senegal. Almost every West African country has experienced strikes resulting in a lost academic year (*année blanche*);[6] the most recent case being Nigeria in

---

jugation with those of spatial circumscription. The term *encadrement* will be used, as it does not have an adequate English translation. Trans.

3. For the francophone situations, see the studies and accounts of the Fédération des Etudiants d'Afrique Noir en France (FEANF): Diane 1990; Dieng 1986; Traoré 1984. On Senegalese students, see Bathily 1992.

4. On the notions of public and private space in totalitarian systems, see Lefort 1983: 53–60. In "Identité et Métissage Politiques," Compte-Rendu de la Séance du 20 février 1991 (*Feuille d'Information No. 16 of Groupe de Travail Cartes d'Identité*), J.-L. Amselle confirms that a group cannot exist socially unless it is able to achieve accreditation, emerging on the public scene through the recourse to spokespeople or proxies, thus creating its own public space.

5. On this subject, see Diouf 1989: 14–24.

6. An *année blanche* is an academic year that has not been officially completed because of the inability to organize year-end examinations and competitions, owing to strikes and the resulting insufficiency of completed class hours. The consequence is a universal repetition of the school year.

1987–88. The recourse to violence, the symbolics of purification by fire, the destruction of the places and monuments of postcolonial munificence—as if to deterritorialize its inscription in space—constitute common elements of the social movements led principally by youth. The project of uprooting the ruling elite's postcolonial style of legitimating itself is legible in numerous developments: the riots orchestrated by Malian students (5 April 1993),[7] the absence, in districts of Lagos and certain Nigerian cities, of any authority on the part of administrators and politicians and their reliance on "area boys";[8] and the crucial role played by "disaffected youth" in the armed struggles in Liberia and Sierra Leone (Richards 1995).

The mise-en-scène and the models for these violent demonstrations seem to have been images of rioting in South African townships and the intifada uprising in Israeli-occupied Palestinian territories, widely diffused through audiovisual media, as well as Hollywood films such as *Rambo* and *Terminator*. Regarding the diffusion and consumption of this culture of the riot, P. Richards writes: "Television does not, in any simple or unproblematic way, transcribe reality. More plausibly, it should be seen as a medium that enhances the scope of human image-making within the range of consumption of a mass audience" (ibid.: 2). This youth is heterogeneous and its manifestations, like the ways it inscribes itself on the urban landscape, are plural. The city, as the scene of its actions, poses numerous problems that the young take into account as actors. Postcolonial urban sociology is dominated by a paradigm in which the rural peasantry is regarded as the fundamental expression of indigenous Africa. As a consequence, the city has long been thought of exclusively in terms of the colonial ethnology of detribalization, rural exodus, and the loss of authentically African traits and values.[9] Before World War II, it was assumed that urban dwellers were rootless; having left their tribal homeland, they were supposed to have lost their traditional reference systems, qualities, and virtues. Colonial and postcolonial literature portray cities as sites of corruption, of moral, sexual, and social deviance, and as sites in which Africans lose their souls and their sense of community. Africans appropriated this colonial

7. For the Malian situation, refer to Diarrah 1993.
8. On the "area boys" Abubakar Momoh writes, "The area boys as a social category become preponderant, popularized and organised from about 1986 when the Structural Adjustment Programme took its full course. Hence today, any form of crime or criminal activity in the entire South-Western Nigeria is identifiable or traceable to the area boys. The area boys are the equivalent of 'Yanbaba' in Hausaland, they are also called *allaayes*, *Omo oni ile* (sons of the soil or landlords), 'street urchins,' 'government pickin,' 'untouchables,' or 'alright sir'" (see Momoh 1993: 28).
9. Colonial novels and the urban sociology of the first two decades of independence are the best illustrations of this point of view. See Laye 1953 and Kane 1961.

representation in their statement that villagers are the "only" full-blooded "Africans" and village values the only authentic ones. The political hegemony of the rural world was reinforced by its demographic domination that, although progressively diminishing, survives in the ruling classes' regime of truth as the popular legitimation of their power. In view of the democratic, essentially urban-rooted contestation, and of the increased urban violence, they regard urban space as lacking both tradition and its logics of supervision and control.

In contrast to a highly legible rural territoriality, the city is a space of superimposed inscriptions and references that appeal to composite memories. The city asserts a cosmopolitan intermingling even as it organizes a geography of territories—simultaneously physical and identity-constituting spaces that continuously reconfigure allegiances, languages, and idioms. Urban territoriality defines itself in relation to a state geometry: the city is the seat of power, the terrain for expressing the imaginary of the ruling class and its ascendence. In this field, there are no possibilities other than confrontation and negotiation. The procedures employed are therefore those of circumvention and, more frequently, of feigned acquiescence and direct confrontation.

In view of the physical breakups and ideological fragmentation ensuing from the economic and political crises, African societies are experiencing major chasms through which new networks—economic, political, ethnic, women's, youth—are stealthily slipping through and enlarging their scope. These networks call for a variety of identity references such as locality, age, gender, common goals, and promotion of former school and university classmates. Their fluidity, flexibility, and often uncertain origin strongly affect social demands and political modes of intervention in the public and private spheres.

With the unity of the missionaries of modernity fizzling out, each of the segments appropriated a specific discourse. Thus, in addition to the physical decay of the space in which power is wielded and displayed is the fragmentation of the ruling social groups (government, unions, students, pupils, entrepreneurs). The reduced capacity of these groups to flaunt themselves and assert their dominance has thereby jeopardized the ability of the ruling class to reproduce itself. Thus the African crisis has paved the way for opening new spaces while promoting deep upheavals that could be briefly summed up as follows: several beliefs including those regarding the homogeneous nature of the urban world and the capacity of cities to construct a homogeneous culture against specificities are being challenged by the ongoing demographic changes. This is related to the demise of the "perception—heretofore unsuspected—of an elite with common interests and values by an urban population that felt that it was a strong minority vis-à-vis the mass of networks."[10]

Thus a new generation emerged on the African political scene, a generation that came into existence in the wake of the foundational event for African nations, namely, independence. A combination of factors led to the invention by this generation of its own sociability which expressed itself in communal and religious enterprises.[11] These factors included the fact that, in addition to holding on tightly to reconstructed traditions mixed up with values of a global world, this new generation felt excluded from the postcolonial munificence and its sites of sociability (e.g., recognition, the rights to free speech, work, and education), and although a numerical majority, as youth, they were reduced to political silence. This youth is actually behind political violence, which ranges from urban riots to Islamic fundamentalist armies, and is spearheading armed conflicts and criminal actions of random violence, looting, and student strikes; it uses violence to express its disillusionment with the outcome of the restoration of democratic rule.

Assessing the Social Conditions

Dakar and its suburb Pikine contain 19 percent of the total population of Senegal and close to 50 percent of the urban population.[12] Dakar accounts for 46 percent of this population, Pikine-Guédiawaye 42 percent, and Rufisque Bargny 12 percent. The Dakar metropolitan area is the principal destination for migrants. It was calculated in 1976 that 51 percent of 630,000 migrants took up residence in Dakar (Antoine et al. 1992: 118).

The selective character of access to property and housing, one of the principal vectors of socialization and means of social differentiation, indicates the precarious situation of the young. The same figures prompted a research team to remark that "the young are under the control [in the total care] of their elders" (ibid.: 75). High unemployment rates profoundly affect the youth of Dakar and reinforce their status as dependents. Newspapers not controlled by the government daily portray a state incapable of assuring a decent quality of life and education for its students or offering them work. The figures published by Le Témoin are a case in point: 100,000 young people enter the job market every year and 4,000 among them have

---

10. OECD/ADB 1994: 6. In terms of the analysis of demographic issues, I benefited from being involved with the CINERGIE/CLUB SAHEL team, which conducted the WALTPS surveys.

11. See Kane 1990: 7–23; Marshall 1993; Otayek 1993; and Brenner 1993.

12. The data used in this chapter are drawn from the IFAN/ORSTROM team (Antoine et al.) 1992; Bocquier 1991; and Sènègal Ministère 1988.

advanced degrees (*Le Témoin* 134: 3). According to Bocquier, 45.2 percent of the employed population of Dakar are younger than thirty years old (Bocquier 1991: 55). This group includes only 15.6 percent apprentices in enterprises in the unregistered sector. He specifies that the unemployed who have never worked are clearly the youngest: 80.8 percent were younger than thirty.

Two component groups of Dakar area youth are markedly distinct. The members of one have been labeled social marginals (*encombrements humains*) by the official ideology.[13] This notion evokes social maladaptation, economic marginalization, and deviance. These social declassés by the regime's standards are equally products of the rural exodus, rejects from the school system, traveling merchants, and beggars. According to a clerk of the Dakar Tribunal,

> minors between 12 and 20 years are found every week of the calendar in the "lockup" for the most varied infractions. Some fist-fight or steal in the markets. Others, girls between 14 and 16 years, are "picked up" along the public thoroughfares. Still others are dedicated to itinerant begging on behalf of charlatan marabouts. Virtually all rural youth without qualifications who "come up" to the capital live in the poorer districts and congregate around the port, the markets, and the stations. (*Le Soleil* 1990: 18)

It is this population in particular that yields those labeled, on the one hand, as vandals and bullies by the militants of the reigning Parti Socialiste (PS) and, on the other, as thugs and mercenaries by the opposition in the wake of demonstrations or punitive expeditions by the PS.

The second group—school-leavers from the high schools, colleges, and universities—is better understood because of the large number of studies devoted to it.[14] The unemployed who have never worked are better educated than the actively employed; this category has more women than men (Antoine et al. 1992: 122). Since 1980, this situation has been aggravated by a generalized crisis of the school and university systems. A. Sylla observes: "A review of the state of the schools in 1990, with the diverse difficulties and problems they have had for a decade—the numerous protest movements and strikes that led to an *année blanche* in 1987–88—makes their future appear quite uncertain, particularly if the causes of distortion and dysfunction are not thoroughly eradicated" (1992: 379).

The consequences of this disastrous situation have been a fierce instructors' strike and a radicalization of the student movement, with a consider-

13. *Encombrements humains*, literally "social obstructions or clutter": see Collignon 1984.
14. See Bathily, Diouf, and Mbodj 1995, and Diop 1992: 431–77.

able increase in the number of university graduates out of work. The defeat of an operation by unemployed holders of master's degrees and the rising failure rate of students, and of unemployed university graduates, usher in new forms of struggle and new groups, for example, the movements of young members of Muslim religious brotherhoods, in the school and university milieux.

These two categories of Dakar area youth—students and social marginals—have always been a central preoccupation of the Senegalese state apparatus and the class that runs it. Since 1966, the Economic and Social Council has considered that the essential problem of the urban youth—whether an intellectual or a manual laborer, employed or unemployed—is that of his social equilibrium (Conseil Economique 1966).

The Senegalese state uses two logics associated with co-optation—repression and *encadrement*—and has consistently attempted to design solutions that integrate the young into the social hierarchy by institutional means, whether political, economic, and/or legal. These strategies have evolved over the years in the attempt to adapt themselves to the plural and multifaceted procedures adopted by the young.

Political Framing versus Mass Movements

There is extensive evidence that shows that the Senegalese state's handling of the youth question has been guided by a vision that, while being tied to the real, emerges more from the repertories of the imaginary and the ideological. Youth and the young are a key theme in the discursive project of nationalist ideology. Although the ideology itself is out of style, it still informs the Senegalese regime's interventions in the management of youth. It is based on the political harnessing of the "vital forces of the nation" and on traditional social values. The ideology of political framing and the extension of the state's domain provide the key references for political, economic, and social activity. This ideology blurs the distinction between the state and the holders of power, on the one hand, and the masses, on the other. It rests on the manipulation of traditions of submission to authority and to elders, thus circumscribing a social and political space from which youth is radically excluded. The monocentric orientation of power and the institutionalization of the de facto single party inspire the creation of public youth organizations.

These organizations are particularly directed at high school and university students and the more or less educated urban young. They have not enjoyed great success. The anti-imperialist trade union organizations were always capable of subverting spectacular demonstrations by the movements affiliated with power. Attempts at political institutionalization were designed to draw youth close to the party in power, and relied heavily on the Ministry of Youth and Sports with its exclusive preoccupation with advanced athletic competition and football (soccer). The failure of these attempts led to an intensification of oblique practices and militancy by the opposition parties, the majority of which were clandestine until political reforms in 1981, which removed restrictions on both the number and ideology of political parties and established integral multipartyism. It is at this stage that student organizations took up the task of spreading the messages of leftist groups, notably Marxists. This same alliance was the beginning of the fragmentation of the student organizations themselves, in the image of the political left, from which they had difficulties distancing themselves in a context of political liberalization.

The Senegalese government has always advocated a political reading of student demonstrations by interpreting student demands as the result of manipulation by opposition parties or outside forces, more precisely Maoist or communist parties or regimes.[15] As a consequence, since the violent student demonstrations in 1968, 1969, and 1971, the state has adopted operating procedures that oscillate between repression and corruption of the student leadership. However, the institution of integral multipartyism in 1981, in opening the public political arena to Marxist parties, provoked a mutation in the student movement: the extraordinary political diversity and confrontations between leftist factions progressively expelled high school and university students from the political scene. The students, in turn, progressively demobilized in order to devote themselves to better defending their standards of living and education—and not only against the regime, but increasingly against the teachers' unions and the opposition parties.[16] This tendency was intensified by the degradation of living and study conditions, with classroom overcrowding, increases in the failure rate, and the abolition of scholarships, grants, and the provision of books and educational materials. This effort to reorganize the student movement resulted in new practices adapted to organizational structures, new forms of struggle, and new modes of mobilization and intervention.

For the second group, those bypassed by the educational system—the unemployed, deviants, beggars, peddlars, informal sector apprentices— who constitute the vast majority of the youth population, the government

15. On the question of the political manipulation of student movements, refer to the interesting analyses of Bathily 1992 and the chapter "Le Syndicalisme Etudiant, Pluralisme et Revendication," in Diop 1992.

16. On the questions of the political and union recompositions of the movement of university and high school students, see Diop 1992.

has always reserved repressive treatment. This treatment has been legitimated by the persistence of the colonial ideology regarding public space and thoroughfares and the nationalist ideology's reading of the rural exodus and its baneful consequences. *Le Soleil* faithfully echoes the discursive complex of the regime:

> Senegalese society has known profound upheavals that occasionally have dramatic repercussions for familial structure. The Senegalese family forms a very important social group in a strongly hierarchical agrarian society. Today, with all order of change, the family has been completely transformed and, with it, parental authority is lax, indeed permissive, if not gone altogether. (*Le Soleil* 1990: 18)

The state assumes the right to substitute itself for parents who have abdicated their responsibilities and to restore traditional values fallen into disuse. With the same gesture, it expels the young marginals from its own space and from that circumscribed for tourism. The notion of "social marginals" permits the state to rank each deviant person according to its own norms or in reference to the traditions it manipulates and continuously reinvents to sustain the total alignment and *encadrement* of society.

The decline of parental authority has become a recurrent theme in political discourses on youth. It is amplified by recourse to marabouts and brotherhood hierarchies and references to the Qu'ran and to the ancestors. Discourses with a high moral tenor support and justify repressive handling of youth. This orientation was aggravated by the surge of "law and order" ideology at the beginning of the 1980s, an ideology that emanated from the ruling class and affected the entire society.

The failure of the policy of *encadrement* of the young by the party in power, the extremely low participation in government-sponsored youth organizations, and youth's extraordinary lack of interest in opposition parties have combined with the effects of the economic crisis to make the youth question the central political issue. Dakar area youth appear to have left the terrain of institutions and formal political organizations for agitational practices outside conventional public frameworks.

Inscribing themselves in heterodox practices (*buissonières*), youth have set about promoting new solidarities and producing new parameters, confronting the state, parents, and educators—or simply ignoring them. They invest their energies in reconstructing urban spaces and practices, challenging the state and municipality's authority over certain districts and their power to name streets and police them. Certain segments assign themselves the role of guardians of Muslim morality to justify their "combing" operations and punitive expeditions against addicts, drunks, and thieves. Since 1988, Le Soleil daily relates the occasionally fatal incidents between "youth gangs" and "thieves or delinquents." In certain parts of Dakar's working-class suburb, Pikine-Guédiawaye, youth gangs organize "moral cleansing" operations in zones reputed to be "places of prostitution, bars, and crime."[17] The young thus become key players in political struggles and the driving force of urban social movements.

Political Idioms: Violence and Heterodox Practices

This section concentrates on the imaginary of the social movement that launched an assault on the ruling class and the history of its dominance as inscribed in urban space with sticks and stones (the electoral riots of 1988), violent pogroms against the Moors (Senegalo-Mauritanian conflict of 1989), and mural painting and clean-up operations (1990), clearing a path through the city and redefining the spaces and logics of sociability and public places.[18] These expressions were in no way violent ruptures, they attest to the long accumulation of heterodox practices (buissonière) that led the young to organize themselves in an autonomous and noninstitutional manner.

The essential characteristic of the crisis of the 1980s is the defiant attitude of the young toward political, economic, social, and cultural institutions. This attitude was manifested in the tendency to create autonomous organizations with strong religious or ethnic connotations, often centered on common origin, region, or locale. This movement affected every segment of the young, rural as well as urban. Two new structures accurately reflect the new tendencies in the urban areas: the Cultural and Athletic Associations (Associations Culturelles et Sportives) and the new coordination between movements of high school students and university students.

Cultural and athletic associations. These associations promote a cultural, social, and athletic life of great intensity. They organize diverse activities such as clean-up operations and vacation classes for children. Faced with the temptations of the neighborhood political leadership to appropriate public playgrounds and to control the fire hydrants, and especially in the wake of trash collecting operations, the young increasingly engage in tests of strength against established public institutions (electricity, water, and transportation companies). Some of these associations are now experi-

17. On the geography of the bars and the violent relations in these troubled areas, see the excellent analysis and eyewitness account of Werner 1994.
18. For the mural paintings and their geography, see Monde 1991; and, for an initial analysis, see Niane, Savané, and Diop 1991.

menting with public libraries and professional training centers. The appearance of the Groupement d'Intérêt Economique (GIE) and *Petites et Moyennes Enterprises* (PME) attests to the evolution of a strongly economic orientation of some associations whose goal is increasing employment among the young.

Through their organizational structures, these far more democratic organizations escape the clientelist logics and the prebendal modalities that have continuously enervated the logics of political integration. They create fissures in which the young elaborate strategies of cooperation and confrontation with the state. In this way, they obtain better results in accomplishing projects and managing communal equipment. Involved with the emergence of a new social conscience and highly critical of governmental plans, the cultural and athletic associations are confronted with the resistance of political entrepreneurs who face the erosion of the effectiveness of their mercenary support. The associations have fostered the progressive dissolution of the logics of centralization and the submission of social actors to the power of the state.

The neighborhood focus of cultural and athletic associations signifies, to a certain extent, the search for a territorial inscription that defies a colonial and postcolonial spatial and institutional arrangement that emphasizes both the symbols of the colony (the builders of the colonial empire) and of the nation (the fathers of the nation). Renaming streets after local figures (football players or marabouts) in the Médina or in Gueule Tapée/Fann-Hock in the place of letters of the alphabet attempts to erase a certain memory. It also unveils self-definitional procedures that create the categories of a new sociability, distinct from those produced by the nation and the ethnic group. Finally, it attacks the state's modalities of management and dismemberment of urban space. The groups that have been founded in the course of the movement have produced private local memories, selecting their own past, their own "founding fathers," and etching their own signs on the sand and the stele. The new constellations of stars (those who have streets named for them) reveal a reconstruction of the past that is a socially revealing elaboration of the present and includes the ubiquitous absence of women being commemorated by this male-dominated movement.

One of the most spectacular forms of this new dynamic was the success of the Cairo '86 operation, which made it possible to put the generous financial contributions of the public, and particularly the young, at the disposal of the national football team to finance its participation in the Africa Cup. The elimination of the national team and Senegal's exclusion from participation in the African competition for more than fifteen years, as well as the rumors of embezzlement, had provoked a collective hysteria.

The year 1986 seemed to mark a turning point in the modes of expression of the young, first by resisting municipal recruitment for the *set weec* or *Augias* community service operations (1987),[19] and then by the progressive appropriation of certain governmental functions.

For example, in various neighborhoods they set up "militias for self-defense and the security of property and the tranquillity of peaceful citizens in the 'hottest' quarters of Dakar."[20] In 1989, the youth of the Médina organized "lynching parties" in the caves of the Corniche along the ocean;[21] these were directed against the thieves and addicts who are blamed for the reign of insecurity in the district bordering on this zone. The raids were designed to compensate for inadequate policing. In 1990 in the same quarter, following a morning assault on a muezzin, fundamentalist youth gangs launched a reprisal operation. Numerous bars and night clubs were burned. In September and October 1993, to fight against the nuisances and accidents caused by collective taxis, the residents bordering Valmy and Petersen streets in the center of Dakar blockaded them and then demanded the governor issue a decree forbidding the circulation of the vehicles, more specifically collective taxis, whose drivers systematically disregard traffic rules.

High school and university student movements. The newest conjuncture of crisis (increasing failure rate, eroding infrastructure, discontinued scholarships) and the democratic opening found new forms of struggle at the heart of the movement of high school and university students. The movements developed an expertise that rendered their leadership less vulnerable to the maneuvers of the authorities through the adoption of a rotating leadership. Their daily submission of negotiations to the sanction of the general assembly imposes a logic more of permanent confrontation than compromise. One of the student movement's most interesting successes is its skill in using the independent press to mobilize public opinion in its support and against the government.

Nevertheless, the students have to a certain extent deserted the terrain of partisan political militancy—at least this no longer exclusively determines

19. *Set weec* and *Augias* were voluntarist clean-up operations, e.g., cleaning streets and planting trees, organized by the Office of the Mayor and the youth branch of the ruling PS party. As such, they were official events and partisan expressions and were markedly unsuccessful in comparison to the community-organized and controlled *Set/Setal* operations. *Set weec* is a generic Wolof term expressing the centrality of investments of human energy as opposed to the capital and technological investments that only developed countries can afford. *Augias* derives from the Augean stables of Herculean legend and, thus, French high culture.
20. The daily reading of *Le Soleil* provides a striking example.
21. Corniche is the designation for the area of the cliffs that run along the seashore on the western side of the Dakar peninsula and contain numerous caves.

their union practices. They have set up coordinating committees (Coordination of Senegalese High School Students and Coordination of Dakar University Students), whose flexibility is testimony to their independence. They present themselves "as rejects of the state, marginalized by civil society, or simply as pawns in the hands of the parties on the political chessboard" (Bathily 1992: 51). The students mounted an intransigent defense of their demands, above all in the context of the massive unemployment of graduates. The slow restructuring of the student movement, its disarticulation from politics *stricto sensu*, has resulted in repeated strikes and the imposition of long and humiliating negotiations on the government. The regime's exasperation has led to a constant and massive utilization of repression. Beginning with the 1987–88 school year, the confrontation led to an *année blanche* and the total paralysis of the Senegalese educational system, with the exception of the private schools, attended by children of the elite.

Sopi: **Violence and political disillusionment.** The context is also that of Abdou Diouf's succession to Senegal's first president, Leopold Sédar Senghor, in 1981 and the difficult democratic transition and contested elections of 1983, at a highly unfavorable economic conjuncture. The state had been progressively disengaging from the sectors of health, education, and sanitation. Public services and public and parapublic institutions "trimmed the fat," and impoverishment ensued. At the same time, the government reinstated the municipal statute of the city of Dakar (1983), which involved the financial disengagement of the state from local structures. In its juridical translation, this returned the administration of public space to the local population, through the intermediary of its elected representatives.

The inefficiency of repression and corruption, the disqualification of social and political intermediaries (parents, teachers' union, marabouts), and the interference of the student demonstrations that began in 1987 with campaigning for the 1988 presidential and legislative election forced the government to negotiate with leaders of youth groups, who obtained concessions that had never before been accorded to social actors. The president of the Republic was obliged to give them an audience after they had repeatedly refused to negotiate with school and university authorities (Diop and Diouf 1990).

In the difficult context of an electoral campaign, the student movement was able to link up with the *Sopi* movement without fear of manipulation.[22]

22. *Sopi* means change in Wolof, the dominant language in Senegal. It is the slogan of the

They filled the streets with their own slogans, which they combined with slogans of the opposition party that had been recast as democratic demands. Their resistance and their autonomy vis-à-vis the political parties were interpreted as "revenge on the state and civil society."

The historic fabric of the electoral and postelectoral violence and the founding events of Set/Setal is woven from the threads of the school and university crises, the année blanche being the catalyst for a series of strikes, demonstrations, and riots in which students, unemployed youth, and marginals attacked urban symbols and the signs of power in the Plateau at the beginning of 1990, before the clean-up operations.[23] The violent assaults against alcohol sales in the Médina and on the fringes of the Plateau together with the operations against the social marginals (robbers, drug addicts, alcoholics) of the Corniche attest to the same movement, in its "moral" and political aspects. The authors of the first work on the movement indicate very clearly this interweaving of motivations:[24]

> The urban riots known as Sopi begin with the advance campaigning for the campaign and elections of February 1988. The announcement of the election results provoked violent riots that shook the principal cities of Senegal for days. The principal authors of the violence, destruction, and resistance to the forces of order were the young: high school and university students and social marginals. February '88 to April '89. Senegalese youth made a dramatic appearance on the political scene. Nobody expected them but they couldn't have cared less. Fear of the future expressed itself in a formidable destructive rage. Between throwing stones a 17-year-old lycée student spits out, "We are going to tear everything down in order to rebuild." Hot air? We shall see. Since July 1990, the juvenile violence has passed over into a sort of dense madness that remains an enigma. Under the eyes of transfixed adults, the erstwhile Mauritanian-hunters, groups of young people put into practice their new credo: order and cleanliness. The most horrible city on the continent, the most infested with squatters and traffic jams is cleaned from top to bottom. Public parks that were no more than sordid urinals are restored to their original role, rehabilitated and beautified. (Niane, Savané, and Diop 1991: foreword)

Parti Démocratique Sénégalais (PDS), the principal opposition party whose leader, Abdoulaye Wade, is the principal rival of President Abdou Diouf. This slogan symbolizes the fight against the regime of the party in power, the Parti Socialiste (PS).

23. The Plateau is the affluent downtown Dakar area where European residences were formerly located.

24. For more details, refer to chapter 12, "Les Emeutes de Février-Mars 1988," in Diop and Diouf 1990: 335–54.

Sopi was the expression of the brutal irruption of these social categories into the tête-à-tête between political parties. It marked the failure of attempts to institutionalize models of political action and definitively consecrated youth as the "accursed share" of Senegalese society. Both the violence of the clashes and the youth of those confronting the forces of order were surprising. It was recorded in the photographic coverage of Le Soleil, accompanied by the following account: "Throughout the day yesterday, Dakar was in an uproar. Cars set on fire and overturned, stores ransacked, gas stations in flames" (Le Soleil 1988a: 11–13).

The principal targets of the young rioters were symbols of the state: the center of the civil administration of greater Dakar was torched; eighty of the public transit company's buses and numerous telephone booths were damaged; government and administration cars were attacked and set on fire (Le Soleil 1988b); these "Black Monday" rioters attacked the homes of militants and individuals close to PS power (Diop and Diouf 1990: 337).

The riots were the consequence of the logic of verbal excesses surrounding the Electoral Code and the partisan position of the administration, denounced by the opposition, and the threats directed at certain opposition leaders. The firm will of the opposition parties, including the recourse to violence, to bar the way to any attempt at electoral fraud, intimidation of PS women, and the closing of schools and universities by the Minister of the Interior all heightened the tension. It was in this "very tense context" that "the Senegalese state let loose in the street a fraction of the young submitted to difficult living and study conditions and to an uncertain future where they joined the ranks of the young unemployed" (ibid.).

The incumbent president Abdou Diouf used pejorative and degrading terms to characterize the youth or one of its component parts—it has never been made clear which—as "unwholesome pseudo-youth." Youth responded to this insult with a total condemnation of the state and the ruling PS and massive support for the Sopi convoys of the electoral campaign. In the same spirit, they attacked and disrupted electoral meetings of the PS and affiliated movements.

A fringe of the urban youth organized the postelectoral riots. The interviews obtained by a journalist from a French radio station during the event give a fairly exact impression of the attitude of this group (Tropic FM 1988). These young people were generally between eleven and eighteen or nineteen years old. They expressed their total refusal to play the classic political game through their violence and in a language of explosive virulence—a language that not only rebelled against politics but even more surely against so-called traditional values. And, even as they clothed themselves in the discourse of the opposition symbolized by the Sopi slogan, they twisted the meaning and preached physical confrontation with the state, a state that, according to their terms, is a regime of robbers divested of its historical legitimacy and its function as principal actor in the building of the nation.

In fact, the irruption of youth into the political arena in such violent modalities establishes an investment in the present and the refusal of the deferment imposed by the nationalist historicity of the ruling class. The state's response to the social movements culminated with the declaration of a state of emergency and the deployment of police throughout Dakar, the goal being to isolate the Plateau and control the strategic points of access to this area along Avenue Malick Sy. The poorer neighborhoods, particularly the Médina, the HLM (Habitations à Loyer Modéré)-subsidized housing development district, and Colobane, were left to the young rebels and to the opposition.

The violence of youth's intervention attests to the furious response to the ongoing attempts at *encadrement* and authoritarianism. The revolt constituted a total refusal of the places assigned to youth not only by political power—first single-party rule and then multiparty democracy—but also, and throughout the revolt, by a tradition whose imperatives of submission to elders are endlessly repeated in radio and television broadcasts as a *crises de valeur* (in French) and an "abdication by parents of the education of children" (in the national languages).

To defuse the crisis that followed the elections, President Abdou Diouf committed his new five-year term to improving the conditions of youth. The constant oscillation in the discourse of the ruling class between a negative pole and a positive pole testifies to its ambivalence toward the practices of the young and its inability to take them in hand, as much in a social and economic register as in an ideological one. The violence seems to have been the sign of enormous distress, profound anguish, and fear in the face of a blocked future and a more and more unequal division of power and riches in a society in crisis.

The profound and lasting disruption by youth and urban marginals of the implementation of the mechanisms for the democratic transition since 1983 (symbolized by *Sopi*) inaugurated a new era: the refusal to allow the institutions established by the new ruling class to direct the process of democratizing Senegalese society. It illustrated the expansive struggles for democracy and, above all, the demand for dialogue, for a hearing without reference to legitimation, henceforth to be backed up by violence on the part of social adults who refused the role of social junior, which no longer offered any benefits in a changing society.

After the state's severe response to the electoral riots and the arrest and subsequent release of the principal opposition leaders, the negotiations of the opposition's most representative fractions and the politicking of *La Table Ronde* discredited the option of a change of political regime.[25] Thus was achieved the unlikely accession of the *Sopi* leaders to power. The controversies within and between the opposition parties and the regime's expert management of the postelectoral crises led to sectors of the opposition (PDS and PIT) joining the government in 1991. The stability of the political configuration, combined with the renewal of structural adjustment programs without political danger to the regime, definitively pushed certain political actors to take shortcuts to achieving a voice; theirs was a discourse refractory to postcolonial sociability and its logics of compromise and accommodation.[26]

The disappointment of the youth in the insignificant role that they were accorded in the postelectoral discussions found a violent outlet during the Senegalo-Mauritanian crisis, provoked by a scuffle between pastoralists and agriculturalists on the banks of the Senegal river. Dakar was the scene for the explosion of a murderous and irrational rage against the Moors. Dozens were mutilated or had their throats slit after Senegalese in certain Mauritanian towns met the same treatment. Youth unleashed an unheard-of violence and threw itself body and soul into campaigns of vengeance that were amplified by more or less fanciful rumors. Mauritanian-owned stores were looted. It required the intervention of the army, rounding up Mauritanians and repatriating them, to put an end to the torrent of violence and hatred.

This extraordinary murderous fury in a society proud of its hospitality (*teranga*) and pacifism seems to have surprised the Senegalese themselves. And, as if to purify themselves, the young threw themselves into the assault against filth, garbage heaps, and stagnant water, following the torrential rains of September 1990. The moral aspect of the movement is reconstructed in this commentary by a young leader: "This massive rain is a sign of purification, so we must clear our neighborhoods, rid them of their recent memory, and of existential dramas of all kinds" (Diallo 1993: 211).

***Set/Setal*: From the political arena to community territory and space.** In its most widely accepted definition, *Set/Setal* is the mobilization of human effort for the purpose of cleansing in the sense of sanitation and hygiene, but also in the moral sense of the fight against corruption, prostitution, and delinquency. The movement's primary concern was to rehabilitate

25. *La Table Ronde* was the Senegalese formula for managing political differences following the electoral riots, which brought together leaders from all the political parties.
26. See, on this subject, Diouf 1992.

local surroundings and remove garbage and filth. It also undertook to embellish these sites, sometimes naming them, often marking them with steles and monuments to bear witness by recalling moments or figures from local history or appealing to the private memories of families or youth associations. *Set/Setal* is clearly a youth movement and a local movement (in opposition to national movements and even to parties and urban sections of parties), that is to say, one centered on the neighborhood. It is a specific response to the accelerated degradation of the urban infrastructure and to the virtual absence of residential garbage collection in the poorer districts, and increasingly in the Plateau, because of the strained relations between the private garbage collection company and the new municipal administration. The new city hall's lack of technical capabilities and financial means lasted until the creation of a new semipublic, semiprivate garbage collection company. The state's desertion of public service and the municipal authority's inability to replace it had plagued Dakar with a repulsive filthiness. Furthermore, political reconfigurations and feuding within the new municipal administration, as well as within the central government, led to conflicts that were accentuated by the recomposition of the ruling class after the legislative and presidential elections of 1983 and again in 1988.[27]

These elements of political crisis were constantly renewed, both through the election of leaders for the majority Socialist Party (PS) and through the regular elections. The ways that violent pitched battles or the riots were brutally dispersed by the forces of order testify to the crisis between 1983 and 1990. And *Sopi* was the rallying cry and banner of these years; it expressed the debasement of political standards, the rise of a new, totally postcolonial generation, and a "crisis of values" intensified by the liberal effect, which resulted from structural adjustment programs and multiparty rule.

Set/Setal possesses historical antecedents for its sanitation and human investment themes, and a genealogy that goes back to the nationalist and voluntarist episode of the first decade of the Senegalese postcolony. These activities were designated as *set weec*, the generic term for human investments, or the *Augias* operations (Monde 1991: 7–8). The *Augias* operations had always been an occasion for the ruling class to affirm its munificence, its incontestable power, and its authority over a population hemmed in on all sides by political *encadrement*. They were the affirmation, at the local level, of the strength of the party in power, of its articulation with the legitimacies of localities and districts, and the expression of the centrality of clientelist constructions and their languages in Senegalese political tra-

27. On all these questions, refer to Diop and Diouf 1990.

jectories. They provided proofs of magnanimity and a reaffirmation of the rule of the nationalists and their heirs.

These practices in the city demand an interrogation of the current political stakes in urban management, that of the worlds of work and of leisure, as well as in the history of the city and the traces left on it by social actors. The morphology of a city, its representation and production, effectively signify the trajectories of the individual and collective lives that unfold there. Does the context of the 1980s and 1990s, marked by the policies of structural adjustment, adequately explain the dynamics of which Set/Setal seems to be the most complete expression? Can we identify relationships between the stylistics of power and the style of Set/Setal? The logics induced by Sopi and the incomplete character of the process of democratizing Senegalese society are developments which proceeded hand in hand with the disengagement of the state and the appeal to continuously reformulated ethnic, religious, and regional identities. Can Set/Setal be read as a strategic syncretism, capable of creating an alternative space for social relations? Does it favor a redefinition of relationships among the state ruling class and the youth? Or is it simply a new tactic by Senegalese youth in the search for a fixed point of reference, as well as a referential matrix in which to ground itself within a changing urban landscape? Set/Setal expresses a harsh critique of the world of adults and politicians by the vast majority of youth. It is an attempt to overcome youth's dependent position and the lack of attention from the adults who provide for them:

> Set/Setal is in the hearts and souls of all young people. If people think that going Set/Setal is simply sweeping the streets and painting the walls, they are mistaken because there are people paid to do that. You can't make street-sweepers out of every one of us. The authorities haven't understood a thing. They don't know how to listen. To do Set/Setal, is to rid ourselves of this colonial heritage that regulates our way of being, of conceptualizing things. Set/Setal is an absolute obligation to find a way out and this necessity to express new concepts in a new language, in this struggle for life. (Diallo 1993: 213)

Whatever the case, taking charge of clean-up and beautification required financial resources that the youth groups obtained either through the organization of public music and dance parties and demonstrations or through the more or less forced solicitation of motorists. According to one of the leaders of these groups, in the HLM district, "The money gathered from the masses, that is to say door to door and by stopping vehicles, was solely designed to make the public participate in our activities, to be independent of the administration and the politicians" (ibid.: 211).

The expression of urban malaise and the malaise of youth has never been experienced in Senegal in such plural and original forms, in this constant oscillation between violence, creativity, and practicality (la débrouille). The educated youth sustain their activities through the uncompromising political struggle to rid Senegal of the PS regime that "prevents us from having a future." During the 1993 elections, the same procedures were again taken up by youth in a different context. The entire political class adopted a consensual political code. Foreign observers were present for the first time to monitor the elections and prevent the PS from manipulating the voting. One of the Senegalese opposition's long-standing demands was thus met.

The youth's enthusiastic engagement in the cause of deposing the head of state, however, did not translate into a massive voter registration. As in 1988, they followed the electoral processions of the opposition, especially M. A. Wade, in large numbers. Students constituted the subgroup of youth that was most engaged in the electoral battle of 1993, in contrast to 1988 when they were less involved than unemployed and uneducated youth. To achieve their objective, the defeat of Diouf and the PS, students organized campus debates and created movements such as La Jeunesse pour l'Alternance (JPA) and Coordination Laye Espoir (CLE).[28] In contrast to the university students, high school students, and especially those from the lycées, demonstrated violently against the regime. The repression against them was ferocious, most notably on 11 February 1993, when Dakar lycéens clashed with the Mobile Intervention Group riot squad of the Senegalese police.

Despite recurrent violence since the elections of 1988, which is, from this point on, the privileged form of expression for youth, the emergence of a tradition of self-reliance on the margin of all systems (educational, economic, parental) is overriding attempts to change the regime through elections. The desertion of the political and of political modes of expression has been the outcome of the crises of Sopi, confirmed by Set/Setal, and this explains perhaps the absence of drama in the 1993 elections.

The failure of Sopi has had contradictory consequences for the political behavior of Senegalese youth, notably affecting their political voice (parole). The most spectacular factor in this evolution is the utter refusal of postcolonial sociability and its logics of compromise and accommodation. The study of the success of this refusal is responsible for Senegal's reputation

28. La Jeunesse pour l'Alternance means Youth for Alternation (rotation of political leadership). "Laye" is the diminutive for Abdoulaye, referring to Abdoulaye Wade, and espoir is hope (salvation).

in West Africa scholarship.[29] This dissonance presupposes plural modes of expression, plural strategies, and above all, new readings of the city—more precisely a counterhistory to nationalist fictions and fables of the radical alterity of African desires, needs, and practices. The dissonance between the style and the discourse of the ruling class, the ruses of democratic opening, and the living conditions of a population on the road to marginalization and impoverishment, provoked the activation and redeployment of powerful new symbolics drawn from both Senegalese nationalism and the globalism made possible by African world music and its Western references.

If political strategy requires an identification, the production of different references proves indispensable in order for those excluded from the political arena, those who express themselves in Set/Setal, to act and think as different kinds of political subjects. The action that aimed at shaking the foundations of the nationalist memory went hand in hand with a new treatment of space that celebrates local memory. Set/Setal expresses the proliferation of new idioms that rest principally on a refusal of traditional political action and assesses new forms and practices of citizenship. These idioms were not accounted for by African nationalist ideologies, which forcefully argued for cultural restoration, including gender and age hierarchies. Set/Setal presents itself as an indigenous appropriation of the city. The human investment, the rehabilitation of neighborhoods, and the murals express a political challenge by the youth and their demand that the political class rethink its actions and its modes of intervention. Through a radical refutation of the modes of political framing, the young have enunciated a new sociability, contradictory to the norms that have presided over the postcolonial compromise.

Multiple paradoxes characterize the situation today. After its association with the government of President Abdou Diouf, the PDS is again in the opposition.[30] It is allied with a religious movement, the Moustachidines wal moustachidati. This religious association is led not by a fundamentalist leader but by Moustapha Sy, a young Tijani marabout who is today in prison for allegedly threatening the security of the state. The Ligue Démo-

29. Refer to D. C. O'Brien 1971, 1975, and 1978. See also Copans 1980 and Coulon 1981.
30. In the period from 1991 to 1993, PDS leaders were members of the government. After the 1993 elections the PDS rejoined the opposition in an alliance with several parties uncompromisingly opposed to the PS (MSU, AJ, etc.), provoked in part by the arrest and detainment of Abdoulaye Wade, and joined in convening a national conference on the model of the democratic conferences being held in a number of West African states. Despite the recent radicalism of its stance, the PDS rejoined the government of President Abdou Diouf in March 1995, deserting its previous allies and provoking a crisis within the Senegalese opposition.

cratique Mouvement pour le Parti de Travail, another opposition party, rejoined the government after the 1993 elections. Currency was devalued despite salaries having been reduced by 15 percent to prevent it. The disenchantment has become so widespread that the unions are unable to mobilize their militants.

This young marabout leads the Moustachidines wal moustachidati and symbolizes the opposition to the regime and its politics. His supporters inaugurate novel forms of expression and resistance, such as challenging judicial authorities. They chant religious poetry instead of responding to questions, thus thwarting the judicial ritual.[31] The young strike a violent blow against the languages of power through the production of synthetic idioms whose elements are borrowed from distant and heterogeneous worlds. They are in the process of creating an urban culture, detached from the colonial and nationalist memories. From the violence of 1987 and 1988 to the flourishing heterodox style (buissonière) of Set/Setal, Senegalese youth express the impossibility of authoritarianism in the period of structural adjustment. And if the murals are the iconographic index of multiple ruptures, can't one discern their history lessons? Has a cultural projection that remodels the imaginary and historical conscience of the generation of independence already come to ill through technocracy and adjustment?

The murals, like mbalax (a form of popular music),[32] express the mobilization of new idioms to capture novel situations. One can support the hypothesis that the Set/Setal movement and its accompanying signs are the indices of a dynamism that was thought to have been suffocated by autocracy and the pervasive mediocrity of an unrealized "democracy of the educated," incapable of managing economic and social crises. The assumption of responsibility for the reconversion of space and its cleansing, as well as the reclaiming of indistinct territories and renaming of streets, have been the vectors for the reintroduction of an excluded youth into a space and a struggle over the city. The youth assumed responsibilities that encroached on the prerogatives of public authority and insisted that accounts be settled. Their actions signify the recuperation of a power that founds and legitimates new discourses of identity. Inasmuch as these orientations are highly local, they are multiple and, therefore, capable of leading to sectarianisms that impede social cohesion.

In the same way, by intervening directly in the organization of space, Set/Setal called into question the subdivision of living spaces in the old lebu

31. See Coulibaly 1993.
32. Mbalax is a Senegalese contribution to world music, diffused worldwide by Youssou N'Dour, Ismail Lo, and other musicians.

quarters of the Plateau—reexamining the spaces set aside not only for work but for innovation (la débrouille) and/or delinquency, spaces for which the city alone offers such diverse possibilities. Each time that the state "unloads" a space, its pretensions to rule are diminished; the liberated space becomes a territory for invention, for dissidence, and for dissonance.

The neighborhood is substituted for the national territory as the canvas for elaborating the symbolic and the imaginary. Discursive and iconographic fables register a local memory that proclaims itself as such against the nationalist memory. This contestation also translates into commemorations and festive demonstrations, of which the music and dance parties and celebrations (furël) are the most obvious signs of the invention of new traditions. To the theatricality of power is opposed the theater of the street, whose young actors and directors invent scenes and texts by drawing on a global repertoire. And, paradoxically, it is along this trajectory that traditional celebrations and games have been rediscovered and re-created, after the state had worn itself out promoting them in vain, in order (it was said) to restore traditional morality.

At stake is the relationship between the national memory and local memories. The new urban order is being elaborated through democratic innovation and the crises that today rock the African postcolonies. Through protests, clean-up campaigns, murals, and memorials, the imaginary and the conscience of the young and marginal of Dakar, who have become a social movement, mark their possession of urban spaces to oppose the state—its official nationalist history and its economic policies in the era of structural adjustment.

At stake here is a form of citizenship that disavows the biases of tradition and challenges authoritarianism, two outstanding features of the African postcolonial states.[33] Through their cold rejection of the modalities of membership in the nation, the youth are redefining the spaces of legal citizenship and erasing their nationalistic attributes and referents, thereby questioning the state's authority to define citizenship (Berlant 1993).

References

Amselle, J.-L. "Identité et métissage politiques." Compte-Rendu de la séance du 20 février 1991. Feuille d'information no. 16. Groupe de Travail Cartes d'identité.

Antoine, P., et al. 1992. "L'Insertion urbaine: Le Cas de Dakar." Unpublished report, Dakar, March.

Anyang'Nyong'o, P., ed. 1992. Thirty Years of Independence in Africa: The Lost Decades? Nairobi: Academy of Science Publishers.

Bathily, A. 1992. Mai 68 à Dakar ou la révolte universitaire et la démocratie. Paris: Editions Chaka.

33. See Mbembe and Roitman 1995 and Devisch 1995.

Bathily, A., M. Diouf, and M. Mbodj. 1995. "The Senegalese Student Movement from Its Inception to 1989." In *African Perspectives in Social Movements and Democracy*, M. Mamdani and E. Wamba-dia-Wamba, eds. Dakar: CODESRIA, 368–407.

Berlant, L. 1993. The "Theory of Infantile Citizenship." *Public Culture* 5(3): 395–410.

Bocquier, P. 1991. "L'Insertion et la mobilité professionelles à Dakar." Ph.D. diss., Université de Paris V.

Brenner, L. 1993. *Muslim Identity and Social Change in Sub-Saharan Africa*. Bloomington: Indiana University Press.

Collignon, R. 1984. "La Lutte des pouvoirs publics contre les encombrements humains à Dakar." *Revue Canadienne des Etudes Africaines* 18(3): 573–82.

Conseil Economique et Social du Sénégal. 1966. "Essai sur la situation actuelle de la jeunesse." Dakar.

Copans, J. 1980. *Les Marabouts de l'Arachide*. Paris: Le Sycamore.

Coulibaly, A. L. 1993. "Evénements du 16 février au Tribunal." *Sud Quotidien*, 19 November.

Coulon, C. 1981. *Le Marabout et le prince*. Paris: Pedone.

Devisch, R. 1995. "Frenzy, Violence, and Ethical Renewal in Kinshasa." *Public Culture* 7(3): 593–629.

Diallo, A. 1993. "L'Experience de *Set/Setal* à Dakar." In *Jeunes, Villes, Emploi: Quel avenir pour la jeunesse Africaine?* E. Le Bris and F. Chaveau, eds. Colloquium papers. Paris: Ministère de la Coopération et du Développement.

Diane, C. 1990. *La FEANF et les grandes heures du mouvement syndical étudiant noire*. Paris: Editions Chaka.

Diarrah, C. O. 1993. "Les Ambiguités et les difficultés de la concrétisation opérationelle du projet démocratique du Mali." Report presented at the Atelier sur les Villes Ouest-Africaines, Dakar, 15–17 November.

Dieng, A. A. 1986. "Histoire des organisations d'étudiants Africains en France (1900–1955)." 2 vols. Dakar: mimeograph.

Diop, M. C., ed. 1992. *Sénégal: Trajectories d'un état*. Dakar: CODESRIA.

Diop, M. C., and M. Diouf. 1990. *Le Sénégal sous Abdou Diouf*. Paris: Karthala.

Diouf, M. 1989. "Représentations historiques et légitimités politiques au Sénégal, 1960–1987." *Revue de la Bibliothèque Nationale* 34 (winter 1989).

——. 1992. "Fresques murales et écriture de l'histoire: Le *Set/Setal* à Dakar." *Politique Africaine* 46 (June): 41–54.

Habib, C., and C. Mouchard, eds. 1993. *La Démocratie à l'oeuvre: Autour de Claude Lefort*. Paris: Edition Esprit.

Kane, C. H. 1961. *L'Aventure ambiguë*. Paris: Julliard.

Kane, O. 1990. "Les Mouvements religieux et le champ politique au Nigéria septentrional: Le Cas du réformisme musulman à Kano." *Islam Sociétés au Sud Sahara* 4 (November 1990).

Laye, C. 1953. *L'Enfant noir*. Paris: Plon.

Lefort, C. 1983. *L'Invention democratique: Les Limites de la domination totalitaire*. Paris: Livre de Poche, Biblio Essais.

Marshall, R. 1993. "Power in the Name of Jesus: Social Transformations and Pentecostalism in Western Nigeria." In *Legitimacy and the State in Contemporary Africa*, T. O. Ranger and O. Vaugh, eds. Oxford: Macmillan, 213–46.

Mbembe, A., and J. Roitman. 1995. "The Figure of the Subject in Times of Crisis." *Public Culture* 7(2): 323–52.

Momoh, A. 1993. "The South-Western Nigeria Case Study. Paper presented at the West African Long-Term Perspective Study." ADB-CINERGIE Conference, Lagos, 11–13 October.

Monde, E.-T. 1991. *Set, des murs qui parlent . . . Nouvelles cultures urbaines à Dakar*. Dakar: Enda.

Niane, J. C., V. Savané, and B. B. Diop. 1991. *Set/Setal: La Seconde Génération des barricades*. Dakar: Sud Editions.

O'Brien, D. C. 1971. *The Murides of Senegal*. Oxford: Oxford University Press.

——. 1975. *Saints and Politicians*. Cambridge: Cambridge University Press.

——. 1978. "Senegal." In *West African States: Promise and Failure*, J. Dunn, ed. Cambridge: Cambridge University Press, 173–88.

OECD/ADB. 1994. "L'Emergence de la compétition: Transformations et déséquilibres dans les sociétés ouest-africaines." Manuscript.

Otayek, R. 1993. "Une relecture islamique du projet révolutionnaire de Thomas Sankara." In *Religion et modernité politique en Afrique noire: Dieu pour tous et chacun pour soi*, J.-F. Bayart, ed. Paris: Karthala, 101–60.

Richards, P. 1995. "Liberia and Sierra Leone." In *Conflict in Africa*, O. W. Furley, ed. London: I. B. Tauris Publishers.

Sénégal Ministère de l'Economie et des Finances, Direction de la Statistique. 1988. "Recensement général de la population et de l'habitat, résultats préliminaires." September.

Le Soleil. 1988a. Special Edition Urnes [election] 88, March.

——. 1988b. 2 March.

——. 1990. La Jeunesse au coeur (special edition), May.

Sylla, A. 1992. "L'Ecole, Quelle réforme?" In *Sénégal: Trajectories d'un état*, M. C. Diop, ed. Dakar: CODESRIA.

Le Témoin. 1993. 134 (23 February).

Traoré, S. 1984. *La Fédération des étudiants d'Afrique noire (FEANF)*. Paris: L'Harmattan.

Tropic FM. 1988. Elections au Sénégal. Radio broadcast. 28 February.

Werner, J. F. 1994. *Marges, sexe et drogue à Dakar*. Paris: Karthala.

Islamic Modernities? Citizenship, Civil Society, and Islamism in a Nigerian City

Michael Watts

Perhaps the feeling that secular beliefs are rationally superior to religious ones is based on the belief that religious convictions are more rigid. But there is no decisive evidence for this. Religious traditions have undergone the most radical transformations over time. Divine texts may be unalterable, but the ingenuities of human interpretation are endless. . . . Fanatics come in all shapes and sizes among skeptics and believers alike. . . . it must be said that the ruthlessness of secular practice yields nothing to the ferocity of the religious. . . . Islamic tradition is the ground on which . . . reasoning takes place [in the Muslim world]. And that is no more than may be said about political and moral reasoning within the modern liberal tradition.—Talal Asad, Genealogies of Religion (emphasis added)

[Islamic] revivalism and reformism are thus a Janus-like creature. . . . Yet [they] . . . maintain a constant ambiguity, for on the one hand they advocate transformations of society, polity and culture that could have been advocated by any Latin American marxist political economist, while on the other they assimilate this to the notion of an independent and invariant [Muslim]

I am deeply indebted to Paul Lubeck and his published work (1985, 1986) on Maitatsine and the Kano economy, and more generally his research on the political economy of fundamentalism during an era of globalization and neoliberal reform. I would also like to acknowledge the assistance and unpublished work of Alan Richards and Terry Burke, both of the University of California, Santa Cruz. Patrick Heller of Columbia University helped with the clarification of the debates over civil society.

historical subject. . . . Islamic radicalism [is] a very recent phenomenon, born of a particular specification. It specified jahiliyya, the non-Islam that is to be converted into Islamic order, as an actual presence.—Aziz Al-Azmeh, *Islams and Modernities*

Implicitly "Christianity" is considered inherent to modern civilization . . . [but] why could Islam not do the same as Christianity? It seems to me rather that the absence of massive ecclesiastical organization of the Christian-Catholic type ought to make this adaptation easier. If it is admitted that modern civilization in its industrial-economic-political manifestation will end up by triumphing in the East . . . why not therefore conclude that Islam will necessarily evolve? Will Islam be able to remain just as it was? No—it is already no longer what it was before the war. Is it possible that it will fall at a stroke? Absurd hypothesis. . . . In actual fact the most tragic difficulty for Islam is given by the fact that a society in a state of torpor . . . has been put into brusque contact with a frenetic civilization already in its phase of dissolution.—Antonio Gramsci, *Further Selections from the Prison Notebooks*

Civil society is a protean term, a characteristic that might go some way toward explaining its current ubiquity in and outside academia. Francis Fukuyama, who not so long ago was proclaiming the end of history, has written a book—*Trust: The Social Virtues and the Creation of Prosperity* (1995)—in which he has rediscovered history in the form of "social capital," that is to say civic institutions, which is going to save capitalism and make us all prosperous. Jean Cohen and Andrew Arato (1992) begin their massively intimidating book *Civil Society and Political Theory* by noting the resurrection, rebirth, and reconstruction of civil society, and its centrality in the post-socialist and postmilitary transitions in Eastern Europe and Latin America. Their concern, unlike Fukuyama, is with democratic theory and with a discourse of civil society oriented to the utopian ideas of modernity. In this sense there is an affinity between Cohen and Arato's project on the re-emergence of civil society and the sea change in contemporary political culture and Habermas's discussion of the modern life-world (which encompasses civil society) and the related concept of the public sphere. Civil society for Habermas is "composed of those associations which, within the framework of the arrangements of public spheres, institutionalize problem-solving discourses for questions of general interest" (1992: 455). The preconditions for the emergence of civil society are a plurality of life-forms, public communications, and the legality of rights and regulation. Habermas too is concerned with democracy, but he emphasizes that it is within civil society that disturbances in the symbolic realm of the life-world are first perceived, experienced, and resisted (Brenner 1993; Calhoun 1992). It is precisely this symbolic realm and its institutional character that has contributed to another aspect of the resurgence of civil society, to which Fukuyama's book speaks, concerned with accumulation and development rather than democracy per se. Social capital—the social norms and institutionalized relationships that underwrite developmental resources—here invokes the networks of civil society as a precondition for trust, duty, and accountability within the domains of welfare and the economy (Putnam 1993; Evans 1995).

In all of this Africa stands as a depressing counterpoint. The conundrum seems to be the coexistence of weak societies and weak states that produces if not the collapse of civil society then something so fractured by cleavages and conflicts that it offers no effective resistance to state hegemony and no semblance of civil society either. One line of popular apocalyptic writing points to a sort of withdrawal and collapse—a combination of war, decay, and anarchy (Kaplan 1994a; Hitchens 1994).[1] It is frequently the African metropolis that appears as the crucible for this decay, for a civil society gone awfully wrong. Lagos, every world traveler's worst nightmare, is naturally the nadir, a city of "capitalism gone wild" as the *Los Angeles Times* (24 February 1983, 10) put it. The *New Republic* was no less enthralled: "Impoverished, filthy, steamy, overcrowded and corrupt, Lagos is the ultimate incarnation of the modern megalopolis gone to hell" (12 July 1993, 11). In some respects these sorts of narratives could be reproduced for most African cities. Here for example is an account of Cairo taken from the *New Yorker* (Weaver 1995: 55), but it could easily be applied to other cities (see Ajami 1995; Kaplan 1994b):

> People seemed to be living on the edge, as much of the city's infrastructure was being reduced to dust. Corruption flourished and political stagnation ossified. . . . Every year Egypt produces more than a hundred thousand university graduates, many of whom cannot find jobs. . . . the city's once astonishing diversity of cultures and social strata has seemingly been reduced to two starkly contrasting poles: poverty, which appeared everywhere, and extraordinary wealth.

I want to explore civil society in metropolitan Africa by taking the case of Kano and by using local Islam as a vehicle for exploring the public spheres in which communicative action and associational life takes place. Kano is in no sense a typical Nigerian city, should such a thing exist; neither is it, in any simple sense, medieval or Islamic. The level of homicide, violence, and robbery is certainly lower than Lagos and probably less than comparable European and American cities (Last 1991: 3). Urban gangs have proliferated

---

1. Kaplan's image of Africa sliding back into Victorian darkness, as he put it, was picked up widely in the U.S. press, but these sentiments also appear within the left community, for example, Christopher Hitchens in *Vanity Fair*: "What if all this bloodshed is for nothing? What if Africa is neither cleansed in blood nor giving birth in blood but just plain *drowning* in blood" (1994: 102).

to the point where the state government declared them unlawful in 1983, and Kano residents complain, as city residents generally do everywhere, about the increase of crime. But this is not the stuff of *Bladerunner* either. Kano, moreover, has a substantial associational life; some 250 associations and self-help groups were registered in 1991, including religious groups, market associations, neighborhood networks, and vigilante groups. But it is the fundamental presence of Islam that dominates the landscape of urban civil society, and it is the growth of Islamism within the city that provides the entrée for my discussion of the Kano public sphere. I shall use the well-documented case of a fundamentalist Muslim movement[2]— Maitatsine—in the 1970s and 1980s (Lubeck 1985, 1986; Watts 1994), a movement that almost pulled Kano city apart in 1980, to explore one small part of the changing landscape of citizenship, identity, and associational life in the city. This story reveals how a distinctive Muslim community was built, as it were, *within* a Muslim community, and to tell it I shall have to trace the dialectical relations between a local social structure of Islam and a local social structure of capitalist accumulation driven by globalization of a certain sort, namely the oil boom. I have employed the metaphor of mapping to inform how these two locally constituted global force fields—Islam and capitalism—informed each other, and thereby challenged, reconfigured, and reconstituted some aspects of urban identity and civil society. To employ the language of Carl Schorske (1981), I want to examine the "reshuffling of the self" associated with an emergent Islamic modernity rooted in the long engagement of Islam with the capitalist "West." In this instance, as in so many others within the contemporary Muslim world, this engagement takes the form of a struggle over Muslim orthodoxy, what Talal Asad calls "a reordering of knowledge that governs the 'correct' form of Islamic practices" (1993: 210), in the context of radical social and economic change in a big, sprawling urban metropolis in northern Nigeria.

My account of the genesis of Maitatsine as a form of revivalism, or political Islam, raises a larger issue of the relations between Islam, civil society, and modernity. "At the heart of the revivalist worldview," says John Esposito, "is the belief that the Muslim world is in a state of decline" (1992:

---

2. By Islamic fundamentalism, Islamism, Islamic revanchism/revivalism and political Islam— terms I take to be roughly interchangeable—I refer to a scripturalist form of religious piety affirming the centrality of the Qu'ran and the hadith for all aspects of life and practice, and the advocacy of a political order whose topos is "none other than the order of rectitude that reigned at the time of the Prophet Mohammed . . . the order described in the voluminous corpus of quasi-sacred narrative scripture called the hadith" (Al-Azmeh 1993: 25). It is, in short, the politicized retrieval of an essence, "that the vicissitudes of time and the designs of enemies, rather than change of any intrinsic nature, had caused to atrophy" (42).

19). But what sort of explanation of, and alternative to, decline does Islamism offer? Specifically, what sort of utopian vision of civil society did Maitatsine contribute, and how does it figure in relation to wide-ranging reformist debates within the Muslim diaspora in Nigeria? These questions tread on territory that cannot be adequately covered here, but it is the widespread essentialist vision of Muslim societies—held even among scholars sympathetic to Islam—that fundamentalisms in particular are "static, reactive, anti-modern and rageful" (cited in Lubeck 1995: 3), that I wish to explore. Central to the relations between the public sphere and Islam is whether Islamism "gives primevalism and primitivism precedence over history" (Al-Azmeh 1993: 93). In this Weberian model of Islam, the prospects for civil society are grim to say the least. Al-Azmeh dismisses Islamism as utopian, ahistorical, and protofascist, wedded to a sort of Romantic hypernationalism; for Turner fundamentalism offers nostalgia, cultural antimodernism, and a limited sense of political pluralism built around "the household of faith" (1994: 93). Ernest Gellner sees the urban ethos and a puritanical, reformed, legally oriented, and powerful clergy (ulama) as conducive to disciplined capitalist accumulation (1983, 1992). But civil society disappears altogether, and politics is condemned to stagnation and eternal elite circulation. It is to these larger questions that I wish to make the Kano case speak.

Refiguring Kano: From Mercantile to Industrial Capitalism

The economic crisis . . . has altered old priorities [in Kano]: the leftover food that could be given as alms is much reduced. . . . the casual jobs are even lower paid if valued in terms of what grain the wages might buy. . . . Marriages are postponed for want of money; fewer wives are taken even by the well-to-do. . . . unemployment for the young seems unremitting. They are not a high priority for food or work; hardship . . . is again attributed to a moral quality.—Murray Last, "Adolescents in a Muslim City"

A bustling, kinetic city forged in the crucible of seventeenth- and eighteenth-century trans-Saharan trade, Kano is the economic fulcrum of northern Nigeria, standing at the heart of the country's most populous state, which currently numbers over ten million people. An ancient walled city whose ironworkings date back to the seventh century, Kano was comparable in size and significance to Cairo and Fez by the mid–sixteenth century, and by 1750 it was a city of international stature and cosmopolitan urbanity. As Murray Last put it, Kano scholars owned books written in Arabic by scholars in southern Russia; its language, Hausa, could be heard in nineteenth-century Brazil and Istanbul (1991: 4). A vital manufacturing center in the precolonial period, Kano's high-quality cloth was exported to

Europe and to other parts of Africa; its pivotal location in long-distance trade facilitated the movement of commodities, ideas, and people from the Muslim diaspora of North Africa to Christian societies along the West African coastal corridor.

Although Islam was adopted in Kano in the fourteenth century, it was not until the reforms of Sarkin Muhammadu Rumfa (1463–1499) that the institutional foundations were laid that would eventually convert the city into a metropolis renowned throughout the Islamic world. The spatial and cultural morphology of the city—its labyrinthine and aleatory structure, its massive mud ramparts, the close juxtaposition of the emir's palace, the central mosque, and the market, as well as its armed forces, shari'ah law, and ward-level policing systems—resembled, in its broad outlines, urban Islamic culture across the Middle East. Until the end of the sixteenth century the leading clerics (*ulama*) in Kano were temporary immigrants, most of whom left the city; by the mid–seventeenth century, however, Kano had firmly secured a reputation for producing its own Muslim clerics and saints (Barkindo 1993; Last 1988). In the wake of the nineteenth-century Sokoto *jihad*, whose leader, Shaikh Usman dan Fodio, adopted Qadiriyya as a kind of official Sufi order, Kano emerged as perhaps the leading urban center of religious scholarship within the Sokoto caliphate, itself the largest pre-colonial state system in all of sub-Saharan Africa, attracting scholars and students from a huge catchment area. As a center of trade, manufacture, learning, and Muslim piety, nineteenth-century Kano was a complexly differentiated, multiethnic, and class-stratified city with a transnational outlook and composition. Islamic affiliation—the majority of Kano residents (*kanawa*) belonged to the Maliki *madhhab* and the Qadiriyya Sufi order—constituted the moral and political compass for the Kano emirate and the caliphal structure of which it was part, providing the ideological blueprint for the city's polity and civil society.

Little more than a half century of British colonial rule (1903–1960) radically refigured the political economy of northern Nigeria, and of Kano in particular, without at all contesting the ideological hegemony of Islam or the institutional dominance of the Sufi orders within civil society. Located at the center of a rich and densely settled (peasant) agricultural and trading system, the city emerged within a decade of colonial conquest as West Africa's preeminent entrepôt, whose mercantile prospects were wrapped up with the fortunes of a single world commodity: the peanut. If the class prerogatives of the Muslim ruling elites (*masu sarauta*) within the old emirate structure were enhanced by their conversion into bureaucrats for the colonial Native Administration system, the economic opportunities afforded by a dynamic import-export trade underwrote the growth of a wealthy and powerful class of local mercantile capitalists, who in some respects stood as a counterweight to the powers of the caliphal system. Furthermore, the social and ethnic composition of the city was transformed as "southerners" (Yoruba, Ibo, and Ibibio peoples in particular) flocked to the city, drawn by an expanding trade economy and by clerical and other jobs within the colonial administration available to English speakers with a secondary-school training. Outside the old walled city (birni), southern Nigerians, Lebanese, North Africans, and a motley group of Europeans settled in a number of new suburbs collectively referred to as waje. To the residents of old Kano, waje was little more than a repository of permissiveness, Westernization in its panoply of forms, and non-Muslim strangers. On the whole, however, the birni passively resisted the European and stranger onslaught (Barkindo 1993). Up until 1970 there was no modern restaurant or bar within the walled city, and the School of Arabic Studies and the Judicial School were the only Western postprimary institutions within the birni proper.

If the cultural and social consequences of peanuts and peanut oil were, to a certain extent, held at arm's length during the colonial epoch, it was oil of an altogether different sort—petroleum—that ushered in a new, and in some respects a more radical transformation of Kano city during the halcyon days of the 1970s. Awash in petro-dollars, urban Kano was transformed during the 1970s from a traditional Muslim mercantile center of 400,000 people at the end of the civil war (1970), into a sprawling, ill-planned, and somewhat anarchic metropolis of over one million ten years later. Seemingly overnight Kano emerged as a fully fledged industrial periphery; employment in the industrial manufacturing sector was roughly 11,000 in 1969 and close to 60,000 before the retrenchments of the mid-1980s (Main 1989). The cultural heart of Kano, the old walled city, was now fully engulfed by the new suburbs sprouting up outside the walls. Suburbanization had its origins earlier in the century, of course, but large-scale immigration, coupled with unplanned state-sponsored urban growth, expanded in the 1970s and thereby eroded the autonomy and social standing of the traditional Hausa core of the city, as ever more yan birni (sons of the city) settled in waje or earned their living there.[3] The relatively impervious membrane that had separated the birni from waje was already porous by the late 1960s. But it was the oil boom that finally marked the blurring of the boundary between the old and the new quarters of the city. At the zenith of

3. For Kano citizens (kanawa), the city's cultural heart is the walled city, the birni. From 1903 onward, the suburbs (waje) outside the walled city expanded, populated in the first instance by Westerners and by Nigerians from the south of the country. As Barkindo notes, waje was an evil to be tolerated, but "this view radically changed from about 1970 onwards" (1993: 94).

the petroleum boom, new industrial estates dotted with Lebanese, Egyptian, and European enterprises sprung up at Challawa and Sharada along the city's periphery, armies of migrants poured into the city, and the icons of urban modernity—massive state-sponsored building and infrastructural projects—reshaped the city skyline (Watts and Lubeck 1983). Kano was part construction site and part theater of orgiastic consumption. It had become a modern city in which "dishes for satellite television dominate the compounds of the rich whose wealth is growing ever more disproportionate as austerity . . . hits the poor. A watch for $17,000; a house for $2 million; private jets to London or the Friday prayer at Mecca" (Last 1991: 4).

The reconfigurations of urban life, community relations, and styles of consumption in urban Kano were driven in the first instance by a ferocious state-led modernization program fueled by petroleum revenues (the 1973–74 and 1978–79 price hikes orchestrated by OPEC leveraged up the price of oil from US$5 to US$40 per barrel). Three times the total gross domestic product of contemporary sub-Saharan Africa—US$140 billion—was banked by the Nigerian state between 1970 and 1983. Government revenues exploded, growing at close to 40 percent per annum during the 1970s (Watts 1994). Oil price hikes in 1973–74 and 1978–79 permitted the Nigerian state to unleash a torrent of federal investments, not least in the industrial sector: the Nigerian national index of manufacturing output, for example, almost tripled between 1972 and 1980. Under a succession of military governments between 1972 and 1979, the absolute number of manufacturing establishments and of industrial wage workers, the scale of direct investment by multinationals, and the shares of federal and regional state capital in industrial output, all witnessed positive growth rates. Black gold promised, for the chosen few at any rate, the "dawn of prosperity and progress for the petroleum rich" (Amuzegar 1982: 814).

Fifteen years later the luster of the oil boom had tarnished. Nigeria's economic future appeared by contrast to be quite bleak, if not altogether austere. Spiraling debt—fueled by a seemingly insatiable appetite for imports—the collapse of oil prices in the early 1980s, and the onslaught of draconian neoliberal programs imposed by the World Bank and the International Monetary Fund contributed to a precipitous recession. The "oil fortress," to employ the language of Le Monde (2 October 1994, 15), had been rocked. Nigeria's roller-coaster economy had irrevocably altered the everyday life of all sectors of society. Like other Nigerian cities, Kano's experience of a rather spectacular commodity boom was felt, and here I borrow from Walter Benjamin (1973), as a "shock" of modernity. Indeed, it was from within this world awash with money and power that—to return to Habermas—the system gradually invaded, and partially colonized the life-world, and in so doing the very idea of Muslim identity and correct Muslim practice came to be challenged and contested.

Changing Identities in the Urban Landscape:
Millenarian Islam and Capitalist Modernity in Kano

Emergent modernism has tended to take the specific form of . . . a "reshuffling of the self." Here historical change not only forces upon the individual a search for a new identity but also imposes upon whole social groups the task of revising or replacing defunct beliefs.—Carl Schorske, Fin de Siècle Vienna: Politics and Culture

Eternal religious truths, like other beliefs, are perceived, understood and transmitted by persons historically situated in "imagined" communities, who knowingly or inadvertently contribute to the reconfiguration or interpretation of those verities, even as their fixed and unchanging natures are affirmed.—Dale Eickelman and James Piscatori, "Social Theory in the Study of Islam Societies"

Born into rural poverty in 1927 in northern Cameroon, Mohammedu Marwa (alias Mallam Maitatsine alias Muhammedu Marwa alias Muhammedu Mai Tabsiri) left his birthplace when he was about sixteen years old. He attached himself to a local Muslim cleric and apparently displayed exceptional brilliance in the Qu'ranic science of exegesis (*tafsir*). His exegetical skills were acquired as a student (*almajirai*) in local Muslim networks and nonformal schools (*makarantar allo*). Settling in Kano city around 1945, he was a regular visitor at the preaching sessions around Shahauci and Fagge grounds in the old quarters of the city, providing unorthodox interpretations of Qu'ranic verses read by an associate, Mallam Aminu Umar or Limanu, who had returned from learning "in the East." Marwa insisted that the Qu'ran was the only valid guide to behavior and belief, and thus rejected both the Sunnah and the Shari'ah.[4] According to the official tribunal on the causes of the Kano riots, Maitatsine preached that "any Muslim who reads any book besides the Koran is a pagan" (Federal Government of Nigeria 1981a: 26). The basis of his inflammatory reading of the Qu'ran rested on a stripping away of the hidden meanings in the sacred text by rooting his analyses of verse in local, that is to say West African, conditions. In particular, by playing on the meanings and phonetic associations of certain Arabic and Hausa words, Marwa, or Maitatsine as he became known locally, provided a powerful literalist and on occasion antimaterial-

4. Shari'ah (the path of God) is Islamic law in the form of a set of divinely revealed principles derived from the Qu'ran, from the example of the Prophet, and from tradition: it is applied by judges in Shari'ah courts. Sunnah customarily refers to good conduct or highly desirable acts based on the example of the Prophet, tradition, and reason. Maitatsine denounced the Sunnah as being made "only for Arabs."

ist thrust to the Qu'ran. His vehement denunciation of bicycles, Western apparel, cigarettes, buttons, cars, and so on brought him his name, Maitatsine, derived from the Hausa adage, "Allah ta tsine" (God will curse). By 1962, Marwa had gained some local notoriety as a troublesome, charismatic, and unorthodox preacher, and Emir Sanusi of Kano actually brought him to trial. He was imprisoned for three months and promptly deported. Marwa's local stature grew substantially, however, following his prediction that Emir Sanusi would fall from power, which came true several years later when the emir was ousted in the wake of the military coup.

Marwa returned to Kano shortly after his deportation—sustaining the popular belief that reactionary forces in high places supported his variety of militant political Islam—and continued to live and preach in the city. He was arrested and imprisoned again in 1966–67 and also in 1973–75, but was not deported. In the period following Marwa's return to Kano city, the open spaces of 'Yan Awaki and Kofar Wombai, liminal neighborhoods within the city that were associated with gangs and a lumpen urban culture, provided a sort of beachhead, a sanctuary in which his students could be housed in makeshift dwellings that by the late 1970s included gardens to sustain the growing numbers of followers. By 1979 something like a community had been built and Maitatsine's compound in 'Yan Awaki housed at least 3,000 persons.[5] Witness number forty-nine to the official Government Tribunal, Uzairu Abdullahi, was one such Hausa disciple recruited from Niger eleven months prior to the insurrection (Federal Government of Nigeria 1981b: 58). At the suggestion of Maitatsine, the followers carried little or no money: to sleep with more than one naira (US$.75) was to exhibit a lack of trust in Allah. They also dressed simply, begged for alms, or worked as transient laborers in occupations typically reserved for dry-season migrants ('yan cin rani) such as cart pushing, tea selling, and petty trade.

Maitatsine's followers ('yantatsine) became increasingly visible around the old city, operating in small groups of three to five people, preaching at major junctions near the Sabon Gari mosque, around Koki, and at Kofar Wombai. Through recitations and unorthodox interpretations of the Qu'ran, the students vigorously attacked materialism, unjust leaders, corrupt ulama, and all followers of the powerful Sufi brotherhoods (darikat) who were deemed to be non-Muslim.[6] Unorthodox behavior fueled rumor

5. Maitatsine's diaspora extended across much of northern Nigeria and into the southern Niger Republic, a region sharing a cultural kinship with the Hausa heartland in Nigeria. These networks provided fertile recruiting grounds for students (almajirai) and aspirant lay clerics (gardawa).

6. Rooted in Muslim mysticism, a Sufi master (shaykh) typically associated himself with a founding saint and a brotherhood or order distinguished by initiation and other rituals. In

on a grand scale. According to popular opinion, Kano's wealthiest contractors and some of the most powerful voices of the northern oligarchy energetically supported the Maitatsine movement. Hearsay had it that Maitatsine was lent support in the period after the return to civilian rule in 1979 by luminaries both within the ruling party, the conservative and northern Muslim-dominated National Party of Nigeria (N P N), and perhaps from the incumbent Kano state administration (the populist Peoples' Redemption Party [P R P]). Local rumor fed the mystique of Maitatsine's magical powers. The tribunal reported grotesque (but largely unsubstantiated) tales of cannibalism, human slaughter (a "human spare parts department" as the local northern press referred to it), mass graves, drugged students, and brainwashed women (Yusuf 1988). At the same time, there were reports in the press of the extraordinary bravery, and impressive self-discipline, of the *'yantatsine*. Indeed, there was something like a moral economy within the community. Sometime in 1979, according to testimony by one of his wives, Marwa apparently declared his own prophethood.

On 26 November 1979, the governor of Kano state wrote to Marwa demanding an evacuation of the quarter within two weeks. Originally intending to vacate 'Yan Awaki, Marwa apparently changed his mind and promptly sent out a letter to diaspora communities calling in reinforcements to fight the "infidels." The *'yantatsine* planned to overrun and take control of the Friday Mosque in Kano, N E PA (the national electricity utility company), and the emir's palace. In their denunciation of the government and their demand to appropriate "all land in the name of Allah," there was an allusion at least to some sort of seizure of state power. On 18 December 1980, four police units were sent to Shahauci playground near the emir's palace to arrest some of Maitatsine's preachers. Disorganized police forces were ambushed by "fanatics"—the language is taken from the influential northern newspapers the *New Nigerian* and *Gaskiya ta fi Kwabo*—armed with bows and arrows, daggers and machetes. According to the official tribunal:

> The fanatics in procession and many more emerging from the cover
> provided by onlookers . . . launched an attack on the Police . . . using
> machetes, bows and arrows, swords and clubs, dane guns, daggers
> and other similar weapons. . . . while attacking they kept shout-

---

northern Nigeria there are two main Sufi orders to which men and women belong: Qadiriyya was founded by Abd al-Qadir Jilani, who lived and taught in Baghdad until his death in 1166, after which his ideas and teachings were introduced into West Africa by Arabo-Berber lineages; and Tijaniyya, which takes its name from Ahman al-Tijani, a cleric of southern Algeria who lived in Fez until his death in 1815. The order was spread in West Africa by El Hajj Umar, who introduced Tijaniyya into Nigeria through the Sultan of Sokoto Muhammed Bello in the first part of the nineteenth century.

ing "Kefri, Kefri" meaning infidels. (Federal Government of Nigeria 1981a: 28)

The 'yantatsine burned police vehicles and seized arms. By late afternoon a huge plume of smoke hung over the city. Over the next few days, in a climate of growing chaos and popular fear, fighting spread and casualties mounted. By 21 December, with the police effectively unable to control the situation, vigilante groups entered the scene, and complex negotiations ensued between local authorities and the Kano state governor Abubakar Rimi, who feared the imposition of martial law by the federal government and hence for his own political survival. On 22 December 'yantatsine were reportedly entering Kano to join the insurrection (six busloads of supporters from Sokoto were intercepted en route to Kano), and trucks full of corpses were seen leaving the city.

After five days of stalemate, confusion, and escalating violence, the army intervened on 29 December with ten hours of mortar barrage, supported by air bombardment. Incurring major losses, the 'yantatsine escaped and marched out of the city in the western districts along the Gwarzo road. Maitatsine led the exit from the 'Yan Awaki quarter following the ferocious bombardment by state security and military forces but was injured and died in the western districts outside the city walls. His body was removed from a shallow grave and kept at a local mortuary for several days before it was cremated at the request of local authorities, presumably to prevent martyrdom among his converts and followers. Within days, photographs of Maitatsine's body (apparently illicitly taken into, and smuggled out of, the Kano police department) were hot-selling items peddled by young boys at busy intersections in the city.[7]

Petrolic Capitalism

Oil creates the illusion of a completely changed life, life without work, life for free. . . . Oil is a resource that anesthetizes thought, blurs vision, corrupts. . . . Look at the ministers from oil countries, how high they hold their heads, what a sense of power.—Ryszard Kapucinski, Shah of Shahs

7. According to the official tribunal figures, 4,177 people died (excluding police and military), but the human toll was clearly much greater. Some quite reliable estimates range as high as 10,000; 15,000 were injured and 100,000 rendered homeless. The physical damage was enormous: in Fagge 82 houses and 249 shops were destroyed; in 'Yan Awaki 165 houses were destroyed and heavily damaged. Of the 917 people arrested, 12 percent were juveniles and 185 were non-Nigerian. Many thousands of Maitatsine's supporters avoided arrest and scattered to various states in the north. Between 1981 and 1985 four more incidents occurred between Maitatsine's followers and state authorities in urban and quasi-urban locations across northern Nigeria; perhaps 4,000 to 5,000 persons died in these conflagrations.

The 1970s was the decade of oil, of bristling petrolic nationalism. Twenty-eight third world states were petroleum exporters; each was able to capture, in varying measure, very substantial oil rents leveraged from a petroleum-dependent world by the success of OPEC's cartel. For OPEC-member states, petroleum became the linchpin of the national economy, representing on average at least three-quarters of national export earnings in 1980. Oil producers were, and remain, however a heterogeneous lot: Lilliputian city-states like Qatar with limited capacity to absorb the revenues locally stand in sharp contrast to populous so-called high-absorbers like Indonesia, Venezuela, and Mexico. Nigeria stands, in this regard, as an archetypical high-absorber, since domestic petroleum output in the 1970s, roughly 1.3 million barrels per day, was sufficient to "absorb" substantial domestic state expenditures. Ironically, as a consequence of the oil boom, Nigeria became more of a monocultural economy than it had ever been in the colonial era: 95.3 percent of total export revenues derived from oil, and almost two-thirds of government revenue was dependent on the petroleum sector. Average annual growth rates for credit, money supply, and state expenditures were exceptional: 45 percent, 66 percent, and 91 percent, respectively, between 1973 and 1980.

How, then, can we begin to grasp the character of Nigeria's petrolic modernization—the fast capitalism unleashed by the oil boom—and its implications for Kano civil society? Two rather obvious points at the outset. First, oil is an, and in some respects *the*, archetypical global commodity. It necessarily projects producers fully into the vortex of international circuits of capital and global finance. To this extent one might talk of a globalization of the Nigerian economy and polity. The second is that the enclave character of the oil industry, combined with the fact that oil revenues typically flow directly into national treasuries, has profound implications for state centralization and for state embeddedness. In this sense, the disposition of oil through fiscal linkages acts as a powerful centralizing force at the level of the state, which is projected into civil society (i.e., localized or domesticated) via expanded forms of public ownership, investment, and service provision. In other words, Nigeria's oil boom was transformative along at least three dimensions: through an ostensibly new relationship with the world economy, through a new strategy of capital accumulation as oil earnings overwhelmed previous sources of state surplus, and through a process of state centralization and state-led import substitution. Each vector directly shaped the contours of civil society, providing the ether in which debates of Islamic modernity were bathed.

The genesis of an enlarged state as the mediator of the oil boom appears with particular clarity in Nigeria in the aftermath of the first oil shock. State centralization had commenced during the civil war, but the creation of new regional states (nineteen states from four autonomous regions) deepened the fiscal dependency on a federal purse through statutory revenue allocation procedures. At the same time, the multiplication of states in the wake of the first oil boom vastly expanded the magnitude of the bureaucracy at all levels of government. Creeping state bureaucratization was seen in a variety of guises: capital expenditures at the federal level increased by 800 percent in real terms between 1973 and 1980, the number of parastatals mushroomed from almost nothing in 1970 to over 800 in 1980; the number of federal employees leapt to 280,000. In the period after 1975 under the Murtala and Obasanjo military administrations (1975–79), the state wage bill and the state-owned industrial sector reached their apotheosis. The federal government encouraged auto-assembly and initiated an ambitious capital and intermediate goods program including an iron and steel sector, petrochemicals, and light engineering. In the same way that oil promised for the Shah of Iran a Great Civilization, so did effortless money produce boundless ambition in Nigeria. El Dorado had been located; it was an oil well.

Naturally the rise of a centralized, bureaucratic petro-state with earnings in 1980 in excess of US$25 billion had serious implications for politics and class rule in Nigeria. The regional elites no longer depended on access to surpluses generated by peasant producers but on oil rents redistributed through the state apparatuses. Indeed, while the military–civil servant alliance maintained its precarious northern political hegemony, the vastly expanded oil revenues bankrolled a huge rent-seeking edifice, a "flabby and heterogeneous dominant coalition preoccupied with a grabbing of public resources . . . through an elaborate network of patronage and subsidies" (Bardhan 1988: 82). Not only did the state embark on a massive program of infrastructural and industrial modernization—attempting to lay the groundwork for systematic capitalist accumulation—but these expenditures became the means by which petrodollars created pacts and coalitions within a national polity sharply divided along regional, ethnic, and religious lines. Patronage, contracting, and subsidies were part and parcel of the desperate political struggle to win control of the state, which was privatized in the specific sense that public office became, to employ Max Weber's language, a prebend, that is, a public position to be used for personal gain. Corruption flourished on a gargantuan scale; in fact the entire local and federal bureaucratic environment was astonishingly undisciplined, chaotic, and venal. In the wake of the return to civilian rule in 1979 these state incapacities reached new levels of malfeasance and inefficiency. Government became more than ever, as Nigerian novelist Chinua

Achebe (1988) observed in his novel *Anthills of the Savannas*, a "crummy family business."

To summarize, there were several key ways in which oil-driven globalization of the boom period fundamentally reconfigured the national, regional, and urban spaces in which Islamism operated and flourished. The first was a commodity boom. Nigeria began to "import all importables," as Frishman put it (1988: 12); Nigerian merchandise imports (capital, intermediary, and consumer goods) increased from N1.1 billion in 1973 to N14.6 billion in 1981. Propelled by new federal and state bureaucracies and the infusion of money unleashed by government-mandated (Udoji Commission) salary increases in 1975, the oil boom became a consumer spending spree. Everything from stallions to stereos exchanged hands in Kano, a sort of commodity fetishism that one commentator aptly described as a Nigerian "cargo cult." The second source of local transformation was a gargantuan state-financed urban construction boom; the capital expenditures of Kano state grew at an average rate of 57 percent between 1973 and 1980. The construction industry (roads, office construction, industrial plant) grew by at least 20 percent per annum in the 1970s, sucking rural labor into dynamic but hopelessly unplanned cities such as Kano.

Furthermore, the boom in oil had the effect of both depressing and distorting non-oil sectors, particularly agriculture and the rural sector. A shortage of labor combined with the inflation of input costs created a profit squeeze for many peasant producers, which was reflected in a depressed agricultural sector and in the collapse of traditional exports (cocoa, groundnuts, and palm oil effectively disappeared). Food imports, particularly wheat, which became a new staple of the urban poor, increased sharply, prompting a series of expensive state irrigation schemes to produce wheat for the local market. Socially disruptive, and a source of lavish rents for contractors, politicians, and the military, these schemes contributed less to national food self-sufficiency than to the growth of land speculation and growing economic inequality in the countryside associated with the rise of so-called overnight farmers and farmer-trader speculators. The oil boom, in short, had manufactured rural-urban drift, social dislocation in the countryside, and a sense—confirmed in many other aspects of social life—of state corruption and violence.

In Nigerian history, the oil boom of the 1970s stands between the first tentative postcolonial efforts at import-substituting industrialization in the 1960s and the oil bust and economic neoliberalism of the 1980s and 1990s. In this sense, petrolic capitalism and Fordist-style state-led industrialization in Nigeria has a much wider resonance. A swath of Middle Eastern political economy can also be located on this larger canvas of the shift from import substitution during the so-called Golden Age of North Atlantic Fordism (1950–70) to the OPEC price revolution from 1973 to 1982 and the surge of state-centered development to the commodity crash, recession, and liberal reforms (infitah) of the last fifteen years.[8] In all such instances, the globalizing impact of the oil boom set the stage for "the crisis of the secular nationalist state once the [oil] rents were spent" (Lubeck 1995: 18). Even before the neoliberal reforms, the oil boom had globalized the economies of oil exporters, disrupted social, cultural, and political economic relations, and laid the foundations for the first Islamic political revolution in Iran in 1979. During the 1980s, globalization took the form not of a commodity boom but of a commodity bust and recession followed by economic liberalization under the auspices of international regulatory institutions. Nigeria, like other oil exporters, experienced 1980s neoliberalism in a particularly savage form because of the precipitous economic decline, itself a function of the fact that the oil rents were unearned windfalls. The chilly winds of adjustment and economic reform that blew into the OPEC world in the 1980s may have stimulated transnational manufacturing and the internationalization of financial activity, but they simultaneously undercut the entire state-led industrial strategy and the rent seeking, that is, politically targeted subsidies, which it sustained. If the crisis of the 1970s was about the failure of state-centered development to deliver improved living standards, public accountability, and democracy, the globalization and radical restructuring of the state that occurred in the name of neoliberal rectitude during the 1980s and 1990s rendered a crisis of another sort: spending cutbacks, the collapse of already tattered social services, declining real wages, public sector layoffs, and the growing presence of foreign transnationals (i.e., the specter of foreign control and Westernization). Islamism clearly predated the oil boom, just as some new forms of political Islam have emerged in the wake of the oil bust. But the central question remains how and whether, in light of the historically contingent forms that globalization assumes, Muslims (radical, militant, or moderate) can make Islamic traditions speak to and interpolate the particular senses of frustration, despondency, and interest thrown up in the interstices of national economies coping with the demands of the new global economy (see Lubeck 1995).

8. The state development occurred against a backdrop of international inflation, declining real incomes, and the dissolution of Keynesian coalitions. Richards (1995) and Richards and Waterbury (1990) have documented for Egypt, for example, the turn from the 1960s (a period of retarded job creation, depressed agriculture, and fostered rural-urban migration) to the oil boom, which raised urban incomes, stimulated inflation and rent seeking, and distorted the economy.

Experiencing Fast Capitalism in Kano City

This letter is from the Prophet Mohammed. It came from Medina to Mecca . . . to Wadi . . . to Kukawa . . . to Bornoland. . . . From there to Hadejia . . . to Kano and from Kano to the whole world. The Prophet said there will be disaster of the wind, poverty, death of sheep and ill-health of women and men. The ill-health of women and men will affect their womanhood and manhood respectively. It would affect the old and the young of women and men East and West, South and North.—Letter circulated by Maitatsine followers and published in *The New Nigerian*, 3 March 1984

How was the peculiar configuration of oil, state, and commodification "experienced" in Kano, and quite specifically how was civil society and the public sphere invaded under the onslaught of what Habermas (1991) calls the "irresistible inner dynamics of the systemic sphere," the "steering media" of power and money? I want to suggest that the question of experience contains two aspects. On the one hand, the oil boom was experienced in class terms, and yet the social and cultural character of this class experience in Kano was, to use Marx's language, inherited from the past and was irreducibly local. The central social class we must consider is the self-conscious popular strata in northern Nigerian society identified locally as commoners, or *talakawa*. On the other hand, the roller-coaster ride on Nigeria's fast capitalist track was experienced explicitly, to employ language from Gramsci's *Prison Notebooks*, in relation to "ethico-political" hegemony, that is to say, on the terrain of civil society and cultural order, and the discursive frame of reference here is Islam itself.

Let's begin with the question of class experience. According to a World Bank study in the early 1980s, 52 percent to 67 percent of Kano's urban population existed at the "absolute poverty level" (cited in Lubeck 1985: 380). At least one-third of the Kano urban labor force was accounted for by the 15,000 or so small-scale enterprises (the vast majority in the trade sector), roughly 10 percent by formal sector industrial workers and perhaps another 20 percent were informal sector workers and the partially or fully unemployed (Frishman 1988). This subaltern class was occupationally diverse but had a social unity in terms of a popular self-identity in Hausa society as commoners. A commoner (*talaka*) is "a person who holds no official position . . . a man in the street . . . a poor person" (Bargery 1934). As an indigenous social category it is of considerable antiquity, emerging from the social division of labor between town and countryside associated with the genesis of political kingdoms (the *sarauta* system) in the fifteenth century, and subsequently the emirate system of the Sokoto caliphate (1806–1902), in which a lineage-based, office-holding class (*masu sarauta*) exercised political authority over subject populations. Talakawa refers, then, to a class relationship of a precapitalist sort but also a political relationship among status-honor groups with distinctive cultural identities and lifestyles. Naturally, the commoners have been differentiated in all sorts of complex ways through the unevenness of proletarianization—the industrial working class, for example, constituting an important social segment of the commoners as such (Lubeck 1985).

Although there is a generic sort of subaltern identity embodied in the notion of commoner, I wish to identify two distinctive social segments that are key to an understanding of Maitatsine's effort to "reshuffle" the Muslim self, namely, to return to a scripturalist form of piety based on the Qu'ran. Both are of some antiquity and are fashioned by locally distinctive social and cultural processes. The first concerns dry-season migrants ('yan cin rani) who circulate through the urban economy during the long dry season, relieving pressures on domestic grain reserves in the countryside, and who may generate limited savings that are typically of great value to dependent sons preparing for marriage. I would include in this category migrants who were, strictly speaking, not participants in seasonal circulatory networks but as a consequence of the urban construction boom and the collapse of agriculture were drawn into the Kano labor market in huge numbers. Almost wholly male, single, and young, and typically drawn from the densely settled and land-scarce northern provinces, they became semipermanent city residents, characteristically working in the so-called traditional occupations such as cart pushers, refuse collectors, and itinerant laborers.

This floating population expanded dramatically in the 1970s not only because of the urban construction boom but also because of rural hardships, notably the devastating impact of drought and food shortage in the early 1970s and the dispossession of peasants because of land speculation, fraudulent land claims, and inadequate state compensations for suburban expansion and state irrigation schemes. In any event, these migrants shuttled into the northern cities such as Kano during the oil boom, filling niches in the secondary labor market and constituting a young and increasingly alienated lumpen proletariat. According to Paul Lubeck (1987) almost 20 percent of the rural migrants who came to Kano during the 1970s were Muslim students (almajirai) or were sons of Islamic scholars. It was, however, precisely this informal sector employment that felt the pinch of declining real wages (because of high inflation) and the gradual displacement of traditional occupations owing in large measure to the import boom and industrial substitution.[9]

9. According to Frishman two-thirds of the small-scale enterprises in Kano disappeared between 1973 and 1980, the lowest survival rates being in traditional occupations such as textiles, leather goods, enamel bowls, and shoe repair (1988: 16).

The second segment of the commoners is associated with the system of informal Muslim schooling (*makarantar allo*), termed "Qu'ranic networks" by Paul Lubeck (1985, 1987), which linked city and country. These networks long predate the nineteenth century *jihad* and refer to a peripatetic tradition, rooted in the human ecology of the Sahel, in which students study with lay clerics (*mallams*) during the dry season. Students migrated to centers of Muslim learning such as Kano and typically studied the Qu'ranic science of exegesis at the feet of notable scholars often living in the entryways of homes of influential merchants and notables. Maitatsine was himself a product of this system. Islamic networks were sustained by a sort of urban moral economy—begging and almsgiving as part of a normative set of relations between rich and poor—that served to both extend Islam into the countryside and provide a measure of social and ideological integration for Hausa society as a whole. The students themselves often worked in the textile industry, acquiring important commercial and craft skills. In Kano these students are referred to as *gardawa*, although this is a semantically dense term that also refers to adult Muslim students, aspirant lay clerics of sorts, who may not be seasoned migrants as such but longer-term urban residents. As an ancient center of learning, of vigorous brotherhood activity, and of enormous mercantile wealth, Kano was quite naturally a major center of *gardawa* activity.

If commoners as a class (and the migrant and *gardawa* segments of it) represent a key set of structural preconditions through which many Kano residents experienced the oil boom, then what were the immediate or proximate qualities of that experience in civil society in urban Kano? I shall focus on three sets of processes that are framed by Cohen and Arato's general definition of civil society as "structures of socialization, association, and organized forms of communication of the lifeworld" (1992: ix, x): state mediation in the form of corruption and violent but undisciplined security forces, urban social processes including the familial and associational spheres, and the return to civilian party politics in 1979.

I have already referred to the growing presence of the local and federal states in social and economic life. To the extent that the state was rendered much more visible in society by virtue of its expanded activities, including road and office construction and contracting of various sorts, its visibility became synonymous with a total lack of moral responsibility and state accountability. In popular discourse, the state and government meant massive corruption on a Hobbesian scale. Graft through local contracts, import speculation, foreign-exchange dealings, drug smuggling, hoarding of food, and so on proliferated on all levels of local and federal officialdom. It was commonplace to hear the governor referred to as a thief, or the lament, "Nigeria ta lalachi" (Nigeria has been ruined). State ownership even implicated Islam itself: the Muslim brotherhoods owned shares in companies while the government was also centrally involved in the annual migration of 100,000 pilgrims who participated in the hadj, a sacred event that was widely seen as a source of corruption and conspicuous consumption rather than as an exercise in Muslim piety. In the return to civilian rule, state corruption reached unprecedented levels; as the commoners put it, "siyasa ta bata duniyo" (politics has spoiled the world). When the home of the governor was searched in Kano in 1983, US$5.1 million was found stacked up in cardboard boxes: primitive accumulation on a grand scale. At around the same time, 10 percent of the Nigerian GDP was "discovered" in an unnamed private bank account in Switzerland.

To put the matter bluntly, state mediation of the oil boom meant corruption, chaos, and bureaucratic undiscipline. Commoners were systematically denied access to a state they experienced as morally bankrupt, illegitimate, and incompetent. The police, who had been placed under federal jurisdiction, and the internal security forces were widely regarded as particularly corrupt, disorganized, and violent; they embodied the moral and political degeneracy of state power. In the context of rising urban crime, it was the police who proved to be the trigger for all sorts of community violence; they were uniformly feared and loathed by Kano's urban poor. Indeed, it was the anti-riot police who perpetrated the slaughter of at least fourteen peasants at the Bakalori irrigation project in a conflict over land compensation, which occurred six months prior to the Maitatsine insurrection. In the popular imagination the police were feared and were explicitly referred to as daggal—literally, the devil.

At another level, the speeding up of Nigerian capitalism—the faster pace and rhythm of life unleashed by oil and state investment—was refracted through the lens of the urban community and associational life. The central issue here is not simply the anarchic and chaotic growth of Kano city— a terrifying prospect in itself—but also the changing material basis of commoners' life and what it implied for the brute realities of urban living. First, urban land became a source of speculation for Kano merchants and civil servants, reflected in the fact that the price of urban plots in the working-class Tudun Wada neighborhood increased twentyfold between 1970 and 1978. Land records invariably disappeared (usually through arson), and compensation for land appropriated by the state was arbitrary and a source of recurrent conflict. Second, the escalation of food prices, typically in the context of price rigging, hoarding, and licensing scandals, far outstripped the growth of urban wages. The inflationary spiral in wage goods went hand in hand with both the internationalization of consumption by Kano's elites—car ownership, for instance, grew by 700 percent in six years—and the erosion of many traditional occupations (mat making, local building, donkey transport, leatherwork, cloth beating [Frishman 1988]) of students and migrants within the secondary labor market.

Furthermore, the state-funded Universal Primary Education (UPE) program represented both an ideological attack by proponents of "Western education" on the Qu'ranic networks and associations, and an assault on the lay clerics and the students who sustained the informal Muslim schooling system. In Kano state, enrollment increased by 491 percent between 1973 and 1977, and in Hadejia emirate the number of primary schools leapt from 36 in 1970 to 392 in 1980. In the 1970s the lay clerics were vigorous critics of UPE, a discontentedness suggestive of a much broader crisis in the Muslim schooling system itself. Broadly put, the lineaments of an urban moral economy—similar in some respects to what Robert Putnam (1993) in a quite different cultural context has referred to as social capital—and of a number of informal public spheres are simultaneously rendered illegitimate and dysfunctional.

One final circumstance is central to an understanding of the discursive space in which Maitatsine could flourish: the return to civilian rule in Nigeria in 1979 following a long period of military governance. In spite of the fact that the National Party of Nigeria (NPN)—the party of the conservative northern oligarchy—was victorious at the federal level and dominated several state legislatures, the populist/socialist People's Redemption Party (PRP) swept to power in Kano state elections. The local government reforms of the 1970s had virtually eliminated the once powerful Native Authority officials who were replaced by the university-educated administrators. However, the triumph of the PRP on a strong antiaristocratic platform marked a qualitatively new political environment for the commoners. Much could be said about the PRP—not least its political split between "radical" and "conservative" factions—but in essence, the assertion of a populist, procommoner state government in Kano provided a political space in which the radical discourse of political Islam could operate and indeed be encouraged, not least insofar as it took as its starting point a critique of those Sufi brotherhoods most closely associated with the traditional emirate authorities and the feudal elements of the old northern ruling classes.

Civil Society and the Definition of Islamic Orthodoxy

Every religion . . . is in reality a multiplicity of distinct and contradictory religions: there is one Catholicism for the peasants, one for women and one for intellectuals which is itself variegated and disconnected.—Antonio Gramsci, Selections from the Prison Notebooks

What the 'ulama [divines] are doing is to attempt a definition of orthodoxy—a (re)ordering of knowledge that governs the "correct" form of Islamic practices. . . . This like all practical criticism seeks to construct a relation of discursive dominance. . . . [But] "Orthodoxy" is not easy to secure in conditions of radical change.—Talal Asad, *Genealogies of Religion*

Let me now turn to the question of capitalist modernity in relation to Islam and the role and character of Islamism within the contours of civil society. In Nigeria, as elsewhere in the Muslim world, Islam is not a monolith but contains important institutional, ideological, and social organizational tensions and contradictions within its circumference.[10] There have been, for example, struggles between and against the Sufi brotherhoods in Nigeria since the 1950s, and the effort by Ahmadu Bello to create the Jama'atu Nasril Islam (Organization for the Victory of Islam) in 1962 can be understood as an attempt to unite a *divided* Muslim community as a way of securing northern political hegemony in the newly independent Nigerian federation. But there is little question that over the past thirty or so years the fissiparous nature of the Muslim community has deepened, and by the 1970s polarization and conflict were increasing. A primary axis of difference and debate links the Sufi orders of brotherhoods—Qadiriyya and Tijaniyya—to which many Nigerian Muslims are aligned, and newer so-called fundamentalist or anti-Sufi groups such as the powerful Jama'atu Izalat Al-Bidah Wa Iqamat Al Sunnah or Izala (roughly translated as the Removal of False Innovations and the Establishment of Orthodox Tradition) headed by Abubakar Gumi with strong connections to King Faisal of Saudi Arabia, and the Muslim Students Society (MSS), the latter being itself split between pro-Iranian and pro-Saudi factions (Ibrahim 1991).

These public debates, which have spilled over on occasion into physical confrontations, are not unrelated to the extraordinary ferment throughout the Muslim world during the last two decades and must be seen as exemplary of a much longer debate over Islamic orthodoxy.[11] Indeed, Islam possesses a long tradition of revival (*tajdid*) and reform (*islah*), which is as much rooted within its own traditions as it is a response to Westernization in its various forms. Clerics, scholars, and religious leaders—representing in the Nigerian case differing Sufi and anti-Sufi constituencies—attempt to redefine Muslim orthodoxy in the context of radical social, economic, and political change by engaging in a long-standing Muslim tradition of public criticism. As Muslims, in other words, "their differences are fought out on

10. There is, of course, a unity within which there are "several traditions related to one another formally through common founding texts and temporally through diverging authoritative interpreters" (Asad 1993: 236).
11. The Aniagolu Tribunal noted 34 clashes between 1978 and 1980 in which "the rival groups were principally Izala, Tijaniyya and Qadiriyya" (Federal Government of Nigeria 1981a: 87).

the ground of [orthodoxy]" (Asad 1993: 210) in an attempt to establish a discursive dominance.

Like other great traditions, Islam is also paradigmatic for its followers, and its origins provide the normative basis of Muslim governance and personal conduct. At the heart of this paradigm, insofar as it shapes attitudes toward the state, society, wealth, and poverty, is the concept of justice. As Burke and Lubeck note, "Popular Islamic ideas of justice . . . inhibit the flaunting of wealth and the taking of interest, and encourage charity. The scripturalist tradition . . . thus constrains the choices open to Muslim actors . . . and also provide repertories of popular action and cultural vocabularies for their expression" (1987: 649). Of course, these abstractions derived from texts and scripturalist discourses are filtered through local experiences and through quite contrary models of the Islamic polity. In the Sunni tradition (of which Nigeria is part), Burke (1986) distinguishes between the Rashidun model, which roots justice and moral virtue in the early Muslim community and the strict application of the Shari'ah, and the imperial model of the later Arab caliphate, which has been typically invoked by incumbent Islamic governments to justify raison d'état policies. Despite the distinctions and historical differences in political practice within the Sunni tradition, a normative thread runs through the great tradition, a search for justice in an unjust world that is analogous to the West European notion of a moral economy (Lubeck 1985, 1986). Like the European counterpart, the Islamic moral economy was a configuration of symbols and traditions to be interpreted, struggled over, and fought for, but it represented a series of cultural and moral norms that imposed particular expectations on the rich, the clergy, and the ruling class more generally, as well as the commoners.

In the light of my emphasis on flexibility, public criticism, and diversity, how might one characterize the communicative and institutional landscape of Islam in northern Nigeria that existed on the eve of the oil boom, when Maitatsine was already active within Kano? I want to draw attention to two basic orientations within Kano Islam. The first concerns the shifting influence of the Sufi brotherhoods, specifically the Qadiriyya, which is associated with the holy war (jihad) of Usman dan Fodio in the early nineteenth century and more generally with the traditional northern Nigerian Hausa-Fulani aristocracy, and the Tijaniyya, which had grown and flourished in the fertile soil of colonial politics and merchant-capitalism. In contradistinction to the Qadiriyya, which was party to a class alliance between the local Muslim ruling class and the colonial state, Tijaniyya contained specific radical, anticolonial beliefs that appealed to a traditional merchant class operating in the interstices of the colonial economy (Paden 1973).

Since the 1960s, however, the hegemony of both brotherhoods has been contested by a number of anti-Sufi reformist sects in northern Nigeria—notably the Izala founded in 1978 by Mallam Idris in Jos in central Nigeria—whose aim is to abolish innovation and to practice Islam in strict accordance with the Qu'ran and the Sunnah. Anti-Sufi sentiment in Nigeria can be traced to the 1930s, but it proliferated during and after World War II with the growth of a class of new elites who articulated both the virtues of the modern social transformations in contradistinction to the vices of tradition and an anticolonial politics that turned on the question of the enhanced powers of "un-Islamic" emirs, imperialist lackeys who had willfully sidelined the legitimate authority and influence of the *ulama* (Umar 1993). Sa'ad Zungur (1915–58) for example was an early critic of Sufi belief and of the colonial support of customary powers insofar as it rested, in his view, on the introjection of superstition (for example, polygamy, saint veneration, wife seclusion) into pristine Islam as practiced by the Prophet and the caliphs.

Since 1960, anti-Sufi movements have proliferated largely through the intellectual leadership and adroit communicational strategies of Sheikh Abubakar Gumi, who has effectively used the Radio Television Kaduna, the Nigerian Television Authority, the Kaduna-based Hausa language newspaper *Gaskiya ta fi Kwabo*, and distributed taped cassettes of his *tafsir* sessions in the Sultan Bello Mosque in Kaduna to promote his message. In Gumi's view, Sufism is not part of Islam because it emerged long after Islam had been completed; saint veneration is denounced as illegitimate, and he rejects key Sufi concepts as invalid innovations, superfluous or un-Islamic (Umar 1993). Gumi argued persuasively for a positivistic conception of Islam, which supersedes any sense of perfection through personal or subjective spiritual experience.

Referred to as the "new jihadists," the doctrines of Izala are identical with Gumi's views. Although critical of the West's decadence, they are neither antimodern nor antimaterialist in any simple sense and hence are widely supported by the northern Nigerian intelligentsia and by aggressive new technocrats and businessmen. In some senses, Izala ideology "is to the Islamic brotherhoods what Protestantism is to Catholicism" (Gregoire 1993: 114). But it is also a form of protest against traditional noncapitalist values and against the perceived corruption of religious values and practices in the context of what Umar calls a "shift from communal to an individual mode of religiosity . . . in tune with the rugged individualism of capitalist social relations" (1993: 178). Whether Izala is simply a cathartic response to the tensions and frustration of Nigerian capitalism is less relevant for my concerns than the fact that its exegetical broadcasts, and its polemics on the need for the separation of mosques, contributed to a growing sense of cleavage and division within Kano city Islam, and to the wider legitimacy of anti-Sufi sentiment.[12] Indeed the very success of Izala had the effect of diluting the earlier tensions between Tijaniyya and Qadiriyya that had developed during a period of Sufi popularization in the 1950s and had unified the orders through new associational forms in 1977.[13] This growing sense of public debate had the joint effect of fueling the fire of so-called Islamic solutions to urban problems and of deepening the Islamic saturation of civil society. Not only were more mosques built in Kano and their activities expanded, but at the same time Muslim institutions such as the Kano Foundation extended their activities to education, assistance for the poor and destitute, social mobilization, and maintaining public order.

The second dimension speaks to the shifting relations among the lay clerics (*ulama*), the teachers (*mallams*), and their associational forms. Many *mallams* are of course spokespersons for the brotherhoods and, to the extent that they are affiliated with state patronage, can be seen as pro-establishment (*malamin soro*). There is nonetheless a relatively independent laity associated in particular with the local Qu'ranic schools, of which there are three different forms. First, the primary schools (*makarantar allo*) for which the Qu'ran is the main (and sometimes the only) text, typically learned by rote at a seminary. Many of Maitatsine's followers were products of this system, in which primary school teachers are typically independent, customarily sustained through alms. Then there is the higher school (*makarantar ilimi*), which ranges widely over theological and legal matters, and interpretation of the religious texts such as the hadith and the Qu'ran. Most higher school teachers are members of the brotherhood orders and are paid for their instructional activities. And third, the so-called Islamiyya schools are primary and secondary, set up in the 1930s and expanded in the 1950s with a syllabus comparable to Western forms of education but focusing on Arabic and Islamic studies.[14] Since the 1970s, they have been funded

12. The critique focuses especially on certain innovations: the folding of arms while praying, not facing Mecca while praying, collections of fees by mallams, and the wearing of amulets. The latter is especially interesting because it speaks to the belief popular in many segments of society in non-Muslim spirits and powers. It is precisely these sources of power (often associated in northern Nigeria with non-Muslim Hausa [Maguzawa] and the urban underworld) that Maitatsine drew upon; indeed, Maitatsine was recognized as a sort of sorcerer. Several of Maitatsine's lieutenants carried talismans (one who is quoted in the *Aniagolu Report* said: "If I were cut into pieces and die I shall come back to life").

13. Specifically Kungiyar Jama'atu Ahlus-Sunnati and Kungiyar Dakarun Dan Fodio. See Umar 1993: 166–67 for an excellent account of these organizations.

14. Islamiyya schools are accredited (i.e., recognized by the state—indeed are state-funded in part), and their graduates are typically employed as judges and scribes in the northern emirates, and normally can gain entry into Nigerian universities. Many of the 'Yan Izalas are in fact

by wealthy Muslim businessmen and by philanthropic groups (for example, the Kano Foundation) with strong affiliations to particular local Muslim constituencies such as Izala.

Key to my argument is the growing tension between these Muslim networks and associations, and how these frictions reside within a larger debate over the differing weight and significance attributed to the Qu'ran, the hadith, the Sunnah, and to distinctive religious practices such as prayer, dress, and ritual. The migrant students (*gardawa*), seen as ignorant and traditional by both the higher school teachers and the Islamiyya scholars, did not enjoy the prestige and patronage of the state and characteristically were not appointed as local judges. The 'Yan Izala and the *gardawa* conversely occupied the same terrain in their antibrotherhood beliefs.[15] Both the *ilimi* and the *gardawa* were marginalized by the fact that the proliferation of Islamiyya schools (in conjunction with the growth of state-funded universal primary education during the oil years) systematically eroded their traditional networks.[16] As Murray Last observes,

> No longer now are there the eventual posts as respected village scholars now that the primary schools have their own religious instructors. No longer is there the ready hospitality (particularly in towns) and the same respect (or casual work) for the migrant students. Worst of all, perhaps, the class of austerely pious, very learned yet public scholars, who once were the models for a particular way of life, has all but disappeared. (quoted in Barkindo 1993: 96)

A longtime resident of Kano, Marwa witnessed these changes in the political and cultural economy of urban Kano during the frenetic oil years. As a charismatic preacher with a compelling, if idiosyncratic, reading of the Qu'ran, he recruited followers from the influx of migrants and students into the city and from the marginal underclass of Kano. Marwa's disciples recruited at the lorry parks and railway stations in Kano where they typically sustained themselves by selling tea and bread (Federal Government of Nigeria 1981b). His followers (migrants, itinerant workers, *gardawa*) were products of the same Qu'ranic system as himself; most of his Kano

---

products of the Islamiyya system, and Sheikh Gumi is perhaps its most distinguished and influential graduate. Many members of the Muslim Students Association are connected to the Islamiyya schools and have a scripturalist reading of Islam.

15. Associated with the brotherhoods, *darikat* practice involved daily prayer and meditation, strict discipline and obedience to saints.

16. I have not mentioned here the tradition of millenarian and Mahdist revolt in Nigeria, which is important. The year 1979 was also the onset of the new century in the Muslim calendar, which was widely held to promise the coming of the Mahdi.

followers were educated in the traditional primary school system. Furthermore, Marwa's use of syncretist and pre-Islamic powers resonated strongly with migrants from the countryside, where vestiges of ancient Hausa metaphysical belief remained quite influential. Slowly Marwa was able to build up an enclave in 'Yan Awaki fashioned around a disciplined, and self-consciously austere, egalitarian community of Muslim brothers who supported themselves largely through alms, although land and urban gardens were appropriated to support the devotees.[17] Marwa's unorthodox and literalist interpretation of the Qu'ran focused specifically on the icons of modernity: bicycles, watches, cars, money. But it would be mistaken to view Maitatsine as antimodern or primevalist in any simple sense. The movement employed modern arms when necessary, and Marwa emphasized the ill-gotten quality of goods and not their inherent illegitimacy. Likewise, his desire to seize key institutions in Kano city—the radio station and the state electricity company—is hardly antimodernist. Kano merchants, bureaucrats, and elites were implicated in his critique, but he targeted the state for its moral bankruptcy and the police as its quintessential representatives. Any affiliation to the state naturally contaminated Islamic practice.

Not surprisingly, commodities and money, in fact, loomed large in Marwa's preaching. The basis of his provocative reading of the Qu'ran as the only valid guide to human conduct rested on the revelation of hidden meanings within the sacred text, and in his rooting of verse in local conditions. Marwa's vehement denunciation of cigarettes, motor vehicles, buttons, and Western-style apparel was revealed through his careful textual analysis. Marwa interpreted Qu'ranic texts in part by playing on the meanings and phonetic associations of certain Hausa and Arabic words. Furthermore, he played creatively with the relations between signs and their referents. In his public preaching he pointed to the physical similarity between the Arabic character for Allah and a simple graphical depiction of a bicycle. This homology not only validated his accusation that all persons who rode bicycles were by definition pagan but also confirmed his far-reaching attack on the corruption and degeneration of Islam at the highest levels. The sense of moral crisis in a curious way lent both credibility and legitimacy to Maitatsine's ideas because there is within Islamic eschatology a strong belief in "Signs of the Hour," the idea that at the end of every century (which in the Muslim calendar fell in 1979) a leader may appear to restore order, to renew and regain the world that has been lost.

17. According to Saad (1988: 118), a survey conducted among the arrested 'yantatsine revealed that 95 percent believed themselves to be Muslim.

To put the argument starkly, Nigeria's oil-based fast capitalism was mapped onto civil society; in practice this produced a gradual colonization of the Kano lifeworld by the steering media of petrolic capitalism. Fast capitalism was experienced by a differentiated, heterogeneous, and transnational Muslim community in Nigeria, which became the forum for a particular sort of public debate.[18] The growing popularity and following of Izala, the Muslim Students Society, and other fundamentalist groups in relation to the powerful brotherhoods suggests that an important struggle over orthodox Islam was already under way in Nigeria by the early 1970s and that cultural and religious capital relevant to these debates was drawn from a transnational Muslim community. Participation in the pilgrimage to Mecca, the geographic circulation of religious elites through transnational networks such as the brotherhoods, and the consumption of new ideas through radio and circulating audio cassettes were all relevant to this vibrant, and not infrequently acrimonious, public discourse—indeed to reasoning within the circumference of a particular tradition—within Islam.

Maitatsine was, in this regard, legitimately part of a wide-ranging public discourse within the public sphere of the northern Nigerian Muslim community. The language of reformism (if not necessarily radical Islamism) resonated with large sections of northern Nigerian society, and Maitatsine enjoyed a hearing and a measure of serious attention, as Bawuro Barkindo properly put it, "partly because many . . . people who did not join him agreed with the *content of his preaching*" (1993: 98; my emphasis). Maitatsine was no more an "isolated fanatic" than the panoply of Islamisms and its complex genesis is simply fundamentalist. Powerful economic and political forces marginalized the popular laity and their followers (*gardawa*) to whom Maitatsine spoke and to some extent represented in Kano city, and this permitted Maitatsine to resurrect a debate dating back at least to the colonial conquest that had in a sense never ceased. This debate condemned the European world and advocated a return to a time in which Islam could be practiced without hindrance. Just as Islam in general had succeeded in penetrating and refiguring civil society in the course of the twentieth century, so too Maitatsine's excavation of and deliberations on an older debate carried a great deal of popular legitimacy and interest. It was the marginalization of a long-standing and institutionalized form of traditional Muslim learning and the exploitation of the Maitatsine movement by larger political forces that ultimately propelled Marwa to both establish and violently

18. This is to make the point that Nigerian clerics, students, and Muslims more generally traveled to North Africa and the Middle East (via the *hadj*) and were familiar with debates within Islam in these places.

defend an independent religious community within the old city walls of Kano that actively pursued and promoted a utopian vision.

The Maitatsine movement had neither the resources nor the organizational capacity of some other forms of political Islam—for example, FIS in Algeria or Musa Sadr's Movement of the Deprived in Lebanon—nor was it capable of seizing state power. But what is known of the followers and of those who tacitly lent their support endorses what seems to be a much broader pattern of the coalitional character of Islamism. Most of these movements are, as Richards (1995) notes, fissiparous and cellular, but they are typically composed of a counterelite of Islamist businessmen and professionals whose opportunities are limited by the old order, a stratum of alienated and frustrated educated young men and women from the larger cities,[19] and a mass of the urban poor who constitute what Roy calls "lumpen-Islamism" (1994: 84). Most students of political sociology agree that the typical profile of the militant is a younger person (usually male) with some education who is a recent urban migrant (Denoeux 1993; Ayubi 1991; Richards 1995; Roy 1994). In this sense the 'yantatsine (Marwa's followers) were almost archetypal: they were uniformly poor (80 percent had income well below the minimum wage) with a not insubstantial tacit support from a number of students, well-placed professionals, businessmen, and commoners at large. In general, however, the genesis of Marwa and his wide-ranging networks of affiliation can only be fully comprehended in terms of the material and status deprivation of 'yantatsine recruits scrambling to survive in an increasingly chaotic and Hobbesian urban environment, punctuated by the unprecedented ill-gotten wealth and corruption of the dominant classes in urban Kano.

Community, Identity, Reason: Islamism and the Very Idea of Civil Society

Islam is taking on new meanings as Muslims assert the centrality of Islam in public and private life. . . . Understanding Islamic fundamentalism as an expression of modernity rather than tradition yields insights into its powerful appeal and draws attention to the social and economic processes associated with its spread.—Victoria Bernal, "Gender, Culture, and Capitalism"

Territorial place-based identity, particularly when conflated with race, gender, religious and class differentiation, is one of the most pervasive bases for both progressive political mobilization and reactionary exclusionary politics.—David Harvey, "From Space to Place and Back Again"

19. Many of these frustrated students suffer from sour grapes: "They hate modernity because they cannot get it! The Islamists are angry not because the aeroplane has replaced the camel; they are angry because they could not get on the aeroplane" (Ayubi 1991: 177).

Maitatsine's Islamism as a particular form of invented tradition represents a dramatic political expression of the changing cultural geography of Nigerian capitalism. It was "fast capitalism" grounded in nonunitary Muslim tradition that provided the material and symbolic raw material from which a distinctive sense of self and of communitarian identity was forged in Kano. The oil boom had fashioned a period of "space-time compression," to use Harvey's (1989) felicitous phrase, and its powers of creative destruction were transmitted through a specific articulation of two world-systemic processes: Islam and capitalism. Each system was both global and local in its constitution; as a global abstraction each force field was experienced, transmitted, and contested in demonstrably local ways.

My concern here has been to say something about the genesis of modern political Islam in relation to globalizations and specific national capitalisms, but in so doing to also explore the relations between Islam and civil society understood in terms of the democratic character of social relations and communications between citizens. It is not simply a question of Tocquevillian notions of association and civility, but also the idea of a public sphere as developed by Habermas and extended by Fraser: namely, a "theater . . . in which political participation is enacted through the medium of talk. It is the space in which citizens deliberate about their common affairs, hence an institutionalized arena of discursive interaction . . . which can on principle be critical of the state" (Bryant 1993: 399). If this public sphere is the site of the production of hegemony (as Gramsci notes in his various discussions of the state), then an understanding of the role of Islam both as a potential source of criticism of the state and as a means by which "philosophies" or "conceptions of the world" assist the ruling bloc in exerting leadership over a variety of groups within political society can provide a counterpoint to the essentialist and Weberian views of Islam. In particular, one can question Ernest Gellner's (1983, 1992) explanation of Islam as an alternative route to modernity in which the urban scripturalism and legalism of the ulama is analogous to Weber's puritan ethic. In this view, puritanical Islam is a modern renewal of its historical essence in which economic development is possible but at the cost of political stagnation and the collapse of civil society (which is subsumed or displaced by religion; see Zabaida 1995).

The Maitatsine insurrection represented a powerful, if counterhegemonic, reading and critique of the Nigerian oil boom and of the Nigerian ruling classes. To this extent one should not be diverted by the syncretist character of the leader, by his purported use of magic, by possible Mahdist overtones, and by accusations of fundamentalist fanaticism. Marwa's self-identity, including his prophethood, is perhaps of less relevance than his antimaterialist, class-based reading of the moral superiority of the Qu'ran, which led him to attack decadence, profligacy, and moral decay. Critical of public corruption, of arbitrary police violence, and of some forms of private property, he fashioned a community largely of young men—unskilled migrants, Qu'ranic scholars, and rural destitutes—who were products of the shifting relations between town and countryside during the 1970s. His critique of materialism and the West was nonetheless ambiguous and contradictory: on the one hand he rejected some aspects of modernity in his invocation of a simple disciplined life, and yet he also invoked a political vision in which the control of modern institutions was central.

Oil and Islam no more determine radical critique or indeed insurrectional politics than does a mixture of copper and Christianity. But Maitatsine's form of Muslim populism possessed a great capacity to resist co-optation, providing in his case a culturally convincing critique of "oil prosperity" and a powerful ideology in weak Islamic states experiencing the radical dislocation of the petrolic capitalism. The Maitatsine followers constituted a certain disenfranchised segment of the northern popular classes who experienced, handled, and resisted a particular form of capitalism through a particular reading of Islamic tradition. It is a truism that Islam is a text-based religion, but we need to grasp the relationships between texts and the meanings they are purported to provide, what Lambek calls local hermeneutics:

> The specific problems raised by the translation of objective meaning of written language into the personal act of speaking . . . [is an act of] appropriation. . . . The nature of texts and the knowledge to be drawn from them in any given historical context are shaped by a sociology or political economy of knowledge: how textual knowledge is reproduced . . . what social factors mediate access to texts, who is able to read and in what manner, who has the authority to represent . . . and how challenges to such authority are manifested. (1990: 23–24)

Islam is a text-based religion made socially relevant through citation, reading, enunciation, and interpretation, and in this sense Islam is not prescriptive, not simply providing unambiguous guidance for its adherents (Fischer and Abedi 1990). Indeed, as Fischer and Abedi have brilliantly shown in their book *Debating Muslims*, there is a dialogic and hermeneutical tradition within Islam rooted in the enigmatic, oral, performative, and esoteric qualities of the Qu'ran. The same religious symbols can be infused with radically different meanings. Tradition itself is constantly negotiated, contested, and reinvented in the context of efforts by rulers and clerics to enforce other meanings in a world turned upside down by oil monies.

There is a multiplicity of Muslim voices, and it was the mapping of local Islam onto local capitalism that threw these religious multiplicities into bold belief, generating intense struggles over the meaning of Islam and the Muslim community.[20]

The community that was built in 'Yan Awaki was a peculiar and parochial affair; little of substance was said about political horizons beyond the ward in which Marwa and his followers resided. Like other oppositional utopian movements (in this case the golden age is the time of Medina), its ability to present a serious and modern Islamic alternative depends on its capacity to "transform cultural solidarity, social discipline and informally organized services into an alliance capable of delivering existing services and a new development strategy capable of coping with the demands of the new global economy" (Lubeck 1995: 53). In this more profound sense Maitatsine was hopelessly inadequate to the modern task of building a transnational, unified community governed by universal Islamic law and underwritten by a state to enforce it. The Maitatsine movement contained, to concur with Harvey's assessment above, both critical and exclusionary politics in a vision that fused religion and class. Its limited perspective and reach—Maitatsine never talked about managing the economy, regulating foreign policy, or processes of globalization—had much to do with a horizon limited by the nationalist sense of political economy associated with informal Muslim schooling. Yet this was not a simple return to some mythical past; rather, it involved contesting some Islamic traditions and creating new ones by a direct engagement with capitalist modernity read through new scripturalist understandings of Islam. At the same time, their projection into the maelstrom of fast capitalism compelled Maitatsine to engage his scripturalist concerns, however inadequately, with the much larger world of contemporary capitalism. To this extent, as Schorske suggests, there was a revising of beliefs and a search for an identity that took the form of a specific, and contradictory, reshuffling of the self. The dramatic way in which oil threw together the old and the new—a sort of combined and uneven development—makes this reshuffling and the place-based identities so produced a curious and in some respects fantastic sort of enterprise.

If Maitatsine appears as a relatively parochial sort of political Islam, it nonetheless contains within it a compelling story with respect to Islam and state-society relations in general and poses a number of fundamental questions about the politics of anti-Sufi movements in Nigeria. On the one

20. For similar arguments within Muslim discourse in relation to capitalism, see Ong 1990 and Lambek 1990.

hand, it is incontestable that Islam had moderated relations between the state and society in postcolonial states. The brotherhoods in this sense exemplify those capacities required of any civil society if it is to curb the hegemony of the state (Villalon 1995: 259): their capacity to aggregate interests, an autonomy that commands the engagement of the state in order to govern, and a strategic flexibility in relation to state action. Further, the anti-Sufi movements in Nigeria began as an anti-imperialist but modernist assault on noncapitalist traditional values, even if in their more recent incarnation, such as Izala, they have assumed a more conservative political cast. Through its prayer meetings, its tafsir, its public debates, and its use of modern communications, the discipline, accessibility, and probity of its institutions, and not least its dense web of associations that provide valued health, welfare, and educational services, Islam acts as both an alternative political and economic platform to the state and a critical oppositional discourse. Islam and Islamism in Nigeria, then, sound a warning to the widespread belief that African societies have tended to be ineffective counterweights to African states.

The Maitatsine and anti-Sufi movements also confirm that Islamism is modern, and as Zabaida says (1995), a political ideology quite distinct from anything in Muslim history. It is not simply that Islam has become the idiom in which a vast array of often contradictory interests and frustrations are discussed in a manner previously associated with secular nationalisms and Marxism. It is also that Islamism has a genealogy that does not simply repeat the essential character of Islam—an unbroken lineage from the eighteenth century or earlier to the contemporary Egyptian brotherhoods—as Gellner and others suggest (Burke 1995). Much of Islamism is new and modern because it engages with and provides a public and reasoned discourse about a number of topics relevant to liberalism, such as constitutionalism, democracy, representative government, economics, and gender. Indeed, as Kramer (1993) points out, Islamist discourse is quite fluid and unstable on issues such as pluralist democracy, protection of human rights, and state accountability. Islamism also innovates in attempting to locate the means by which it can articulate a vision that simultaneously claims membership in a transnational community and a national polity (Lubeck 1995).

Villalon (1995: 265) is surely right to express skepticism about any claim that purports to see an intrinsically democratic relationship in the ways in which Islam links state and society. Religious criticism within the Kano and anti-Sufi sphere is limited and limiting; there are things that cannot be criticized and choices that are not permitted. But as Asad says, these limitations are "due not to a permanent incapacity to contemplate change, still less to an intrinsic contradiction between religion and reason" (1993: 232). This observation was of course at the heart of Gramsci's interest in religion, and it is to Gramsci that I turn for insight into the conditions under which religion can challenge dominant hegemonies and create an oppositional culture based on what he called "critical understanding." It is my claim that the foundation of this critical understanding—free spaces and autonomous organizations, organic intellectuals, and social interaction to ensure the plausibility and sustenance of new worldviews (see Billings 1990)—can be read into Kano Islamism, and even into the myopia of the Maitatsine movement itself.

References

Achebe, C. 1988. Anthills of the Savannas. New York: Vintage.

Ajami, F. 1995. "The Sorrows of Egypt." Foreign Affairs (September): 2–88.

Al-Azmeh, A. 1993. Islams and Modernities. London: Verso.

Amuzegar, J. 1982. "Oil Wealth: A Very Mixed Blessing." Foreign Affairs (spring): 814–35.

Asad, T. 1993. Genealogies of Religion. Baltimore: Johns Hopkins University Press.

Ayubi, N. 1991. Political Islam: Religion and Politics in the Arab World. London: Routledge.

Bardhan, P. 1988. "Dominant Proprietory Classes and India's Democracy." In India's Democracy, A. Kohli, ed. Princeton: Princeton University Press, 76–83.

Bargery, G. 1934. Hausa-English Dictionary. London: Oxford University Press.

Barkindo, B. 1993. "Growing Islamism in Kano since 1970." In Muslim Identity and Social Change in Sub-Saharan Africa, L. Brenner, ed. Bloomington: University of Indiana Press, 91–105.

Benjamin, W. 1973. Charles Baudelaire. London: Verso.

Bernal, V. 1994. "Gender, Culture, and Capitalism." Comparative Studies in Society and History 36(1): 36–67.

Billings, D. 1990. "Religion as Opposition: A Gramscian Analysis." American Journal of Sociology 96(1): 1–31.

Brenner, N. 1993. "The Limits of Civil Society in the Age of Global Capitalism." M.A. thesis, University of Chicago.

Bryant, C. 1993. "Social Organization, Civility, and Sociology." British Journal of Sociology 44(3): 397–401.

Burke, E. 1986. "Understanding Arab Protest Movements." Arab Studies Quarterly 8(4): 333–45.

———. 1995. "Orientalism and World History." Paper presented at the Theory and Society Conference, University of California, Davis, February 24–26.

Burke, E., and P. Lubeck. 1987. "Explaining Social Movements in Two Oil-Exporting States." Comparative Studies in Society and History 29(4): 643–65.

Calhoun, C., ed. 1992. Habermas and the Public Sphere. Cambridge: MIT Press.

Cohen, J., and A. Arato. 1992. Civil Society and Political Theory. Cambridge: MIT Press.

Denoeux, G. 1993. Urban Unrest in the Middle East. Albany: SUNY Press.

Eickelman, D., and J. Piscatori. 1990. "Social Theory in the Study of Muslim Societies." In Muslim Travelers, D. Eickelman and J. Piscatori, eds. Berkeley: University of California Press, 3–28.

Esposito, J. 1992. The Islamic Threat. New York: Oxford University Press.

Evans, P. 1995. *Embedded Autonomy: States and Industrial Transformation.* Princeton: Princeton University Press.

Federal Government of Nigeria. 1981a. *[Aniagolu] Report of Tribunal of Inquiry on Kano Disturbances.* Lagos: Federal Government Press.

——. 1981b. *Views of the Government of the Federation on the Report of the Kano Disturbances Tribunal of Inquiry.* Lagos: National Assembly Press.

Fischer, M., and A. Abedi. 1990. *Debating Muslims.* Madison: University of Wisconsin Press.

Frishman, A. 1988. "The Survival and Disappearance of Small Scale Enterprises in Urban Kano, 1973–1980." Unpublished manuscript, Hobart and William Smith Colleges.

Fukuyama, F. 1995. *Trust: The Social Virtues and the Creation of Prosperity.* New York: Free Press.

Gellner, E. 1983. *Muslim Society.* Cambridge: Cambridge University Press.

——. 1992. *Postmodernism, Reason, and Religion.* London: Routledge.

Gramsci, A. 1971. *Selections from the Prison Notebooks.* New York: International Publishers.

——. 1995. *Further Selections from the Prison Notebooks.* Minneapolis: University of Minnesota Press.

Gregoire, E. 1993. "Islam and Identity of Merchants in Maradi (Niger)." In *Muslim Identity and Social Change in Sub-Saharan Africa,* L. Brenner, ed. Bloomington: University of Indiana Press, 106–15.

Habermas, J. 1991. *The Structural Transformation of the Public Sphere.* Trans. Thomas Burger. Cambridge: MIT Press.

——. 1992. "Further Reflections on the Public Sphere." In *Habermas and the Public Sphere,* C. Calhoun, ed. Cambridge: MIT Press, 421–61.

Harvey, D. 1989. *The Condition of Postmodernity.* Oxford: Basil Blackwell.

——. 1993. "From Space to Place and Back Again." In *Mapping the Futures,* J. Bird et al., eds. London: Routledge, 3–29.

Hitchens, C. 1994. "African Gothic." *Vanity Fair* (November): 90–117.

Ibrahim, J. 1991. "Religion and Political Turbulence in Nigeria." *Journal of Modern African Studies* 29(1): 115–36.

Kaplan, R. 1994a. "The Coming Anarchy." *Atlantic Monthly* (February): 44–76.

——. 1994b. "Eaten from Within." *Atlantic Monthly* (November): 26–44.

Kapucinski, R. 1982. *Shah of Shahs.* New York: Harcourt.

Kramer, G. 1993. "Islamist Notions of Democracy." MERIP 23: 2–8.

Lambek, M. 1990. "Certain Knowledge, Contestable Authority." *American Ethnologist* 17(1): 23–40.

Last, M. 1988. "Charisma and Medicine in Northern Nigeria." In *Charisma and Brotherhood in African Islam,* D. Cruise O'Brien and C. Coulon, eds. London: Oxford University Press, 188–201.

——. 1991. "Adolescents in a Muslim City." *Kano Studies* (special issue): 1–22.

Lubeck, P. 1984. "Islamic Networks and Urban Capitalism: An Instance of Articulation from Northern Nigeria." *Cahiers d'Etudes Africaines* 81(83): 67–78.

——. 1985. "Islamic Protest under Semi-Industrial Capitalism." *Africa* 55(4): 369–89.

——. 1986. *Islam and Labor.* Cambridge: Cambridge University Press.

——. 1987. "Islamic Protest and Oil-Based Capitalism." In *State, Oil, and Agriculture,* M. Watts, ed. Berkeley: Institute of International Studies, 268–90.

——. 1995. "Globalization and the Islamist Moment." Unpublished paper, Department of Sociology, University of California, Santa Cruz.

Lucas, J. 1994. "The State, Civil Society, and Regional Elites: A Study of Three Associations in Kano." *African Affairs* 93: 21–38.

Main, H. 1989. "Workers Retrenchment and Urban-Rural Linkages in Kano, Nigeria." In *Inequality and Development*, K. Swindell et al., eds. London: Macmillan, 223–42.

Ong, A. 1990. "State versus Islam." *American Ethnologist* 17(2): 258–76.

Paden, J. 1973. *Religion and Political Culture in Kano*. Berkeley: University of California Press.

Putnam, R. 1993. *Making Democracy Work*. Cambridge: Harvard University Press.

Richards, A. 1995. "Toward a Political Economy of Islamism." Unpublished paper, Department of Economics, University of California, Santa Cruz.

Richards, A., and J. Waterbury. 1990. *A Political Economy of the Middle East*. Boulder, Colo.: Westview.

Roy, O. 1994. *The Failure of Political Islam*. London: Tauris.

Saad, H. 1988. "Urban Blight and Religious Uprising in Northern Nigeria." *Habitat International* 12(2): 111–28.

Schorske, Carl. 1981. *Fin de Siècle Vienna: Politics and Culture*. New York: Vintage.

Turner, B. 1994. *Orientalism, Postmodernism, and Globalism*. London: Routledge.

Umar, M. 1993. "Changing Islamic Identity in Nigeria from the 1960s to 1980s." In *Muslim Identity and Social Change in Sub-Saharan Africa*, L. Brenner, ed. Bloomington: University of Indiana Press, 154–78.

Villalon, L. 1995. *Islamic Society and State Power in Senegal*. Cambridge: Cambridge University Press.

Watts, M. 1994. "The Devil's Excrement." In *Money, Power, and Space*, S. Corbridge, R. Martin, and N. Thrift, eds. Oxford: Blackwell, 406–45.

Watts, M., and P. Lubeck. 1983. "The Popular Classes and the Oil Boom: A Political Economy of Rural and Urban Poverty." In *The Political Economy of Nigeria*, I. W. Zartman, ed. New York: Praeger, 105–44.

Weaver, M. 1995. "The Novelist and the Sheik." *New Yorker*, 30 January, 52–69.

Williams, R. 1973. *The Country and the City*. New York: Oxford University Press.

Yusuf, A. 1988. *Maitatsine: Peddler of Epidemics*. Syneco: Kano.

Zabaida, S. 1989. *Islam, People, and the State*. London: Routledge.

———. 1995. "Islam, Is There a Muslim Society?" *Economy and Society* 24(2): 151–88.

São Paulo

Cristiano Mascaro

São Paulo is today a city of over fifteen million people. They travel its streets incessantly, streets illuminated here and there by cracks of light passing between its enormous buildings. I feel the need to roam these places—exhaustively, often circling around the same block—in the hope of being surprised by a luminous moment that gives me the illusion of being before an exclusive apparition. I capture these moments as images, and through this hunt for the revealed forms, I imagine myself inserted more fully into the everyday life of the city.

Fortified Enclaves: The New Urban Segregation

Teresa P. R. Caldeira

In the last few decades, the proliferation of fortified enclaves has created a new model of spatial segregation and transformed the quality of public life in many cities around the world. Fortified enclaves are privatized, enclosed, and monitored spaces for residence, consumption, leisure, and work. The fear of violence is one of their main justifications. They appeal to those who are abandoning the traditional public sphere of the streets to the poor, the "marginal," and the homeless. In cities fragmented by fortified enclaves, it is difficult to maintain the principles of openness and free circulation that have been among the most significant organizing values of modern cities. As a consequence, the character of public space and of citizens' participation in public life changes.

In order to sustain these arguments, this essay analyzes the case of São Paulo, Brazil, and uses Los Angeles as a comparison. São Paulo is the largest metropolitan region (it has more than sixteen million inhabitants) of a society with one of the most inequitable distributions of wealth in the

This article is based on the analysis developed in my book *City of Walls: Crime, Segregation, and Citizenship in São Paulo* (Berkeley: University of California Press, forthcoming), copyright by the Regents of the University of California. I thank the University of California Press for the permission to use material from the book.

world.[1] In São Paulo, social inequality is obvious. As a consequence, processes of spatial segregation are also particularly visible, expressed without disguise or subtlety. Sometimes, to look at an exaggerated form of a process is a way of throwing light onto some of its characteristics that might otherwise go unnoticed. It is like looking at a caricature. In fact, with its high walls and fences, armed guards, technologies of surveillance, and contrasts of ostentatious wealth and extreme poverty, contemporary São Paulo reveals with clarity a new pattern of segregation that is widespread in cities throughout the world, although generally in less severe and explicit forms.

In what follows, I describe the changes in São Paulo's pattern of spatial segregation that have occurred in the last fifteen years. I show how the fortified enclaves became status symbols and instruments of social separation and suggest their similarities with other enclaves around the world. I examine Los Angeles as an example to illustrate both the type of architectural design and urban planning that the enclaves use and evaluate the effects of this design. Finally, I discuss how the new public space and the social interactions generated by the new pattern of urban segregation may relate to experiences of citizenship and democracy.

Building Up Walls:
São Paulo's Recent Transformations

The forms producing segregation in city space are historically variable. From the 1940s to the 1980s, a division between center and periphery organized the space of São Paulo, where great distances separated different social groups; the middle and upper classes lived in central and well-equipped neighborhoods and the poor lived in the precarious hinterland.[2] In the last fifteen years, however, a combination of processes, some of them similar to those affecting other cities, deeply transformed the pattern of distribution of social groups and activities throughout the city. São Paulo continues to be a highly segregated city, but the way in which inequalities are inscribed into urban space has changed considerably. In the 1990s, the physical distances separating rich and poor have decreased at the same time that the mechanisms to keep them apart have become more obvious and more complex.

1. In Brazil in 1989, the proportion of income in the hands of the poorest 50 percent of the population was only 10.4 percent. At the same time, the richest 1 percent had 17.3 percent of the income. Data is from the National Research by Domicile Sample (PNAD) undertaken by the Census Bureau. The distribution of wealth has become more inequitable since the early 1980s (Lopes 1993; Rocha 1991).

2. For an analysis of the various patterns of urban segregation in São Paulo from the late nineteenth century to the present, see Caldeira (forthcoming and 1996).

The urban changes that occurred in the 1980s and 1990s in São Paulo, and the new pattern of spatial segregation they generated, cannot be separated from four different processes that became intertwined during this period. First, the 1980s and early 1990s were years of economic recession, with very high rates of inflation and increasing poverty. The 1980s are known in Brazil and in Latin America as the "lost decade." Contrary to the "miracle" years of the 1970s, economic growth was very low, the gross national product dropped 5.5 percent during the 1980s, unemployment rose, and inflation went up dramatically. For several years after the mid-1980s, inflation was higher than 1,000 percent a year, and successive economic plans to deal with it failed. Inflation was only controlled after 1994 with the Plano Real. However, the previous decade of inflation, unemployment, and recession has brought poverty to alarming dimensions. Recent research shows that the effects of the economic crisis were especially severe for the poor population and aggravated the already iniquitous distribution of wealth in Brazil (Rocha 1991; Lopes 1993).[3]

This process of impoverishment has had serious consequences for the position of the poor in urban space. The periphery of the city became unaffordable for the poorest. Since the 1940s, the working classes had been building their own houses in the periphery of the city in a process called "autoconstruction" (see Caldeira 1984; Holston 1991). In this process, they bought cheap lots in distant areas of the city without any infrastructure and services, and frequently involving some illegality, and spent decades building their dream houses and improving their neighborhoods. In this way, they both constructed their homes and expanded the city. However, their generally successful efforts to improve the quality of life in the periphery through the organization of social movements—which I discuss below—occurred at a moment when the economic crisis denied upcoming generations of workers the same possibility of becoming homeowners, even in precarious and distant areas of town. Consequently, the poorest population has to move either to *favelas* and *cortiços* in the central areas of town, or to distant municipalities in the metropolitan region.[4] According to a recent study by the office of São Paulo's Secretary of Housing, residents in *favelas* represented 1.1 percent of the city's population in 1973, 2.2 percent in 1980, 8.8 percent in 1987, and 19.4 percent in 1993— that is, 1,902,000 people in 1993 (O Estado de S. Paulo, 15 October 1994, C-1).

3. Although the Metropolitan Region of São Paulo has one of the best situations in Brazil, the Gini coefficient increased from 0.516 in 1981 to 0.566 in 1989 (Rocha 1991: 38). The Gini coefficient varies from zero to one. It would be zero if all people had the same income, and one if one person concentrated the whole national income. For Brazil, the Gini coefficient was 0.580 in 1985 and 0.627 in 1989 (ibid.).

4. A *favela* is a set of shacks built on seized land. A *cortiço* is a type of tenement housing.

Second, these changes during the 1980s accompanied the consolidation of a democratic government in Brazil after twenty-one years of military rule. On the one hand, elections were held peacefully, regularly, and fairly, and political parties organized freely. On the other hand, trade unions and all types of social movements emerged onto the political scene, bringing the working classes and dominated groups to the center of politics and transforming the relationship between politicians and citizens. This is not a small achievement in a country with a tradition of high social inequality, elitism, and authoritarianism. This process of democratic consolidation has had many consequences and limits (see Holston and Caldeira, forthcoming). It is important to note the consequences of this process in terms of the urban environment. Since the mid-1970s, social movements organized by homeowners associations in the periphery have pressured local administrations both to improve the infrastructure and services in their neighborhoods and to legalize their land. Combined with changes in political groups in office brought about by free elections, this pressure transformed the priorities of local administration, making the periphery the site of much investment in the urban infrastructure. Moreover, during two decades of land disputes, social movements forced municipal governments to offer various amnesties to illegal developers, which resulted in the regularization of lots and their insertion into the formal land market. However, these new achievements also diminished the supply of irregular and cheap lots on the market. Since legal developments and lots in areas with a better infrastructure are obviously more expensive than illegal lots in underdeveloped areas, it is not difficult to understand that the neighborhoods that achieved these improvements came to be out of the reach of the already impoverished population, who were therefore pushed into *favelas* and *cortiços.*

Third, during the 1980s, São Paulo's economic activities started to be restructured. Following the same pattern of many metropolises around the world, São Paulo is under a process of expansion of tertiary activities, or tertiarization. In the last decade, the city lost its position as the largest industrial pole of the country to other areas of the state and to the Metropolitan Region as a whole, becoming basically a center of finance, commerce, and the coordination of productive activities and specialized services—in a pattern similar to what is happening in the so-called global cities (Sassen 1991). This process has various consequences for the urban environment. The oldest industrial areas of the city are going through combined processes of deterioration and gentrification. In some of them, especially in districts in the inner part of town where various sectors of the middle classes live, abandoned houses and factories were transformed into *cortiços.* Concomitantly, both the opening of new avenues and of a subway line in the eastern zone generated urban renewal and the construction of new apartment buildings for the middle classes, some of which conform to the model of closed condominiums discussed below. The most recent process, however, concerns the displacement of services and commerce from the inner city to districts on the periphery, especially to the western and southern zones of the metropolitan region. The new tertiary jobs are located in recently built, enormous office and service centers that have multiplied in the last fifteen years. At the same time, spaces of commerce are changing as immense shopping malls are created in isolated areas of the old periphery, and as some old shopping areas are abandoned to homeless people and street vendors.

Finally, the fourth process of change relates most directly to the new pattern of urban residential segregation because it supplies the justifying rhetoric: the increase in violent crime and fear. Crime has been increasing since the mid-1980s, but, more important, there has been a qualitative change in the pattern of crime. Violent crime in the 1990s represents about 30 percent of all crime, compared with 20 percent in the early 1980s. Murder rates in the 1990s have oscillated between 30 and 50 per 100,000 people in São Paulo.[5] However, the most serious element in the increase of violence in São Paulo is police violence. In the early 1990s, São Paulo's military police killed more than 1,000 suspects per year, a number that has no comparison in any other city in the world.[6] The increase in violence, insecurity, and fear comes with a series of transformations, as citizens adopt new strategies of protection. These strategies are changing the city's landscape, patterns of residence and circulation, everyday trajectories, habits, and gestures related to the use of streets and of public transportation. In sum, the fear of crime is contributing to changes in all types of public interactions.

As a result, São Paulo is today a city of walls. Physical barriers have been constructed everywhere—around houses, apartment buildings, parks, squares, office complexes, and schools. Apartment buildings and houses that used to be connected to the street by gardens are now everywhere

5. Violent crime has been growing in various metropolises around the world. In the United States, the number of violent crimes per capita grew by 355 percent between 1960 and 1990, according to FBI reports. However, murder has decreased in the U.S. in the last five years. In 1993, rates of murder per 100,000 population in several American cities were higher than or comparable to those of São Paulo. The highest rate was 80.3 in New Orleans, followed by 78.5 in Washington, D.C. It was 34.0 in Miami, 26.5 in New York City, and 30.5 in Los Angeles (Uniform Crime Reports for the United States).

6. In 1992, São Paulo's military police killed 1,470 civilians, including 111 prisoners killed inside the city's main prison. In that year, Los Angeles police killed 25 civilians, and the New York police killed 24 civilians. For a complete analysis of the pattern of police violence and of the increase in violence and crime in São Paulo, see Caldeira forthcoming.

separated by high fences and walls, and guarded by electronic devices and armed security men. The new additions frequently look odd because they were improvised in spaces conceived without them, spaces designed to be open. However, these barriers are now fully integrated into new projects for individual houses, apartment buildings, shopping areas, and work spaces. A new aesthetics of security shapes all types of constructions and imposes its new logic of surveillance and distance as a means for displaying status, and is changing the character of public life and public interactions.

Among the diverse elements changing the city, the new enclaves for residence, work, and consumption of the middle and upper classes are provoking the deepest transformations. Although they have different uses and many specializations (some for residence, others for work, leisure, or consumption; some more restricted, others more open), all types of fortified enclaves share some basic characteristics. They are private property for collective use; they are physically isolated, either by walls or empty spaces or other design devices; they are turned inward and not to the street; and they are controlled by armed guards and security systems that enforce rules of inclusion and exclusion. Moreover, these enclaves are very flexible arrangements. Because of their size, the new technologies of communication, the new organization of work, and security systems, they possess all that is needed within a private and autonomous space and can be situated almost anywhere, independent of the surroundings. In fact, most of them have been placed in the old periphery and have as their neighbors either *favelas* or concentrations of autoconstructed houses. Finally, the enclaves tend to be socially homogeneous environments, mostly for the middle and upper classes.

Fortified enclaves represent a new alternative for the urban life of these middle and upper classes. As such, they are codified as something conferring high status. The construction of status symbols is a process that elaborates social distance and creates means for the assertion of social difference and inequality. In the next section, I examine real estate advertisements as one way of analyzing this process for the case of São Paulo's enclaves. After that, I analyze the characteristics of the enclaves that make them an urban form that creates segregation and reproduces social inequality while transforming the character of public life.

Advertising Segregated Enclaves for the Rich

Real estate advertisements tell us about the lifestyles of the middle and upper classes and reveal the elements that constitute current patterns of social differentiation. The ads not only reveal a new code of social distinction, but also explicitly treat separation, isolation, and protection as a matter of status. The following interpretation is based on the analysis of real estate advertisements for closed condominiums published in the newspaper O Estado de S. Paulo between 1975 and 1995. I analyze the advertisements in order to try to discover what is capturing the imagination and desires of São Paulo's middle and upper classes and to highlight some of the main images they are using in order to construct their place in society. I am particularly interested in uncovering how, in the last twenty years, the advertisements elaborated the myth of what they call "a new concept of residence" on the basis of the articulation of images of security, isolation, homogeneity, facilities, and services.[7] I argue that the image that confers the highest status and is most seductive is that of an enclosed and isolated community, a secure environment in which one can use various facilities and services and live only among equals. The advertisements present the image of islands to which one can return every day, in order to escape from the city and its deteriorated environment and to encounter an exclusive world of pleasure among peers. The image of the enclaves, therefore, is opposed to the image of the city as a deteriorated world pervaded by not only pollution and noise but, more important, confusion and mixture, that is, social heterogeneity.

Closed condominiums are supposed to be separate worlds. Their advertisements propose a "total way of life" that would represent an alternative to the quality of life offered by the city and its deteriorated public space. The ads suggest the possibility of constructing a world clearly distinguishable from the surrounding city: a life of total calm and security. Condominiums are distant, but they are supposed to be as independent and complete as possible to compensate for it; thus the emphasis on the common facilities they are supposed to have that transform them into sophisticated clubs. In these ads, the facilities promised inside closed condominiums seem to be unlimited—from drugstores to tanning rooms, from bars and saunas to ballet rooms, from swimming pools to libraries.

In addition to common facilities, São Paulo's closed condominiums offer a wide range of services. The following are some of the services (excluding security) mentioned in the advertisements: psychologists and gymnastic teachers to manage children's recreation, classes of all sorts for all ages, organized sports, libraries, gardening, pet care, physicians, message centers, frozen food preparation, housekeeping administration, cooks, cleaning personnel, drivers, car washing, transportation, and servants to

---

7. Expressions in quotation marks are taken from the advertisements.

do the grocery shopping. If the list does not meet your dreams, do not worry, for "everything you might demand" can be made available. The expansion of domestic service is not a feature of Brazil alone. As Sassen (1991: chaps. 1, 8) shows for the case of global cities, high-income gentrification requires an increase in low-wage jobs; yuppies and poor migrant workers depend on each other. In São Paulo, however, the intensive use of domestic labor is a continuation of an old pattern, although in recent years some relationships of labor have been altered, and this work has become more professional.

The multiplication of new services creates problems, including the spatial allocation of service areas. The solutions for this problem vary, but one of the most emblematic concerns the circulation areas. Despite many recent changes, the separation between two entrances—in buildings and in each individual apartment—and two elevators, one labeled "social" and the other "service"—seems to be untouchable; different classes are not supposed to mix or interact in the public areas of the buildings.[8] Sometimes, the insistence on this distinction seems ridiculous, because the two elevators or doors are often placed side-by-side, instead of being in distinct areas. As space shrinks, and the side-by-side solution spreads, the apartments that have totally separate areas of circulation advertise this fact with the phrase, "social hall independent from service hall." The idea is old: class separation as a form of distinction.

Another problem faced by the new developments is the control of a large number of servants. As the number of workers for each condominium increases, as many domestic jobs change their character, and as "creative services" proliferate for middle and upper classes who cannot do without them, so also the mechanisms of control diversify. The "creative administrations" of the new enclaves in many cases take care of labor management and are in a position to impose strict forms of control that would create impossible daily relationships if adopted in the more personal interaction between domestic servants and the families who employ them. This more "professional" control is, therefore, a new service and is advertised as such. The basic method of control is direct and involves empowering some workers to control others. In various condominiums, both employees of the condominium and maids and cleaning workers of individual apartments (even those who live there) are required to show their identification tags to go in and out of the condominium. Often they and their personal belongings are searched when they leave work. Moreover, this control usually involves men exercising power over women.

8. See Holston 1989 for an analysis of this system of spatial separation.

The middle and upper classes are creating their dream of independence and freedom—both from the city and its mixture of classes, and from everyday domestic tasks—on the basis of services from working-class people. They give guns to badly paid working-class guards to control their own movement in and out of their condominiums. They ask their badly paid "office-boys" to solve all their bureaucratic problems, from paying their bills and standing in all types of lines to transporting incredible sums of money. They also ask their badly paid maids—who often live in the *favelas* on the other side of the condominium's wall—to wash and iron their clothes, make their beds, buy and prepare their food, and frequently care for their children all day long. In a context of increased fear of crime in which the poor are often associated with criminality, the upper classes fear contact and contamination, but they continue to depend on their servants. They can only be anxious about creating the most effective way of controlling these servants, with whom they have such ambiguous relationships of dependency and avoidance, intimacy and distrust.

Another feature of closed condominiums is isolation and distance from the city, a fact presented as offering the possibility of a better lifestyle. The latter is expressed, for example, by the location of the development in "nature" (green areas, parks, lakes), and in the use of phrases inspired by ecological discourses. However, it is clear in the advertisements that isolation means separation from those considered to be socially inferior and that the key factor to assure this is security. This means fences and walls surrounding the condominium, guards on duty twenty-four hours a day controlling the entrances, and an array of facilities and services to ensure security—guardhouses with bathrooms and telephones, double doors in the garage, and armed guards patrolling the internal streets. "Total security" is crucial to "the new concept of residence." Security and control are the conditions for keeping the others out, for assuring not only isolation but also "happiness," "harmony," and even "freedom." In sum, to relate security exclusively to crime is to fail to recognize all the meanings it is acquiring in various types of environments. The new systems of security not only provide protection from crime but also create segregated spaces in which the practice of exclusion is carefully and rigorously exercised.

The elaboration of an aesthetics of security and the creation of segregation on the basis of building enclaves is a widespread process, although not necessarily occurring elsewhere in the same obvious ways as in São Paulo. Fortified enclaves are not unique to São Paulo. In October 1993, a large advertising campaign in São Paulo elaborated on the similarities with enclaves in U.S. cities. It was a campaign to sell the idea of an "edge city" (an expression used in English) as a way of increasing the appeal and price of specific enclaves. One main character of this campaign was Joel Garreau, the U.S. journalist and author of the book *Edge City—Life on the New Frontier*. His photograph appeared in full-page ads in national magazines and newspapers, he came to São Paulo to talk to a select group of realtors, and he was one of the main participants in a thirty-minute television program advertising some enclaves. Garreau was helping market three huge real estate developments—Alphaville, Aldeia de Serra, and Tamboré—which combined closed condominiums, shopping centers, and office complexes as if they were a piece of the first world dropped into the metropolitan region of São Paulo.

The paulista "edge city" was not created from scratch in 1993. The Western zone in which these developments are located is the part of the metropolitan region most affected by transformations in the last two decades. Until the 1970s this area was a typical poor periphery of the metropolitan region. Since then, real estate developers who benefited from the low price of land and facilities offered by local administrations have invested heavily in this area. Over fifteen years, they built large areas of walled residences adjacent to office complexes, service centers, and shopping malls. The area had among the highest rates of population growth in the metropolitan region during 1980–90, a period when the growth rate in the city of São Paulo declined sharply. Because the new residents are largely from the upper social groups, this area today has a concentration of high-income inhabitants, who, before the 1980s, would have lived in central neighborhoods (Metrô 1989). In other words, this area clearly represents the new trend of movement of wealthy residents as well as services and commerce to the periphery of the city and to enclosed areas. The 1993 campaign used many images already old in real estate advertisements of closed condominiums, but gave to them a touch of novelty by baptizing its product as "edge city." Its aim was to launch new projects in the area, and for this they used Garreau's expertise on suburban development.

The television program, broadcast in São Paulo on Saturday, 16 October 1993, illustrates very well the connections with the first world model as well as the local peculiarities. The program combined scenes from U.S. edge cities (Reston, Virginia, and Columbia, Maryland) and the three developments being advertised in São Paulo. In this program, Garreau—speaking in English with Portuguese subtitles—described edge cities as the predominant form of contemporary urban growth and used Los Angeles and its multicentered form as an example. The program had interesting differences in the way it presented Brazilian as opposed to U.S. edge cities. Residents from enclaves in both countries were interviewed in front of swimming pools, lakes, and in green areas, emphasizing both the luxurious and the antiurban character of the developments. However, if the U.S. edge cities have external walls and controls in their entrance gates, they are not shown, and their security personnel is not visibly present either. In the paulista case, on the contrary, they are crucial and emphasized. At one point, the program shows a scene shot from a helicopter: the private security personnel of a condominium intercept a "suspect car" (a popular vehicle, a Volkswagen bus) outside the walls of the condominiums; they physically search the occupants, who are forced to put their arms up against the car. Although this action is completely illegal for a private security service to perform on a public street, this together with scenes of visitors submitting identification documents at the entrance gates reassures the rich residents (and spectators) that "suspect" (poor) people will be kept away. Another revealing scene is an interview in English with a resident of a U.S. edge city. He cites as one of his reasons for moving there the fact that he wanted to live in a racially integrated community. This observation is censored in the Portuguese subtitles, which say instead that his community has "many interesting people." In São Paulo, the image of a racially integrated community would certainly devalue the whole development. For the paulista elites, first world models are good insofar as they may be adapted to include outright control (especially of the poor) and the eradication of racial and social difference.

To use first world elements in order to sell all types of commodities is a very common practice in third world countries. However, contrasting the different situations may be especially revealing. In this case, the need to censor a reference to racial integration indicates that the paulista system of social inequality and distance is indeed obvious and that race is one of its most sensitive points.[9] Moreover, the parallel between the Brazilian and the American examples suggests that although the degree of segregation may vary in different contexts, it is present in similar forms in both cases. It is worth then investigating the characteristics of this form and its effects on the organization of public life.

Attacking Modern Public Space

The new residential enclaves of the upper classes, associated with shopping malls, isolated office complexes, and other privately controlled en-

9. Although many people like to think of Brazilian society as a "racial democracy," any reading of available social indicators shows pervasive discrimination against the Black population. For example, a recent study by Lopes (1993) on poverty shows that 68 percent of the urban households below the indigent line have a Black or Mulatto person as its head, whereas Black or Mulatto households represent only 41 percent of the total urban households.

vironments, represent a new form of organizing social differences and creating segregation in São Paulo and in many other cities around the world. The characteristics of the paulista enclaves that make their segregationist intentions viable may be summarized in four points. First, they use two instruments in order to create explicit separation: on the one hand, physical dividers such as fences and walls; on the other, large empty spaces creating distance and discouraging pedestrian circulation. Second, as if walls and distances were not enough, separation is guaranteed by private security systems: control and surveillance are conditions for internal social homogeneity and isolation. Third, the enclaves are private universes turned inward with designs and organization making no gestures toward the street. Fourth, the enclaves aim at being independent worlds that proscribe an exterior life, evaluated in negative terms. The enclaves are not subordinate either to public streets or to surrounding buildings and institutions. In other words, the relationship they establish with the rest of the city and its public life is one of avoidance: they turn their backs on them. Therefore, public streets become spaces for elite's circulation by car and for poor people's circulation by foot or public transportation. To walk on the public street is becoming a sign of class in many cities, an activity that the elite is abandoning. No longer using streets as spaces of sociability, the elite now want to prevent street life from entering their enclaves.

Private enclaves and the segregation they generate deny many of the basic elements that constituted the modern experience of public life: primacy of streets and their openness; free circulation of crowds and vehicles; impersonal and anonymous encounters of the pedestrian; unprogrammed public enjoyment and congregation in streets and squares; and the presence of people from different social backgrounds strolling and gazing at those passing by, looking at store windows, shopping, and sitting in cafes, joining political demonstrations or using spaces especially designed for the entertainment of the masses (promenades, parks, stadiums, exhibitions).[10] The new developments in cities such as São Paulo create enclosures that contradict both the prototype of modern urban remodeling, that of Baron Haussmann, and basic elements of the modern conception of public life. Haussmann's state-promoted transformations of Paris were strongly criticized and opposed, but no one denied that the new boulevards were readily appropriated by huge numbers of people eager to enjoy both the street's public life, protected by anonymity, and the consumption possi-

10. Analyses of various dimensions of the modern experience of urban life are found in Benjamin 1969, Berman 1982, Clark 1984, Harvey 1985, Holston 1989, Rabinow 1989, Schorske 1961, Sennett 1974, Vidler 1978.

bilities that came with it. The *flâneur* described by Baudelaire and the consumer of the new department stores each became symbols of the modern appropriation of urban public space, as Paris became the prototype of the modern city.

At the core of the conception of urban public life embedded in modern Paris are notions that city space is open to be used and enjoyed by anyone, and that the consumption society it houses may become accessible to all. Of course, this has never been entirely the case, neither in Paris nor anywhere else, for modern cities have always remained marked by social inequalities and spatial segregation, and are appropriated in quite different ways by diverse social groups, depending on their social position and power. In spite of these inequalities, however, modern Western cities have always maintained various signs of openness related especially to circulation and consumption, which contributed to sustaining the positive value attached to the idea of an open public space accessible to all.

These modern urban experiences were coupled with a political life in which similar values were fostered. The modern city has been the stage for all types of public demonstrations. In fact, the promise of incorporation into modern society included not only the city and consumption but also the polity. Images of the modern city are in many ways analogous to those of the modern liberal-democratic polity, consolidated on the basis of the fiction of a social contract among equal and free people, which has shaped the modern political sphere. This fiction is quite radical—like that of the open city—and helped to destroy the hierarchical social order of feudal statuses preceding it. But, clearly, it was only with severe struggles that the definitions of those who could be considered "free and equal" have been expanded. As with the open city, the polity incorporating all equal citizens has never occurred, but its founding ideals and its promise of continuous incorporation have retained their power for at least two centuries, shaping people's experience of citizenship and city life and legitimating the actions of various excluded groups in their claims for incorporation.[11]

In sum, the images of openness, freedom, and possibilities of incorporation that constituted modernity have never been completely fulfilled, but have never completely lost their referential role either. In cities such as São Paulo and Los Angeles, however, various aspects of public experience are now contradicting those images. One challenge to basic concepts sustaining these fictions comes from some minority groups. They question

11. A powerful image of progressive incorporation is offered in the classic essay by T. H. Marshall ([1950] 1965) on the development of citizenship. For recent critiques of Marshall's optimistic and evolutionary view, see Hirschman 1991 and Turner 1992; Turner 1992 also criticizes the universality of Marshall's model.

the liberal principle of universalism, arguing that the social contract has always been constituted on the basis of the exclusion of some, and that the rights of minority groups can only be addressed if approached from the perspective of difference rather than that of commonality.[12] This is what we might call a positive attack on modern liberal ideals: its aim is still to expand rights, freedom, and equality, and it searches for models that may achieve these goals in a more effective way. However, the transformations going on at the level of the urban environment represent an attack of a different kind. They reject the principles of openness and equality, and take inequality and separation as their values. While minority groups criticize the limitations of liberal fictions in terms of the creation of equality and justice, recent urban transformations materially build a space with opposite values. And this new type of urban form shapes public life and everyday interactions of millions of people around the world. In what follows I discuss in more detail the instruments used by enclaves to produce segregation.

Modernist Instruments, Segregated Spaces

In order to achieve their goals of isolating, distancing, and selecting, the fortified enclaves use some instruments of design that are, in fact, instruments of modernist city planning and architectural design. Various effects of modernist city planning are similar to those of the new enclaves, suggesting that we should look at their similarities more carefully. One strikingly similar effect of both modernist city planning and the fortified enclaves is their attack on streets as a type and concept of public space. In Brazil, the construction of modernist Brasília in the late 1950s crystallized an international modernism and its transformation of public space and relayed it to the rest of the country (see Holston 1989). In modernist Brasília as in new parts of São Paulo and Los Angeles, pedestrians and anonymous interactions in public life that marked modern Paris tend to be eliminated. However, if the results tend to be the same, the original projects of modernism and current enclosures are radically different. It is worth, then, investigating how such different projects ended up producing similar effects.

Modernist architecture and city planning were elaborated on the basis of a criticism of industrial cities and societies and intended to transform them through the radical remodeling of space. Their utopia was clear: the erasure of social difference and creation of equality in the rational city of the

12. See, for example, the feminist critique of the social contract (Pateman 1988) and of the legal understanding of equality as sameness (Eisenstein 1988).

future mastered by the avant-garde architect. Modernist attacks on the streets were central to its criticism of capitalism and its project of subversion. They perceived the corridor street as a conduit of disease and as an impediment to progress, because it would fail to accommodate the needs of the new machine age. Moreover, modernist architecture attacks the street because "it constitutes an architectural organization of the public and private domains of social life that modernism seeks to overturn" (Holston 1989: 103). In capitalist cities, the organization of the public and private domains is best expressed in the corridor street and its related system of public spaces including sidewalks and squares: a solid mass of contiguous private buildings frames and contains the void of public streets. Modernist planning and architecture inverted these solid-void/ figure-ground relationships that have been the basis for the physical structure of Western cities since the fifth century B.C. In the modernist city, "streets appear as continuous voids and buildings as sculptural figures" (ibid.: 125). By subverting the old code of urban order, modernist planning aims at and succeeds in erasing the representational distinction between public and private. When all buildings—banks, offices, apartments—are sculptural, and all spaces are nonfigural, "the old architectural convention for discriminating between the public and the private is effectively invalidated" (ibid.: 136).

Modernist city planning aspired to transform the city into a single homogeneous state-sponsored public domain, to eliminate differences in order to create a universal rationalist city divided into functional sectors such as residential, employment, recreational, transportation, administrative, and civic. Brasília is the most complete embodiment of both the new type of city and public life created by modernist city planning. This new type of city space, however, turned out to be the opposite of the planner's intentions. Brasília is today Brazil's most segregated city, not its most egalitarian. Ironically, the instruments of modernist planning, with little adaptation, become perfect instruments to produce inequality, not to erase difference. Streets only for vehicular traffic, the absence of sidewalks, enclosure and internalization of shopping areas, and spatial voids isolating sculptural buildings and rich residential areas are great instruments for generating and maintaining social separations. These modernist creations radically transform public life not only in cities such as Brasília, but in other contexts and with different intentions. In the new fortified enclaves they are used not to destroy private spaces and produce a total unified public, but to destroy public spaces. Their objective is to enlarge specific private domains so that they will fulfill public functions, but in a segregated way.

Contemporary fortified enclaves use basically modernist instruments of planning with some notable adaptations. First, the surrounding walls: unlike in modernist planning, such as for Brasília, where the residential areas were to have no fences or walls but only to be delimited by expressways, in São Paulo the walls are necessary to demarcate the private universes. However, this demarcation of private property is not supposed to create the same type of (nonmodernist) public space that characterizes the industrial city. Because the private universes are kept apart by voids (as in modernist design), they no longer generate street corridors. Moreover, pedestrian circulation is discouraged and shopping areas are kept away from the streets, again as in modernist design. The second adaptation occurs in the materials and forms of individual buildings. Here there are two possibilities: buildings may completely ignore the exterior walls, treating façades as their backs; or, plain modernist façades may be eliminated in favor of ornament, irregularity, and ostentatious materials that display the individuality and status of their owners. These buildings reject the glass and transparency of modernism and their disclosure of private life. In other words, internalization, privacy, and individuality are enhanced. Finally, sophisticated technologies of security assure the exclusivity of the already isolated buildings.

Analyzing what is used from modernist architecture and city planning and what is transformed in the new urban form generated by the private enclaves, one arrives at a clear conclusion: the devices that have been maintained are those that destroy modern public space and social life (socially dead streets transformed into highways, sculptural buildings separated by voids and disregarding street alignments, enclaves turned inside); the devices transformed or abandoned are those intended to create equality, transparency, and a new public sphere (glass façades, uniformity of design, absence of material delimitations such as walls and fences). Instead of creating a space in which the distinctions between public and private disappear—making all space public as the modernists intended— the enclaves use modernist conventions to create spaces in which the private quality is enhanced beyond any doubt and in which the public, a shapeless void treated as residual, is deemed irrelevant. This was exactly the fate of modernist architecture and its "all public space" in Brasília, a perversion of initial premises and intentions. The situation is just the opposite with the closed condominiums and other fortified enclaves of the 1980s and 1990s. Their aim is to segregate and to change the character of public life by bringing to private spaces constructed as socially homogeneous environments those activities that had been previously enacted in public spaces.

Today, in cities such as São Paulo we find neither gestures toward openness and freedom of circulation regardless of differences, nor a technocratic universalism aiming at erasing differences. Rather, we find a city space whose old modern urban design has been fragmented by the insertion of independent and well-delineated private enclaves (of modernist design), which pay no attention to an external overall ordination and which are totally focused on their own internal organization. The fortified fragments are no longer meant to be subordinated to a total order kept together by ideologies of openness, commonality, or promises of incorporation. Heterogeneity is to be taken more seriously: fragments express radical inequalities, not simple differences. Stripped of the elements that in fact erased differences such as uniform and transparent façades, modernist architectural conventions used by the enclaves are helping to ensure that different social worlds meet as infrequently as possible in city space, that is, that they belong to different spaces.

In sum, in a city of walls and enclaves such as São Paulo, public space undergoes a deep transformation. Felt as more dangerous, fractured by the new voids and enclaves, broken in its old alignments, and privatized with chains closing streets, armed guards, guard dogs, guardhouses, and walled parks, public space in São Paulo is increasingly abandoned to those who do not have a chance of living, working, and shopping in the new private, internalized, and fortified enclaves. As the spaces for the rich are enclosed and turned inside, the outside space is left for those who cannot afford to go in. A comparison with Los Angeles shows that this new type of segregation is not São Paulo's exclusive creation and suggests some of its consequences for the transformation of the public sphere.

São Paulo, Los Angeles

Compared to São Paulo, Los Angeles has a more fragmented and disperse urban structure.[13] São Paulo still has a vivid downtown area and some central neighborhoods concentrating commerce and office activities, which are shaped on the model of the corridor street and which, in spite of all transformations, are still crowded during the day. Contemporary Los Angeles is "polynucleated and decentralized" (Soja 1989: 208). And its renovated downtown, one of the city's economic and financial centers, does not

13. It is not my intention to give a detailed account of Los Angeles's recent pattern of urbanization. I will only point out some of its characteristics that, by comparison with São Paulo's process, allow me to raise questions about new forms of social segregation that seem to be quite generalized. For analyses of Los Angeles, see Banham 1971; Davis 1990; Soja 1989, 1992.

have much street life: people's activities are contained in the corporate buildings and their under- and overpass connections to shopping, restaurants, and hotels.[14] São Paulo's process of urban fragmentation by the construction of enclaves is more recent than Los Angeles's, but it has already changed the peripheral zones and the distribution of wealth and economic functions in ways similar to that of the metropolitan region of Los Angeles. According to Soja (1989), the latter is a multicentered region marked by a "peripheral urbanization," which is created by the expansion of high-technological, post-Fordist industrialization and marked by the presence of high-income residential developments, huge regional shopping centers, programmed environments for leisure (theme parks, Disneyland), links to major universities and the Department of Defense, and various enclaves of cheap labor, mostly immigrants. Although São Paulo lacks the high-technology industries found in Los Angeles, its tertiarization and distribution of services and commerce are starting to be organized according to the Los Angeles pattern.

Although we may say that São Paulo expresses Los Angeles's process of economic transformation and urban dispersion in a less explicit form, it is more explicit and exaggerated in the creation of separation and in the use of security procedures. Where rich neighborhoods such as Morumbi use high walls, iron fences, and armed guards, the West Side of Los Angeles uses mostly electronic alarms and small signs announcing "Armed Response." While São Paulo's elites clearly appropriate public spaces—closing public streets with chains and all sorts of physical obstacles, installing private armed guards to control circulation—Los Angeles elites still show more respect for public streets. However, walled communities appropriating public streets are already appearing in Los Angeles, and one can wonder if its more discrete pattern of separation and of surveillance is not in part associated with the fact that the poor are far from the West Side, whereas in Morumbi they live beside the enclaves. Another reason must surely be the fact that the Los Angeles Police Department—although considered one of the most biased and violent of the United States—still appears very effective and nonviolent if compared with São Paulo's police (see Caldeira forthcoming: chap. 4). São Paulo's upper classes explicitly rely on the services of an army of domestic servants and do not feel ashamed to transform the utilization of these services into status symbols, which in turn are incorporated in newspaper advertisements for enclaves. In West Los Angeles, although the domestic dependence on the services of immi-

14. See Davis 1991 and Soja 1989 on the importance of downtown Los Angeles in the structuring of the region.

grant maids, nannies, and gardeners seems to be increasing, the status associated with employing them has not yet become a matter for advertisement. In São Paulo, where the local government has been efficient in approving policies to help segregation, upper-class residents have not yet started any important social movement for this purpose. But in Los Angeles residents of expensive neighborhoods have been organizing powerful homeowner associations to lobby for zoning regulations that would maintain the isolation their neighborhoods now enjoy (Davis 1990: chap. 3).

Despite the many differences between the two cases, it is also clear that in both Los Angeles and São Paulo conventions of modernist city planning and technologies of security are being used to create new forms of urban space and social segregation. In both cities, the elites are retreating to privatized environments that they increasingly control and are abandoning earlier types of urban space to the poor and their internal antagonisms. As might be expected given these common characteristics, in both cities we find debates involving planners and architects in which the new enclaves are frequently criticized, but also defended and theorized. In São Paulo, where modernism has been the dominant dogma in schools of architecture up to the present, the defense of walled constructions is recent and timid, using as arguments only practical reasons such as increasing rates of crime and of homelessness. Architects tend to talk about walls and security devices as an unavoidable evil. They talk to the press, but I could not find either academic articles or books on the subject. In Los Angeles, however, the debate has already generated an important literature, and both the criticism and the praise of "defensible architecture" are already quite elaborated.

One person voicing the defense of the architectural style found in the new enclaves is Charles Jencks. He analyzes recent trends in Los Angeles architecture in relation to a diagnosis of the city's social configuration. In his view, Los Angeles's main problem is its heterogeneity, which inevitably generates chronic ethnic strife and explains episodes such as the 1992 uprising (1993: 88). Since he considers this heterogeneity as constitutive of L.A.'s reality, and since his diagnosis of the economic situation is pessimistic, his expectation is that ethnic tension increases, that the environment becomes more defensive, and that people resort to more diverse and nastier measures of protection. Jencks sees the adoption of security devices as inevitable and as a matter of realism. Moreover, he discusses how this necessity is being transformed into art by styles that metamorphose hard-edged materials needed for security into "ambiguous signs of inventive beauty and 'keep out'" (ibid.: 89), and which design façades with their backs to the street, camouflaging the contents of the houses. For him, the response to ethnic strife is "defensible architecture and riot realism" (ibid.). The "realism" lies in architects looking at "the dark side of division, conflict, and decay, and represent[ing] some unwelcome truths" (ibid.: 91). Among the latter is the fact that heterogeneity and strife are here to stay, that the promises of the melting pot can no longer be fulfilled. In this context, boundaries would have to be both clearer and more defended.

> Architecturally it [Los Angeles] will have to learn the lessons of Gehry's aesthetic and en-formality: how to turn unpleasant necessities such as chain-link fence into amusing and ambiguous signs of welcome/keep out, beauty/defensive space. . . . Defensible architecture, however regrettable as a social tactic, also protects the rights of individuals and threatened groups. (ibid.: 93)

Jencks targets ethnic heterogeneity as the reason for Los Angeles's social conflicts and sees separation as a solution. He is not bothered by the fact that the intervention of architects and planners in L.A.'s urban environment reinforces social inequality and spatial segregation. He also does not interrogate the consequences of these creations for public space and political relationships. In fact, his admiration of the backside-to-the-street solution indicates a lack of concern with the maintenance of public streets as spaces that embed the values of openness and conviviality of the heterogeneous masses.

But Los Angeles's defensible architecture also has its critics, and the most famous of them is Mike Davis, whose analysis I find illuminating, especially for thinking about the transformations in the public sphere. For Davis (1990, 1991, 1993), social inequality and spatial segregation are central characteristics of Los Angeles, and his expression, "Fortress L.A.," refers to the type of space being presently created in the city.

> Welcome to post-liberal Los Angeles, where the defense of luxury lifestyles is translated into a proliferation of new repressions in space and movement, undergirded by the ubiquitous "armed response." This obsession with physical security systems, and, collaterally, with the architectural policing of social boundaries, has become a zeitgeist of urban restructuring, a master narrative in the emerging built environment of the 1990s. We live in "fortress cities" brutally divided between "fortified cells" of affluent society and "places of terror" where the police battle the criminalized poor. (Davis 1990: 223–24)

For Davis, the increasingly segregated and privatized Los Angeles is the result of a clear master plan of postliberal (i.e., Reagan-Bush Republican) elites, a theme he reiterates in his analysis of the 1992 riots (Davis 1993). To talk of contemporary Los Angeles is for him to talk of a new "class war at the level of the built environment" and to demonstrate that "urban form is indeed following a repressive function in the political furrows of the Reagan-Bush era. Los Angeles, in its prefigurative mode, offers an especially disquieting catalogue of the emergent liaisons between architecture and the American police state" (Davis 1990: 228).

Davis's writing is marked by an indignation fully supported by his wealth of evidence concerning Los Angeles. Nevertheless, sometimes he tends to collapse complex social processes into a simplified scenario of warfare that his own rich description defies. Despite this tendency to look at social reality as the direct product of elite intentions, Davis elaborates a remarkable critique of social and spatial segregation, and associates the emerging urban configuration with the crucial themes of social inequality and political options. For him, not only is there nothing inevitable about "fortress architecture," but also it has deep consequences for how the public space and public interactions are shaped.

My analysis of São Paulo's enclaves coincides with Davis's analysis of Los Angeles as far as the issue of the public space is concerned. It is clear in both cases that the public order created by private enclaves of the "defensible" style has inequalities, isolation, and fragmentation as starting points. In this context, the fiction of the overall social contract and the ideals of universal rights and equality that legitimated the modern conception of public space vanish. We should ask, then, if there is already another political fiction organizing inequalities and differences at the societal level, and how to best conceive this new configuration as the old modern model loses its explanatory value. If social differences are brought to the center of the scene instead of being put aside by universalistic claims, then what kind of model for the public realm can we maintain? What kind of polity will correspond to the new fragmented public sphere? Is democracy still possible in this new public sphere?

Public Sphere: Inequalities and Boundaries

People attach meanings to the spaces where they live in flexible and varying ways, and the factors influencing these readings and uses are endless.[15] However, cities are also material spaces with relative stability and rigidity that shape and bound people's lives and determine the types of encounters possible in public space. When walls are built up, they form the stage for public life regardless of the meanings people attach to them and regardless

15. On this theme, see Certeau 1984: part 3.

of the multiple "tactics" of resistance people use to appropriate urban space.

In this essay, I have been arguing that in cities where fortified enclaves produce spatial segregation, social inequalities become quite explicit. I have also been arguing that in these cities, residents' everyday interactions with people from other social groups diminish substantially, and public encounters primarily occur inside protected and relatively homogeneous groups. In the materiality of segregated spaces, in people's everyday trajectories, in their uses of public transportation, in their appropriations of streets and parks, and in their constructions of walls and defensive façades, social boundaries are rigidly constructed. Their crossing is under surveillance. When boundaries are crossed in this type of city, there is aggression, fear, and a feeling of unprotectedness; in a word, there is suspicion and danger. Residents from all social groups have a sense of exclusion and restriction. For some, the feeling of exclusion is obvious, as they are denied access to various areas and are restricted to others. Affluent people who inhabit exclusive enclaves also feel restricted; their feelings of fear keep them away from regions and people that their mental maps of the city identify as dangerous.

Contemporary urban segregation is complementary to the issue of urban violence. On the one hand, the fear of crime is used to legitimate increasing measures of security and surveillance. On the other, the proliferation of everyday talk about crime becomes the context in which residents generate stereotypes as they label different social groups as dangerous and therefore as people to be feared and avoided. Everyday discussions about crime create rigid symbolic differences between social groups as they tend to align them either with good or with evil. In this sense, they contribute to a construction of inflexible separations in a way analogous to city walls. Both enforce ungiving boundaries. In sum, one consequence of living in cities segregated by enclaves is that while heterogeneous contacts diminish, social differences are more rigidly perceived and proximity with people from different groups considered as dangerous, thus emphasizing inequality and distance.

Nevertheless, the urban environment is not the only basis of people's experiences of social differences. If fact, there are other arenas in which differences tend to be experienced in almost opposite ways, offering an important counterpoint to the experience of the urban environment. This is the case of the perceptions of social difference forged through the intensification of communication networks and mass media (international news, documentaries about all types of lives and experiences), through mass movements of populations, through tourism, or through the consumption of ethnic products (food, clothes, films, music). In these contexts, boundaries between different social universes become more permeable and are constantly crossed as people have access to worlds that are not originally their own.

Thus, the perception and experience of social differences in contemporary cities may occur in quite distinct ways. Some tame social differences, allowing their appropriation by various types of consumers. Other experiences, such as those of emerging urban environments, characterized by fear and violence, magnify social differences and maintain distance and separateness. If the first type of experience may blur boundaries, the second type explicitly elaborates them. Both types of experience constitute the contemporary public sphere, but their consequences for public and political life are radically distinct. On the one hand, the softening of boundaries may still be related to the ideals of equality of the liberal-democratic polity and may serve as the basis of claims of incorporation. The tamed differences produced to be consumed do not threaten universalist ideals, and in their peculiar way put people into contact. On the other hand, the new urban morphologies of fear give new forms to inequality, keep groups apart, and inscribe a new sociability that runs against the ideals of the modern public and its democratic freedoms. When some people are denied access to certain areas and when different groups are not supposed to interact in public space, references to a universal principle of equality and freedom for social life are no longer possible, even as fiction. The consequences of the new separateness and restriction for public life are serious: contrary to what Jencks thinks (1993), defensible architecture and planning may only promote conflict instead of preventing it, by making clear the extension of social inequalities and the lack of commonalities.

Among the conditions necessary for democracy is that people acknowledge those from different social groups as co-citizens, that is, as people having similar rights. If this is true, it is clear that contemporary cities that are segregated by fortified enclaves are not environments that generate conditions conducive to democracy. Rather, they foster inequality and the sense that different groups belong to separate universes and have irreconcilable claims. Cities of walls do not strengthen citizenship but rather contribute to its corrosion. Moreover, this effect does not depend either on the type of political regime or on the intentions of those in power, since the architecture of the enclaves entails by itself a certain social logic.

Discussions about cities such as Los Angeles, London, or Paris, that is, cities populated by people from the most diverse cultural origins, commonly invoke the theme of the limits of modern citizenship based on affiliation to a nation-state. One might rethink the parameters of citizenship in those cities and suggest that the criterion for participation in political life could be local residence rather than national citizenship. Moreover, it would be possible to argue that this local participation is increasingly necessary to make those cities livable and to improve the quality of life of the impoverished population, increasingly consisting of immigrants. The contrast between this alternative political vision and the reality of fortified cities allows for at least two conclusions, one pessimistic and one more optimistic.

The pessimistic would say that the direction of new segregation and the extension of social separation already achieved would make impossible the engagement of a variety of social groups in a political life in which common goals and solutions would have to be negotiated. In this view, citizenship in cities of walls is meaningless. The optimistic interpretation, however, would consider that the change in the criteria for admission to political life, and the consequent change in status of a considerable part of the population, would generate a wider engagement in the search for solutions to common problems and would potentially bridge some distances. There are many reasons to be suspicious of such optimism; studies of homeowner associations in Los Angeles remind us how local democracy may be used as an instrument of segregation (Davis 1990: chap. 3). However, the boom of social movements in São Paulo after the mid-1970s suggests a cautious optimism. Where excluded residents discover that they have rights to the city, they manage to transform their neighborhoods and to improve the quality of their lives. That fortified enclaves in part counteracted this process should not make us abandon this qualified optimism. The walls were not able to totally obstruct the exercise of citizenship, and poor residents continue to expand their rights.

References

Banham, Reyner. 1971. *Los Angeles: The Architecture of Four Ecologies*. Baltimore: Pelican.

Benjamin, Walter. 1969. *Illuminations*. Harry Zohn, trans. Hannah Arendt, ed. New York: Schocken.

Berman, Marshall. 1982. *All That Is Solid Melts into Air*. New York: Penguin.

Caldeira, Teresa Pires do Rio. 1984. *A Política dos Outros*. São Paulo: Brasiliense.

——. 1996. "Building Up Walls: The New Pattern of Spatial Segregation in São Paulo." *International Social Science Journal* 147: 55–66.

——. forthcoming. *City of Walls: Crime, Segregation, and Citizenship in São Paulo*. Berkeley: University of California Press.

Certeau, Michel de. 1984. *The Practice of Everyday Life*. Berkeley: University of California Press.

Clark, T. J. 1984. *The Painting of Modern Life: Paris in the Art of Manet and His Followers*. Princeton: Princeton University Press.

Davis, Mike. 1990. *City of Quartz: Excavating the Future in Los Angeles*. London: Verso.

——. 1991. "The Infinite Game: Redeveloping Downtown L.A." In *Out of Site: Social Criticism of Architecture*, Diane Ghirardo, ed. Seattle: Bay Press, 77–113.

——. 1993. "Who Killed Los Angeles? Part Two: The Verdict Is Given." *New Left Review* 199: 29–54.

Eisenstein, Zillah R. 1988. *The Female Body and the Law*. Berkeley: University of California Press.

Harvey, David. 1985. *Consciousness and the Urban Experience: Studies in History and Theory of Capitalist Urbanization*. Baltimore: Johns Hopkins University Press.

Hirschman, Albert O. 1991. *The Rhetoric of Reaction: Perversity, Futility, Jeopardy*. Cambridge: Belknap Press of Harvard University Press.

Holston, James. 1989. *The Modernist City: An Anthropological Critique of Brasília*. Chicago: University of Chicago Press.

——. 1991. "Autoconstruction in Working-Class Brazil." *Cultural Anthropology* 6(4): 447–65.

Holston, James, and Teresa P. R. Caldeira. "Democracy, Law, and Violence: Disjunctions of Brazilian Citizenship." In *Fault Lines of Democratic Governance in the Americas*. Felipe Agüero and Jeffrey Stark, eds. Boulder, Colo.: Lynne Rienner Press.

Jencks, Charles. 1993. *Heteropolis: Los Angeles, the Riots, and the Strange Beauty of Hetero-Architecture*. London: Ernst and Sohn.

Lopes, Juarez Brandão. 1993. "Brasil 1989: Um estudo sócioeconômico da indigência e da pobreza urbanas." NEEP: *Cadernos de Pesquisa* 25.

Marshall, T. H. [1958] 1965. "Citizenship and Social Class." In *Class, Citizenship, and Social Development*, T. H. Marshall. New York: Doubleday.

Metrô—Companhia do Metropolitano de São Paulo. 1989. *Pesquisa OD/87: Síntese das Informações*. São Paulo: Metrô.

Pateman, Carole. 1988. *The Sexual Contract*. Stanford: Stanford University Press.

Rabinow, Paul. 1989. *French Modern: Norms and Forms of the Social Environment*. Cambridge: MIT Press.

Rocha, Sonia. 1991. "Pobreza metropolitana e os ciclos de curto prazo: balanço dos anos 80." IPEA: *Boletim de Conjuntura* 12.

Sassen, Saskia. 1991. *The Global City: New York, London, Tokyo*. Princeton: Princeton University Press.

Schorske, Carl E. 1961. *Fin-de-Siècle Vienna: Politics and Culture*. New York: Vintage.

Sennett, Richard. 1974. *The Fall of Public Man: On the Social Psychology of Capitalism*. New York: Vintage.

Soja, Edward W. 1989. *Postmodern Geographies: The Reassertion of Space in Critical Social Theory*. London: Verso.

——. 1992. "Inside Exopolis: Scenes from Orange County." In *Variations on a Theme Park: The New American City and the End of Public Space*, Michael Sorkin, ed. New York: Noonday.

Turner, Bryan. 1992. "Outline of a Theory of Citizenship." In *Dimensions of Radical Democracy: Pluralism, Citizenship, Community*, Chantal Mouffe, ed. London: Verso.

Vidler, Anthony. 1978. "The Scenes of the Street: Transformation in Ideal and Reality, 1750–1871." In *On Streets*, Stanford Anderson, ed. Cambridge: MIT Press.

Genealogy: Lincoln Steffens on New York

Selected, with an introductory note by Dilip Parameshwar
Gaonkar and Christopher Kamrath

gen·e·al·o·gy, n.: the descent of three keywords: *public, publicity,* and *public opinion.*

"New York: Good Government to the Test" is the final chapter of Lincoln Steffens's *The Shame of the Cities,* a 1904 volume that reprinted a series of *McClure's Magazine* exposés of municipal corruption in American cities. These articles provide a detailed investigative account of how rapidly growing turn-of-the-century cities were actually run. The carefully researched and artfully told stories of boodling, graft, and mismanagement recount how an apathetic public in city after city endures (and accedes to) its elected officials, who routinely sacrifice the public interest in favor of "big business" interests and brazenly collude with the criminal elements in vice racketeering.

Steffens argues that the lawlessness in American cities is not a contingent and variable local phenomenon but a systemic failure rooted in the readiness with which the "good and law-abiding" citizens cede their civic responsibilities to anyone who offers to discharge those responsibilities on their behalf—be it the "boss," the "machine," or the "business mayor."

And this makes the American claim to self-government a travesty. Steffens hoped that his articles would not only expose the general structure and the hidden practices of municipal corruption but also challenge "the civic pride of an apparently shameless citizenship" (Steffens [1904] 1957: 1). With tales and tropes of shame, he thought he could catch the conscience of a wayward public and spur it to civic action.

It is a historical commonplace that the January 1903 issue of *McClure's* inaugurated a "literature of exposure" that Theodore Roosevelt would later label "muckraking."[1] The issue contained three long articles: Steffens's second piece on municipal corruption, titled "The Shame of Minneapolis"; the third chapter of Ida Tarbell's book, *The History of the Standard Oil Company*, a monumental case study of how John D. Rockefeller built one of the largest trusts of the time; and Ray Stannard Baker's "The Right to Work," an account of the violence directed at nonstriking workers during the 1902 United Mine Workers strike in the coal fields of Pennsylvania. Samuel McClure's brief framing editorial for this issue described its content as "such an arraignment of American character as should make every one of us stop and think."[2] And it did. These articles are remarkable for their relentless pursuit of detail and complete rendering of the social problem that each of them addressed. Their rhetorical power stems from an effective combination of extensive field research characteristic of the newly emerging social sciences and a mode of narrative composition drawn from the genre of "social realism" in literature. Baker was a novelist and Steffens aspired to be one.

The article reprinted here was written after Steffens had exposed various forms of corruption in Saint Louis (boodle), Minneapolis (police graft), Pittsburgh (a political and industrial machine), and Philadelphia (general civic corruption) (Steffens 1957 [1904]: 10–11). In the last two installments of the series, Steffens examines attempts at reform in Chicago and New York. In his autobiography, Steffens describes these two cities as illustrating two distinct approaches to reform: one aims at "representative government" and the other at "good government" (Steffens 1931: 430). In the article on Chicago, Steffens documents the efforts by a municipal league to reform the city by exposing corrupt politicians, nominating better candidates, and educating the citizenry. This type of reform, slow and requiring continuous vigilance, seeks to ensure that elected officials act in the public interest and uphold the law. The article reprinted here analyzes the then prevalent "good government" model of reform as it was practiced in New

1. Roosevelt's speech, "The Man with the Muckrake," was delivered on 14 April 1906; reprinted in Weinberg and Weinberg 1961: 58–65.
2. "McClure Editorial: Concerning three articles in this number of *McClure's*, and a coincidence which may set us thinking"; reprinted in Weinberg and Weinberg 1961: 4–5.

York City. This type of reform, allegedly swift and efficient, attempts to wipe out corruption and mismanagement by electing a businessman as mayor to run the city. However, this type of reform neglects politics, and such neglect eventually catches up with it at the polls. Seth Low, the businessman whom New Yorkers had selected to cleanse their city, lost his mayoral reelection campaign shortly after Steffens's article was published.

For Steffens, the failure of cities to obtain lasting reform was a direct result of reformers' neglect of politics. He describes the citizens' involvement in most reform movements as mere revolt. The revolts are part of a regular pattern. Faced with rampant and overt corruption, citizens form coalitions to clean out the city, to enact strict laws and charters, and to elect a business mayor. Initially they succeed. Soon the indignation that fueled the revolt subsides, citizens return to their usual concerns, the new laws are not enforced, and the mayor is either turned out, baffled by the "machine," or simply becomes corrupt himself. Steffens argues that such revolts merely strengthen organizations such as Tammany by forcing them, through periodic exiles, to refine their methods and consolidate their control. At the end of the essay Steffens suggests that, by abdicating politics to the businessman, New York may have "worked for thirty years along the wrong road—crowded with unhappy American cities—the road to Philadelphia and despair."[3]

In the 1990s, New York has found new and different ways of turning government over to business. Business people throughout Manhattan have organized business-improvement districts (BIDs), charged with the task of urban reform and maintenance of property values. As corporate versions of the neighborhood association, BIDs are chartered by state law and can assess taxes on property within the district.[4] These taxes are used to support public improvements, sanitation services, and private security forces. Several BIDs have even become welfare providers for the purpose of clearing the streets of the homeless. Recent allegations that the homeless-outreach program of the "Grand Central Partnership"—a well-entrenched BID praised as an alternative to "the welfare state" by Speaker of the House Newt Gingrich—deployed "goon squads" to clear out homeless people from contested public places like ATM vestibules does, indeed, suggest grim possibilities about such quasi–public welfare programs dedicated to the needs of commerce.[5]

3. Steffens [1904] 1957: 214. Philadelphia, in Steffens's view, was the most corrupt of the cities.
4. Traub 1995c: 36–40. We are indebted to Robert J. McCarthy Jr. for drawing our attention to Traub's piece.
5. For an account of these allegations, see Lambert 1995: B-1; Lueck, 1995a: B-1; New York Times 1995: A-30; Lueck, 1995b: 1, 27. For an earlier article, see Lueck 1994: A-1.

BIDs, unlike the "machine" of Steffens's time, are forthright and proud about their undemocratic nature. Gretchen Dykstra, the president of the Times Square BID, admits: "We control the money, we get things done, and we are outside of democratic oversight and accountability" (Traub 1995c: 37). The eclipse of the civic rights and responsibilities of the public who inhabits the metropolis, an eclipse of private citizens by the corporate giants who own real estate, is now being advocated and celebrated as "urban reform" and a source of civic pride.

For the introduction to his next book, *The Struggle for Self-Government* (1906), which extends the investigation of corruption to the level of state governments, Steffens composed a satirical dedicatory epistle to the embattled czar of Russia, Nicholas the Second (Steffens 1906 [1968]: iii–xxiii). Here Steffens tells the czar that he should grant, instead of resisting, his subjects' demand for a representative government similar to the one in the United States. Once given the representative government, Steffens assures the czar that the Russian people would quickly turn over their civic responsibilities to a boss such as the czar. Steffens thus satirically recommends democracy as a prophylaxis to revolution. It is a grim irony today that BIDs publicly advertise their plutocratic political structure as a model for civic virtue. And what tales of shame—if shame still be a public emotion—would stir today's sleeping citizens to action?

New York: Good Government to the Test
Lincoln Steffens

Just about the time this article will appear,* Greater New York will be holding a local election on what has come to be a national question—good government. No doubt there will be other "issues." At this writing (September 15 [1903]) the candidates were not named nor the platforms written, but the regular politicians hate the main issue, and they have a pretty trick of confusing the honest mind and splitting the honest vote by raising "local issues" which would settle themselves under prolonged honest government. So, too, there will probably be some talk about the effect this election might have upon the next presidential election; another clever fraud which seldom fails to work to the advantage of rings and grafters, and to the humiliation and despair of good citizenship. We have nothing to do with these deceptions. They may count in New York, they may determine the result, but let them. They are common moves in the corruptionist's game, and, therefore, fair tests of citizenship, for honesty is not the

*First published in *McClure's Magazine*, November 1903. Reprinted here from Steffens 1989 [1957]: 195–214.

sole qualification for an honest voter; intelligence has to play a part, too, and a little intelligence would defeat all such tricks. Anyhow, they cannot disturb us. I am writing too far ahead, and my readers, for the most part, will be reading too far away to know or care anything about them. We can grasp firmly the essential issues involved and then watch with equanimity the returns for the answer, plain yes or no, which New York will give to the only questions that concern us all. [Tammany tried to introduce national issues, but failed, and "good government" was practically the only question raised.]

Do we Americans really want good government? Do we know it when we see it? Are we capable of that sustained good citizenship which alone can make democracy a success? Or, to save our pride, one other: Is the New York way the right road to permanent reform?

For New York has good government, or, to be more precise, it has a good administration. It is not a question there of turning the rascals out and putting the honest men into their places. The honest men are in, and this election is to decide whether they are to be kept in, which is a very different matter. Any people is capable of rising in wrath to overthrow bad rulers. Philadelphia has done that in its day. New York has done it several times. With fresh and present outrages to avenge, particular villains to punish, and the mob sense of common anger to excite, it is an emotional gratification to go out with the crowd and "smash something." This is nothing but revolt, and even monarchies have uprisings to the credit of their subjects. But revolt is not reform, and one revolutionary administration is not good government. That we free Americans are capable of such assertions of our sovereign power, we have proven; our lynchers are demonstrating it every day. That we can go forth singly also, and, without passion, with nothing but mild approval and dull duty to impel us, vote intelligently to sustain a fairly good municipal government, remains to be shown. And that is what New York has the chance to show; New York, the leading exponent of the great American anti–bad government movement for good government.

According to this, the standard course of municipal reform, the politicians are permitted to organize a party on national lines, take over the government, corrupt and deceive the people, and run things for the private profit of the boss and his ring, till the corruption becomes rampant and a scandal. Then the reformers combine the opposition: the corrupt and unsatisfied minority, the disgruntled groups of the majority, the reform organizations; they nominate a mixed ticket, headed by a "good business man" for mayor, make a "hot campaign" against the government with "Stop, thief!" for the cry, and make a "clean sweep." Usually, this affects only the disciplining of the reckless grafters and the improvement of the graft system of corrupt government. The good mayor turns out to be weak or foolish or "not so good." The politicians "come it over him," as they did over the business mayors who followed the "Gas Ring" revolt in Philadelphia, or the people become disgusted as they did with Mayor Strong who was carried into office by the anti-Tammany rebellion in New York after the Lexow exposures. Philadelphia gave up after its disappointment, and that is what most cities do. The repeated failure of revolutionary reform to accomplish more than the strengthening of the machine have so discredited this method that wide-awake reformers in several cities— Pittsburgh, Cincinnati, Cleveland, Detroit, Minneapolis, and others—are following the lead of Chicago.

The Chicago plan does not depend for success upon any one man or any one year's work, nor upon excitement of any sort of bad government. The reformers there have no ward organizations, no machine at all; their appeal is solely to the intelligence of the voter and their power rests upon that. This is democratic and political, not bourgeois and business reform, and it is interesting to note that whereas reformers elsewhere are forever seeking to concentrate all the powers in the mayor, those of Chicago talk of stripping the mayor to a figurehead and giving his powers to the aldermen who directly represent the people, and who change year by year.

The Chicago way is but one way, however, and a new one, and it must be remembered that this plan has not yet produced a good administration. New York has that. Chicago, after seven years' steady work, has a body of aldermen honest enough and competent to defend the city's interests against boodle capital, but that is about all; it has a wretched administration. New York has stuck to the old way. Provincial and self-centered, it hardly knows there is any other. Chicago laughs and other cities wonder, but never mind, New York, by persistence, has at last achieved a good administration. Will the New Yorkers continue it? That is the question. What Chicago has, it has secure. Its independent citizenship is trained to vote every time and to vote for uninteresting, good aldermen. New York has an independent vote of 100,000, a decisive minority, but the voters have been taught to vote only one in a long while, only when excited by picturesque leadership and sensational exposures, only *against*. New York has been so far an anti–bad government, anti-Tammany, not a good-government town. Can it vote, without Tammany in to incite it, for a good mayor? I think this election, which will answer this question, should decide how other cities go about reform.

The administration of Mayor Seth Low may not have been perfect, not in the best European sense: not expert, not co-ordinated, certainly not wise. Nevertheless, for an American city, it has been not only honest, but able, undeniably one of the best in the whole country. Some of the departments have been dishonest; others have been so inefficient that they made the whole administration ridiculous. But what of that? Corruption also is clumsy and makes absurd mistakes when it is new and untrained. The "oaths" and ceremonies and much of the boodling of the St. Louis ring seemed laughable to my corrupt friends in Philadelphia and Tammany Hall, and New York's own Tweed regime was "no joke," only because it was so general, and so expensive to New York. It took time to perfect the "Philadelphia plan" of misgovernment, and it took time to educate Croker and develop his Tammany Hall. It will take time to evolve masters of the (in America) unstudied art of municipal government—time and demand. So far there has been no market for municipal experts in this country. All we are clamoring for today in our meek, weak-hearted way, is that mean, rudimentary, virtue miscalled "common honesty." Do we really want it? Certainly Mayor Low is pecuniarily honest. He is more; he is conscientious and experienced and personally efficient. Bred to business, he rose above it, adding to the training he acquired in the conduct of an international commercial house, two terms as mayor of Brooklyn, and to that again a very effective administration, as president, of the business of Columbia University. He began his mayoralty with a study of the affairs of New York; he has said himself that he devoted eight months to its finances: and he mastered this department and is admitted to be the master in detail of every department which has engaged his attention. In other words, Mr. Low has learned the business of New York; he is just about competent now to become the mayor of a great city. Is there a demand for Mr. Low?

No. When I made my inquiries—before the lying had begun—the Fusion leaders of the anti-Tammany forces, who nominated Mr. Low, said they might renominate him. "Who else was there?" they asked. And they thought he "might" be re-elected. The alternative was Richard Croker or Charles F. Murphy, his man, for no matter who Tammany's candidate for mayor was, if Tammany won, Tammany's boss would rule. The personal issue was plain enough. Yet there was no assurance for Mr. Low.

Why? There are many forms of the answer given, but they nearly all reduce themselves to one—the man's personality. It is not very engaging. Mr. Low has many respectable qualities, but these never are amiable. "Did you ever see his smile?" said a politician who was trying to account for his instinctive dislike for the mayor. I had; there is no laughter back of it, no humor, and no sense thereof. The appealing human element is lacking all through. His good abilities are self-sufficient; his dignity is smug; his courtesy seems not kind; his self-reliance is called obstinacy because, though he listens, he seems not to care; though he understands, he shows no sympathy, and when he decides, his reasoning is private. His most useful virtues—probity, intelligence, and conscientiousness—in action are often an irritation; they are so contented. Mr. Low is the bourgeois reformer type. Even where he compromises he gets no credit; his concessions make the impression of surrenders. A politician can say "no" and make a friend, where Mr. Low will lose one by saying "yes." Cold and impersonal, he cools even his heads of departments. Loyal public service they give, because his taste is for men who would do their duty for their own sake, not for his, and that excellent service the city has had. But members of Mr. Low's administration helped me to characterize him; they could not help it. Mr. Low is not a lovable character.

But what of that? Why should his colleagues love him? Why should anybody like him? Why should he seek to charm, win affection, and make friends? He was elected to attend to the business of his office and to appoint subordinates who should attend to the business of their offices, not to make "political strength" and win elections. William Travers Jerome, the picturesque District Attorney, whose sincerity and intellectual honesty made sure the election of Mr. Low two years ago, detests him as a bourgeois, but the mayoralty is held in New York to be a bourgeois office. Mr. Low is the ideal product of the New York theory that municipal government is business, not politics, and that a business man who would manage the city as he would a business corporation, would solve for us all our troubles. Chicago reformers think we have got to solve our own problems; that government is political business; that men brought up in politics and experienced in public office will make the best administrators. They have refused to turn from their politician mayor, Carter H. Harrison, for the most ideal business candidate, and I have heard them say that when Chicago was ripe for a better mayor they would prefer a candidate chosen from among their well-tried aldermen. Again, I say, however, that this is only one way, and New York has another, and this other is the standard American way.

But again I say, also, that the New York way is on trial, for New York has what the whole country has been looking for in all municipal crises—the non-political ruler. Mr. Low's very faults, which I have emphasized for the purpose, emphasize the point. They make it impossible for him to be a politician even if he should wish to be. As for his selfishness, his lack of tact, his coldness—these are of no consequence. He has done his duty all the better for them. Admit that he is uninteresting; what does that matter? He has served the city. Will the city not vote for him because it does not like the way he smiles? Absurd as it sounds, that is what all I have heard against Low amounts to. But to reduce the situation to a further absurdity, let us eliminate altogether the personality of Mr. Low. Let us suppose he has no smile, no courtesy, no dignity, no efficiency, no personality at all; suppose he were an It and had not given New York a good administration, but had only honestly tried. What then?

Tammany Hall? That is the alternative. The Tammany politicians see it just as clear as that, and they are not in the habit of deceiving themselves. They say "it is a Tammany year," "Tammany's turn." They say it and they believe it. They study the people, and they know it is all a matter of citizenship; they admit that they cannot win unless a goodly part of the independent vote goes to them; and still they say they can beat Mr. Low or any other man the anti-Tammany forces may nominate. So we are safe in eliminating Mr. Low and reducing the issue to plain Tammany.

Tammany is bad government; not inefficient, but dishonest; not a party, not a delusion and a snare, hardly known by its party name—Democracy; having little standing in the national councils of the party and caring little for influence outside of the city. Tammany is Tammany, the embodiment of corruption. All the world knows and all the world may know what it is and what it is after. For hypocrisy is not a Tammany vice. Tammany is for Tammany, and the Tammany men say so. Other rings proclaim lies and make pretensions; other rogues talk about the tariff and imperialism. Tammany is honestly dishonest. Time and time again, in private and in public, the leaders, big and little, have said they are out for themselves and their own; not for the public, but for "me and my friends"; not for New York, but for Tammany. Richard Croker said under oath once that he worked for his own pockets all the time, and Tom Grady, the Tammany orator, has brought his crowds to their feet cheering sentiments as primitive, stated with candor as brutal.

The man from Mars would say that such an organization, so self-confessed, could not be very dangerous to an intelligent people. Foreigners marvel at it and at us, and even Americans—Pennsylvanians, for example—cannot understand why we New Yorkers regard Tammany as so formidable. I think I can explain it. Tammany is corruption with consent; it is bad government founded on the suffrages of the people. The Philadelphia machine is more powerful. It rules Philadelphia by fraud and force and does not require the votes of the people. The Philadelphians do not vote for their machine; their machine votes for them. Tammany used to stuff the ballot boxes and intimidate voters; to-day there is practically none of that. Tammany rules, when it rules, by right of the votes of the people of New York.

Tammany corruption is democratic corruption. That of the Philadelphia ring is rooted in special interests. Tammany, too, is allied with "vested interests"—but Tammany labors under disadvantages not known in Philadelphia. The Philadelphia ring is of the same party that rules the State and the nation, and the local ring forms a living chain with the State and national rings. Tammany is a purely local concern. With a majority only in old New York, it has not only to buy what it wants from the Republican majority in the State, but must trade to get the whole city. Big business everywhere is the chief source of political corruption, and it is one source in New York; but most of the big businesses represented in New York have no plants there. Offices there are, and head offices, of many trusts and railways, for example, but that is all. There are but two railway terminals in the city, and but three railways use them. These have to do more with Albany than New York. So with Wall Street. Philadelphia's stock exchange deals largely in Pennsylvania securities, New York's in those of the whole United States. There is a small Wall Street group that specializes in local corporations, and they are active and give Tammany a Wall Street connection, but the biggest and the majority of our financial leaders, bribers though they may be in other cities and even in New York State, are independent of Tammany Hall, and can be honest citizens at home. From this class, indeed, New York can, and often does, draw some of its reformers. Not so Philadelphia. That bourgeois opposition which has persisted for thirty years in the fight against Tammany corruption was squelched in Philadelphia after its first great uprising. Matt Quay, through the banks, railways, and other business interests, was able to reach it. A large part of his power is negative; there is no opposition. Tammany's power is positive. Tammany cannot reach all the largest interests and its hold is upon the people.

Tammany's democratic corruption rests upon the corruption of the people, the plain people, and there lies its great significance; its grafting system is one in which more individuals share than any I have studied. The people themselves get very little; they come cheap, but they are interested. Divided into districts, the organization subdivides them into precincts or neighborhoods, and their sovereign power, in the form of votes, is bought up by kindness and petty privileges. They are forced to a surrender, when necessary, by intimidation, but the leader and his captains have their hold because they take care of their own. They speak pleasant words, smile friendly smiles, notice the baby, give picnics up the River or the Sound, or a slap on the back; find jobs, most of them at the city's expense, but they have also newsstands, peddling privileges, railroad and other business places to dispense; they permit violations of the law, and, if a man has broken the law without permission, see him through the court. Though a blow in the face is as readily given as a shake of the hand, Tammany kindness is real kindness, and will go far, remember long, and take infinite trouble for a friend.

The power that is gathered up thus cheaply, like garbage, in the districts is concentrated in the district leader, who in turn passes it on through a general committee to the boss. This is a form of living government, extra-legal, but very actual, and, though the beginnings of it are purely democratic, it develops at each stage into an autocracy. In Philadelphia the boss appoints a district leader and gives him power. Tammany has done that in two or three notable instances, but never without causing a bitter fight which lasts often for years. In Philadelphia the State boss designates the city boss. In New York, Croker has failed signally to maintain vice-bosses whom he appointed. The boss of Tammany Hall is a growth, and just as Croker grew, so has Charles F. Murphy grown up to Croker's place. Again, whereas in Philadelphia the boss and his ring handle and keep almost all of the graft, leaving little to the district leaders, in New York the district leaders share handsomely in the spoils.

There is more to share in New York. It is impossible to estimate the amount of it, not only for me, but for anybody. No Tammany man knows it all. Police friends of mine say that the Tammany leaders never knew how rich police corruption was till the Lexow committee exposed it, and that the politicians who had been content with small presents, contributions, and influence, "did not butt in" for their share till they saw by the testimony of frightened police grafters that the department was worth from four to five millions a year. The items are so incredible that I hesitate to print them. Devery told a friend once that in one year the police graft was "something over $3,000,000." Afterward the syndicate which divided the graft under Devery took in for thirty-six months $400,000 a month from gambling and poolrooms alone. Saloon bribers, disorderly house blackmail, policy, etc., etc., bring this total up to amazing proportions.

Yet this was but one department, and a department that was over-looked by Tammany for years. The annual budget of the city is about $100,000,000, and though the power that comes of the expenditure of that amount is enormous and the opportunities for rake-offs infinite, this sum is not one-half of the resources of Tammany when it is in power. Her resources are the resources of the city as a business, as a political, as a social power. If Tammany could be incorporated, and all its earnings, both legitimate and illegitimate, gathered up and paid over in dividends, the stockholders would get more than the New York Central bond- and stock-holders, more than the Standard Oil stockholders, and the controlling clique would wield a power equal to that of the United States Steel Company. Tammany, when in control of New York, takes out of the city un-believable millions of dollars a year.

No wonder the leaders are all rich; no wonder so many more Tammany men are rich than are the leaders in any other town; no wonder Tammany is liberal in its division of the graft. Croker took the best and the safest of it, and he accepted shares in others. He was "in on the Wall Street end," and the Tammany clique of financiers have knocked down and bought up at low prices Manhattan Railway stock by threats of the city's power over the road; they have been let in on Metropolitan deals and on the Third Avenue Railroad grab; the Ice trust is a Tammany trust; they have banks and trust companies, and through the New York Realty Company are forcing alliances with such financial groups as that of the Standard Oil company. Croker shared in these deals and businesses. He sold judgeships, taking his pay in the form of contributions to the Tammany campaign fund, of which he was treasurer, and he had the judges take from the regular real estate exchange all the enormous real estate business that passed through the courts, and give it to an exchange connected with the real estate business of his firm, Peter F. Meyer and Co. This alone would maintain a ducal estate in England. But his real estate business was greater than that. It had extraordinary legal facilities, the free advertising of abuse, the prestige of political privilege, all of which brought in trade; and it had advance information and followed with profitable deals, great public improvements.

Though Croker said he worked for his own pockets all the time, and did take the best of the graft, he was not "hoggish." Some of the richest graft in the city is in the Department of Buildings: $100,000,000 a year goes into building operations in New York. All of this, from outhouses to skyscrapers, is subject to very precise laws and regulations, most of them wise, some impossible. The Building Department has the enforcement of these; it passes upon all construction, private and public, at all stages, from plan-making to actual completion; and can cause not only "unavoidable delay," but can wink at most profitable violations. Architects and builders had to stand in with the department. They called on the right man and they settled on a scale which was not fixed, but which generally was on the basis of the department's estimate of a fair half of the value of the saving in time or bad material. This brought in at least a banker's percentage on one hundred millions a year. Croker, so far as I can make out, took none of this! It was let out to other leaders and was their own graft.

District Attorney William Travers Jerome has looked into the Dock Department, and he knows things which he yet may prove. This is an important investigation for two reasons. It is very large graft, and the new Tammany leader, Charlie Murphy, had it. New York wants to know more about Murphy, and it should want to know about the management of its docks, since, just as other cities have their corrupt dealings with railways and their terminals, so New York's great terminal business is with steamships and docks. These docks should pay the city handsomely. Mr. Murphy says they shouldn't; he is wise, as Croker was before he became old and garrulous, and, as Tammany men put it, "keeps his mouth shut," but he did say that the docks should not be run for revenue to the city, but for their own improvement. The Dock Board has exclusive and private and secret control of the expenditure of $10,000,000 a year. No wonder Murphy chose it.

It is impossible to follow all New York graft from its source to its final destination. It is impossible to follow here the course of that which is well known to New Yorkers. There are public works for Tammany contractors. There are private works for Tammany contractors, and corporations and individuals find it expedient to let it go to Tammany contractors. Tammany has a very good system of grafting on public works; I mean that it is "good" from the criminal point of view—and so it has for the furnishing of supplies. Low bids and short deliveries, generally speaking (and that is the only way I can speak here), is the method. But the Tammany system, as a whole, is weak.

Tammany men as grafters have a confidence in their methods and system, which, in the light of such perfection as that of Philadelphia, is amusing, and the average New Yorker takes in "the organization" a queer sort of pride, which is ignorant and provincial. Tammany is way behind the times. It is growing; it has improved. In Tweed's day the politicians stole from the city treasury, divided the money on the steps of the City Hall, and, not only the leaders, big and little, but heelers and outsiders; not only Tweed, but ward carpenters robbed the city; not only politicians, but newspapers and citizens were "in on the divvy." New York, not Tammany alone, was corrupt. When the exposure came, and Tweed asked his famous question, "What are you going to do about it?" the ring mayor, A. Oakey Hall, asked another as significant. It was reported that suit was to be brought against the ring to recover stolen funds. "Who is going to sue?" said Mayor Hall, who could not think of anybody of importance sufficiently without sin to throw the first stone. Stealing was stopped and grafting was made more businesslike, but still it was too general, and the boodling for the Broadway street railway franchise prompted a still closer grip on the business. The organization since then has been gradually concentrating the control of graft. Croker did not proceed so far along the line as the Philadelphia ring has, as the police scandals showed. After the Lexow exposures, Tammany took over that graft, but still let it go practically by districts, and the police captains still got a third. After the Mazet exposures, Devery became Chief, and the police graft was so concentrated that the division was reduced to fourteen parts. Again, later, it was reduced to a syndicate of four or five men, with a dribble of miscellaneous graft for the police. In Philadelphia the police have nothing to do with the police graft; a policeman may collect it, but he acts for a politician, who in turn passes it up to a small ring. That is the drift in New York. Under Devery the police officers got comparatively little, and the rank and file themselves were blackmailed for transfers and promotions, for remittances of fines, and in a dozen other petty ways.

Philadelphia is the end toward which New York under Tammany is driving as fast as the lower intelligence and higher conceit of its leaders will let it. In Philadelphia one very small ring gets everything, dividing the whole as it pleases, and not all those in the inner ring are politicians. Trusting few individuals, they are safe from exposure, more powerful, more deliberate, and they are wise as politicians. When, as in New York, the number of grafters is large, this delicate business is in some hands that are rapacious. The police grafters, for example, in Devery's day, were not content with the amounts collected from the big vices. They cultivated minor vices, like policy, to such an extent that the Policy King was caught and sent to prison, and Devery's wardman, Glennon, was pushed into so tight a hole that there was danger that District Attorney Jerome would get past Glennon to Devery and the syndicate. The murder of a witness the night he was in the Tenderloin police station served to save the day. But, worst of all, Tammany, the "friend of the people," permitted the organization of a band of so-called Cadets, who made a business, under the protection of the police, of ruining the daughters of the tenements and even of catching and imprisoning in disorderly houses the wives of poor men. This horrid traffic never was exposed; it could not and cannot be. Vicious women were "planted" in tenement houses and (I know this personally) the children of decent parents counted the customers, witnessed their transactions with these creatures, and, as a father told with shame and tears, reported totals at the family table.

Tammany leaders are usually the natural leaders of the people in these districts, and they are originally goodnatured, kindly men. No one has a more sincere liking than I for some of those common but generous fellows; their charity is real, at first. But they sell out their own people. They do give them coal and help them in their private troubles, but, as they grow rich and powerful, the kindness goes out of the charity and they not only collect at their saloons or in rents—cash for their "goodness"; they not only ruin fathers and sons and cause the troubles they relieve; they sacrifice the children in the schools; let the Health Department neglect the tenements, and, worst of all, plant vice in the neighborhood and in the homes of the poor.

This is not only bad; it is bad politics; it has defeated Tammany. Woe to New York when Tammany learns better. Honest fools talk of the reform of

Tammany Hall. It is an old hope, this, and twice it has been disappointed, but it is not vain. That is the real danger ahead. The reform of a corrupt ring means, as I have said before, the reform of its system of grafting and a wise consideration of certain features of good government. Croker turned his "best chief of police," William S. Devery, out of Tammany Hall, and, slow and old as he was, Croker learned what clean streets were from Colonel Waring, and gave them. Now there is a new boss, a young man, Charles F. Murphy, and unknown to New Yorkers. He looks dense, but he acts with force, decision, and skill. The new mayor will be his man. He may divide with Croker and leave to the "old man" all his accustomed graft, but Charlie Murphy will rule Tammany and, if Tammany is elected, New York also. Lewis Nixon is urging Murphy publicly, as I write, to declare against the police scandals and all the worst practices of Tammany. Lewis Nixon is an honest man, but he was one of the men Croker tried to appoint leader of Tammany Hall. And when he resigned Mr. Nixon said that he found that a man could not keep that leadership and his self-respect. Yet Mr. Nixon is a type of the man who thinks Tammany would be fit to rule New York if the organization would "reform."

As a New Yorker, I fear Murphy will prove sagacious enough to do just that: stop the scandal, put all the graft in the hands of a few tried and true men, and give the city what it would call good government. Murphy says he will nominate for mayor a man so "good" that his goodness will astonish New York. I don't fear a bad Tammany mayor; I dread the election of a good one. For I have been to Philadelphia.

Philadelphia had a bad ring mayor, a man who promoted the graft and caused scandal after scandal. The leaders there, the wisest political grafters in this country, learned a great lesson from that. As one of them said to me:

> The American people don't mind grafting, but they hate scandals. They don't kick so much on a jiggered public contract for a boulevard, but they want the boulevard and no fuss and no dust. We want to give them that. We want to give them what they really want, a quiet Sabbath, safe streets, orderly nights, and homes secure. They let us have the police graft. But this mayor was a hog. You see, he had but one term and he could get his share only on what was made in his term. He not only took a hog's share off what was coming, but he wanted everything to come in his term. So I'm down on grafting mayors and grafting office holders. I tell you it's good politics to have honest men in office. I mean men that are personally honest.

So they got John Weaver for mayor, and honest John Weaver is checking corruption, restoring order, and doing a great many good things, which it is "good politics" to do. For he is satisfying the people, soothing their ruffled pride, and reconciling them to machine rule. I have letters from friends of mine there, honest men, who wish me to bear witness to the goodness of Mayor Weaver. I do. And I believe that if the Philadelphia machine leaders are as careful with Mayor Weaver as they have been and let him continue to give to the end as good government as he has given so far, the "Philadelphia plan" of graft will last and Philadelphia will never again be a free American city.

Philadelphia and New York began about the same time, some thirty years ago, to reform their city governments. Philadelphia got "good government"—what the Philadelphians call good—from a corrupt ring and quit, satisfied to be a scandal to the nation and a disgrace to democracy. New York has gone on fighting, advancing and retreating, for thirty years, till now it has achieved the beginnings, under Mayor Low, of a government for the people. Do the New Yorkers know it? Do they care? They are Americans, mixed and typical; do we Americans really want good government? Or, as I said at starting, have they worked for thirty years along the wrong road—crowded with unhappy American cities—the road to Philadelphia and despair?

Post Scriptum: Mayor Low was nominated on the Fusion ticket. Tammany nominated George B. McClellan. The local corporations contributed heavily to the Tammany campaign fund and the people of New York elected the Tammany ticket by a decisive majority of 62,696. The vote was: McClellan, 314,782; Low, 252,086.

Spaces of Insurgent Citizenship

James Holston

Cities are plugged into the globe of history like capacitors: they condense and conduct the currents of social time. Their layered surfaces, their coats of painted stucco, their wraps of concrete register the force of these currents both as wear and as narrative. That is, city surfaces tell time and stories. Cities are full of stories in time, some sedimented and catalogued; others spoorlike, vestigial, and dispersed. Their narratives are epic and everyday; they tell of migration and production, law and laughter, revolution and art. Yet, although obvious, their registry is never wholly legible, because each foray into the palimpsest of city surfaces reveals only traces of these relations. Once lived as irreducible to one another, they are registered as part of the multiplicity and simultaneity of processes that turn the city into an infinite geometry of superimpositions. Their identities, modes, forms, categories, and types recombine in the gray matter of streets. City narratives are, as a result, both evident and enigmatic. Knowing them is always experimental.

It must have been with considerable exasperation, therefore, that the Dutch architect Aldo van Eyck asserted in the mid-1960s that "we know nothing of vast multiplicity—we cannot come to grips with it—not as architects, planners or anybody else. . . . [But] if society has no form—how can architects build its counterform?" (quoted in Frampton 1980: 276–77). This confession of illiteracy is especially striking not only because it abandons the narrative of cities but also because it does so by declaring the dissolution of the social within the disciplines of modern architecture and planning. This declaration is particularly bitter because it signals the end of a century in which modernist doctrine posed the urban questions of our time precisely by advancing planning and architecture as solutions to the *social* crises of industrial capitalism. At least in its European and Latin American versions, modernism forged what we could call this imaginary of planning by developing its revolutionary building types and planning conventions as instruments of social change and by conceiving of change in terms of the imagined future embodied in the narratives of its master plans.[1]

But is van Eyck's inability to find form in society—that is, to read its multiplicity—a problem of society as he implies or a consequence of a theoretical position that rejects the redemptive claims and social engagements of modernism? Given the human capacity for narrative, and its ineluctable registry in artifact, I conclude the latter. Moreover, I would argue that van Eyck's consternation is representative of the estrangement of the social in modern architecture and its related modes of planning generally. I suggest that this estrangement is a consequence of a number of theoretical conditions that structure the current production of concepts in

1. Van Eyck's conjunction of "architect or planner" suggests a potentially confusing use of terms. I am grateful to John Friedmann for having urged, in a conversation about this essay, that I clarify my own sense of this problem. If we look at the use of the terms planner and planning in the various professions and disciplines that claim them, we see two distinct but, I will argue, related meanings. On the one hand, planning is very generally used to refer to urban design, derived in large measure from architectural theory and practice. In this form, the dominant mode of planning in modern times is that developed by CIAM. As I discuss, this model is predicated on an idealist project of alternative futures. On the other hand, since the consolidation of the modern state, planning is also widely used to refer to the application of social science to the management of society. Indeed, some applied social scientists, like Friedmann, who call themselves planners, are deeply critical of modernist urban design and its modes of planning. Very often, however, these two senses of planning share a notion of alternative futures and a reliance on the state that relate them both historically and theoretically. It is this relation that interests me and that permits a broader argument about modernity and planning in its various forms. Thus, I use the CIAM model of urban design as paradigmatic of modernist planning. However, I also consider applied social science as a related version when it is based on a similar ideal of the future.

these fields about the urban landscape: (1) the rejection of the redemptive power of modernism deriving not only from the perceived failures of its utopian mode but also from the more general dissolution of the idea of the social itself in planning, architecture, government, and social science; (2) the inability of the professions of planning and architecture to move beyond that rejection to develop a new activist social imagination; and (3) the preoccupation in postmodern theory with aesthetic formalism, technologies of communication, and concepts of virtual reality, which tends to disembody the social and rematerialize it as commodity images.[2] If my conclusion is correct, then the problem van Eyck poses is more anthropological than morphological. That is, it is a question of learning to interpret anew what appears to him now thoroughly defamiliarized; in a word, society itself, or, better, aspects of the social that indicate its dynamism.

As I do not believe that "society has no form" or that "we know nothing of vast multiplicity," I want to argue that one of the most urgent problems in planning and architectural theory today is the need to develop a different social imagination—one that is not modernist but that nevertheless reinvents modernism's activist commitments to the invention of society and to the construction of the state. I suggest that the sources of this new imaginary lie not in any specifically architectural or planning production of the city but rather in the development of theory in both fields as an investigation into what I call the spaces of insurgent citizenship—or insurgent spaces of citizenship, which amounts to the same thing. By insurgent, I mean to emphasize the opposition of these spaces of citizenship to the modernist spaces that physically dominate so many cities today. I also use it to emphasize an opposition to the modernist political project that absorbs citizenship into a plan of state building and that, in the process, generates a certain concept and practice of planning itself. At the heart of this modernist political project is the doctrine—also clearly expressed in the tradition of civil or positivist law—that the state is the only legitimate source of citizenship rights, meanings, and practices. I use the notion of insurgent to refer to new and other sources and to their assertion of legitimacy.[3]

2. These concerns receive such extensive discussion in the literature on postmodernism that I cannot comment on them here without being superficial. In addition to the well-known studies of the glorification of consumption in postmodernist theory and description of contemporary society by Jean Baudrillard or Paul Virilio, for example, see the recent (and fun, if not always accurate) work by Celeste Olalquiaga (1992). For a recent attempt to dematerialize the city itself, see Sorkin 1992.

3. See Holston 1989 and 1995 for further discussion of, respectively, this modernist political and planning project and the notion of an insurgent urbanism. I would like to thank the organizers of two conferences for inviting me to present early versions of this essay, "New

The Alternative Futures of Modernism

The spaces of an insurgent citizenship constitute new metropolitan forms of the social not yet liquidated by or absorbed into the old. As such, they embody possible alternative futures. It is important to distinguish this concept of the possible from the fundamentally different idea of alternative futures inherent in modernist planning and architectural doctrine. Both express the basic paradigm of modernity that emphasizes that alternative futures are indeed possible. But the insurgent and the modernist are competing expressions, which I will distinguish as ethnographic and utopian, respectively. In modern architecture and urban design, the latter derives specifically from the model city of the Congrès Internationaux d'Architecture Modern (CIAM). Since the 1920s, its manifestos have called for the state to assert the priority of collective interests over private interests by imposing on the chaos of existing cities the construction of a new type of city based on its master plans (Figure 1). But that model derives in turn from the pervasive ideal of modernity that the state, usually in the form of a national government, can change society and manage the social by imposing an alternative future embodied in plans. In this Faustian sense, the project of modernist planning is to transform an unwanted present by means of an imagined future. Whether in the form of urban design or applied social science, this idea of planning is central to the identity of the modern state: it motivates political authorities to attempt to create and legitimate new kinds of public spheres, with new subjects and subjectivities for them. The instruments of these initiatives define not only the development agenda of the state but also its accredited liberal professions and social sciences—architecture, urban design, demography, bureaucratic administration, sociology, criminology, epidemiology, and so forth—through which governments try to forge new forms of collective association and personal habit as the basis of propelling their societies into a proclaimed future.

This ideology of planning is utopian not because it is critical of the present or because it has as its objective the disruption of taken-for-granted norms. It shares these characteristics with the ethnographic mode I propose. Rather, it is utopian because its notion of alternative futures is based on absent causes and its methods on a theory of total decontextualization. The CIAM version of modernist planning is an instructive example. The key features of its theory of alternative features are four. First, it is

Metropolitan Forms" at Duke University and "Art, Architecture, and Urbanism" in Brasília. I am grateful to Teresa Caldeira for her suggestions on the final version and to Leonie Sandercock for encouraging its original publication.

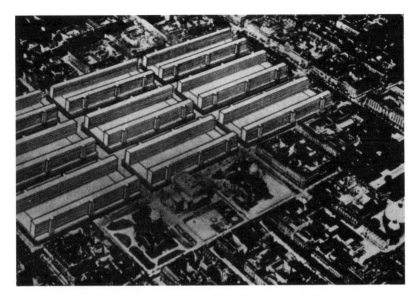

Figure 1. Berlin: Project for center city, Ludwig Hilberseimer, 1927.

based on a tension between existing social conditions and their imagined opposite. Second, this opposite is conceived in terms of absent causes, present nowhere in the world but existing only in plans and their technologies that are supposed to colonize the old and create the new in relation to which they then appear as natural offspring. Lúcio Costa, planner of Brasília, clearly expressed this concept of generative absent causes when he wrote the following in "Razões da nova arquitetura" in 1930: "There exists, already perfectly developed in its fundamental elements . . . an entire new constructive know-how, paradoxically still waiting for the society to which, logically, it should belong" ([1930] 1980: 15). Costa conceived of this technology as embodying the imagined principles of a society that did not yet exist but that it would help bring into being precisely by giving embodiment to those principles in built form.

The third and fourth aspects of the model constitute a theory of colonization to implement the new architecture-planning-technology. Its aim is to achieve both an objective and a subjective transformation of existing conditions. In terms of the former, colonization depends on the force of the state to create objective conditions for the imposition of a new order of urban life. The CIAM model appeals directly to state authority to institute the total planning of the built environment that, according to the theory, constitutes these conditions and permits the implementation of its blueprints of the future. This appeal privileges the development of the apparatus of the modern state itself as the supreme planning power. Precisely because of that emphasis, state-building elites of every kind of political persuasion have embraced the CIAM model of urban development, as the history of city planning around the world attests.

The model also relies on a subjective transformation of existing conditions. In this case, borrowing from other avant-garde movements of the early twentieth century, it uses techniques of shock to force a subjective appropriation of the new social order inherent in its plans. These techniques emphasize decontextualization, defamiliarization, and dehistoricization. Their central premise of transformation is that the new architecture/urban design would create set pieces within existing cities that would subvert and then regenerate the surrounding fabric of denatured social life. El Lissitzky explained this premise concisely in 1929: "The introduction of new building types into the old fabric of the city affects the whole by transforming it" ([1929] 1970: 52). It is a viral notion of revolution, a theory of decontextualization in which the radical qualities of something totally out of context infect and colonize that which surrounds it. This something may be a single building conceived as an instance of the total plan, that is, as a fragment of its radical aesthetics and social practices. Or it may be an entire city designed as an exemplar, as in the case of Brasília (Figure 2). Either way, the radical fragment is supposed to create new forms of social experience, collective association, perception, and personal habit. At the same time, it is supposed to preclude those forms deemed undesirable by negating previous social and architectural expectations about urban life.

This use of decontextualization ultimately springs from the conviction that it is possible to extract antithetically from existing conditions an absent ideal as a new positive entity—that is to say, to extract an imagined social and aesthetic order "from [the] estranged and splintered reality by means of the will and power of the individual," as Theodor Adorno once described this process in a discussion of Schönberg's music (quoted in Buck-Morss 1977: 57). This extraction is achieved, in other words, through subjective synthesis. Such synthesis is reached through the shock of defamiliarization during which the subject identifies with the ideal in the dialectic as the means necessary to bridge the now evident gap between his or her local and splintered situation and the proposed future plenitude.

CIAM doctrine maintained that these proposals of transformation would create a city embodying revolutionary premises of work, housing, transportation, and recreation. It argued that this embodiment would redefine the social basis of urban organization. These propositions were not, I would hold, wrong. Indeed, over the course of this century, CIAM's new building types, urban structures, and planning conventions triumphed to

Figure 2. Brasília: South Wing of the Plano Piloto, 1981. Photo by James Holston.

such an extent that they became standard practice in the professions of architecture and planning around the world. Moreover, I would argue that they remain so today, even where their derivation from the CIAM model is unrecognized and their use has nothing to do with its social agenda, as is often the case, for example, in the United States.[4]

4. I cannot discuss more fully the CIAM model city here, but I refer readers to my 1989 study of Brasília for a historical and critical analysis (esp. pp. 31–58). Nor can I discuss its relation to postmodernism, which I would have to do to substantiate my claim of its continued dominance. The outline of my argument would be to distinguish the planned and embodied spatial logic of the built environment of the contemporary city—its patterns of urbanization— from the architecture of its individual buildings. I would also distinguish the city's spatial logic from its modes of social change and capital accumulation, through the two are related. Many authors have described both recent architecture and modes of social change and capital accumulation in terms of new patterns of representing and consuming "space, time, and identity," which they call postmodern. Be that as it may, I would call the urban landscape postmodern only where I could identify new modes and processes of developing the city that generate both spatial and social counterformations to the modernist urbanism that already dominates most cities. From that perspective, I detect little in the spatial production of Los Angeles, for example, that could constitute a postmodern urbanism beyond limited exercises in historical preservation or citation (often related to shopping or elite residence). As I suggest later, there are some examples of what I call insurgent urbanism (i.e., the spaces of insurgent citizenship) that might qualify in this sense. But, overwhelmingly, I see the built Los Angeles metropolitan region as a consequence, more or less explicit, of modernist doctrines. Moreover, I would argue that recent patterns of urbanization—for example, the

However, if few promises for change have captured the world's imagination to a greater degree than this idealist project of alternative futures, few have yielded greater perversity. A fundamental dilemma inevitably dominates this project if it is to have any substance beyond the imaginary world of plans. It is one inherent in all forms of planning—both as urban design and as applied social science—that propose an alternative future based on absent totalities: the necessity of having to use what exists to achieve what is imagined destroys the utopian difference between the two that is the project's premise. Worse, examples such as Brasília show that attempts to maintain the plan in spite of the corrosive effects of this utopian paradox exacerbate the very conditions that generate the desire for change. Perversely, they tend to turn the project into an exaggerated version of what its planners wanted to preclude in the first place (Figures 3 and 4).[5]

Consider, for example, the modernist system of traffic circulation. When we analyze it in terms of what it systematically set out to abolish—the traditional street system of public spaces that it considered too congested and unhealthy for the modern machine age—its social consequence becomes clear. By eliminating this kind of street, it also eliminates the urban crowds and the outdoor political domain of social life that the street traditionally supports. Estranged from the no-man's land of outdoor public space that results, people stay inside. But the consequent displacement of social life from the outdoor public "rooms" of streets and squares to the indoor rooms of malls, clubs, homes, and cars does not merely reproduce the outdoor city public and its citizenry in a new interior setting. Rather, this interiorization encourages a privatizing of social relations. Privatization allows greater control over access to space, and that control almost invariably stratifies the public that uses it. The empty no-man's spaces and privatized interiors that result contradict modernism's declared intentions to revitalize the urban public and render it more egalitarian. This interiorization is not an extraneous consequence or a by-product of some other process. Rather, it is a direct entailment of the solid/void–figure/ground conventions of modernism's spatial logic, as I have demonstrated else-

<hr />

downtown "renaissance" developments and the urbanization of suburbia into "edge cities"— are further consecrations of these doctrines.

5. In Brasília, for example, such attempts led urban designers and other kinds of planners to respond to the inevitable deformations of their plans (such as illegal squatter settlements, chaotic growth, and organized political opposition) with dystopic measures that characterized the rest of Brazil they wanted to exclude. These measures reproduced that Brazil at the foundations of Brasília. They included the denial of political rights, the repression of voluntary associations, and the restricted distribution of public goods, especially housing, on the basis of status discriminations (see Holston 1989: chaps. 6–8).

Figure 3. (above) Vila Chaparral, Brasília: Insurgent squatter settlement on the periphery of the periphery of the Plano Piloto, that is, near the legal housing track QSC of the satellite-city Taquatinga, 1981. Photo by James Holston.

Figure 4. (left) Vila Chaparral, Brasília: Internal street, 1981. Photo by James Holston.

Spaces of Insurgent Citizenship   163

Figure 5. (above) Morumbi, São Paulo: Guardhouse of residential building in a neighborhood where all street activity is suspect, 1994. Photo by Teresa Caldeira.

Figure 6. (above) Morumbi, São Paulo: The elite urban periphery—a new urbanism of closed condominiums for the rich mixed with squatters settlements for the poor, 1994. Photo by Teresa Caldeira.

where (1989: 101–44). Significantly, it is this logic that motivates today's developers to use the vocabulary of modernist architecture and urban design to create the new fortified spaces of contemporary urbanism (see Figure 5).[6]

6. See Caldeira's essay in this volume and her forthcoming book for a discussion of the reuse of modernist design in generating contemporary forms of segregation in Los Angeles and São Paulo.

The imagined future of modernism raises a further dilemma. On the one hand, it always runs the risk of the utopian paradox I just described: either it remains without substance and thus disconnected from the conditions that generate a desire for it; or, in gaining history, it exacerbates the very issues it intends to negate. On the other hand, a second conclusion is also apparent: without a utopian factor, plans remain locked in the prisonhouse of unacceptable existing conditions. Is not the elimination of the desire for a different future as oppressive as the modernist perversion of it? To exclude the imaginary and its inherently critical perspective in that way is to condemn planning to accommodations of the status quo, and I reject such paralysis. Hence, a difficult question remains: if the notion of alternative futures is both indispensable and yet, in its utopian form, perverse, what kind of intervention in the city could construct a sense of emergence without imposing a teleology that disembodies the present in favor of a utopian difference?

Insurgent Citizenship

My criticism of modernist planning is not that it presupposes a nonexistent egalitarian society or that it dreams of one. To deny that dream is also to conceal or encourage a more totalitarian control of the present. It is rather that modernist planning does not admit or develop productively the para-

Figure 7. Jardim das Camélias, São Paulo: The working-class urban periphery—autoconstructed houses with high security gates and yet lots of street life, 1994. Photo by Teresa Caldeira/James Holston.

doxes of its imagined future. Instead, it attempts to be a plan without contradiction, without conflict. It assumes a rational domination of the future in which its total and totalizing plan dissolves any conflict between the imagined and the existing society in the imposed coherence of its order. This assumption is both arrogant and false. It fails to include as *constituent* elements of planning the conflict, ambiguity, and indeterminacy characteristic of actual social life. Moreover, it fails to consider the unintended and the unexpected as part of the model. Such assumptions are common to master plan solutions generally and not only to those in urban planning. Their basic feature is that they attempt to fix the future—or the past, as in historical preservation—by appealing to precedents that negate the value of present circumstance. The crucial question for us to consider, therefore, is how to include the ethnographic present in planning, that is, the possibilities for change encountered in existing social conditions.

Not all master plans negate the present as a means to get to the imagined future (or past) of planning. A powerful counterexample is the U.S. Constitution. It is certainly a master plan and certainly modern in proposing a system of national government "in order to form a more perfect union" (Preamble). Yet its great strength is precisely that its provisions are imprecise and incomplete. Moreover, it is distrustful of the very institutions of government it creates. As a blueprint, it does not try to legislate the future. Rather, its seven original articles and twenty-six amendments embody a few guiding principles—for example, federalism, separation of powers, and checks and balances—that not only channel conflict into mediating institutions but also protect against possible abuses of the governmental powers they create. Above all, they establish a trust that future generations of citizens have the ability and the right to make their own histories by interpreting what the master plan means in light of their own experience.[7]

The U.S. Constitution has, therefore, two kinds of planning projects: state building and citizenship building. The key point for our discussion is that the latter is conditioned by the former but not reducible to it because the Constitution secures for citizens a real measure of insurgence against the state. On the one hand, it designs a state with the *minimum* conditions necessary to institutionalize both order and conflict. On the other hand, it guarantees the necessary conditions for social mobilization as a means to include the unintended and the unforeseeable as possible sources of new constitutional interpretation.

This frame of complementary perspectives offers an important sugges-

7. Thus, for example, the Supreme Court has at different times both upheld and prohibited race discrimination.

tion for thinking about a new production of the city. If modernist planning relies on and builds up the state, then its necessary counteragent is a mode of planning that addresses the formations of insurgent citizenship. Planning theory needs to be grounded in these antagonistic complements, both based on ethnographic and not utopian possibility: on one side, the project of state-directed futures, which can be transformative but which is always a product of specific politics; and, on the other, the project of engaging planners with the insurgent forms of the social that often derive from and transform the first project but are in important ways heterogeneous and outside the state. These insurgent forms are found both in organized grassroots mobilizations and in everyday practices that, in different ways, empower, parody, derail, or subvert state agendas. They are found, in other words, in struggles over what it means to be a member of the modern state—which is why I refer to them with the term citizenship. Membership in the state has never been a static identity, given the dynamics of global migrations and national ambitions. Citizenship changes as new members emerge to advance their claims, expanding its realm, and as new forms of segregation and violence counter these advances, eroding it. The sites of insurgent citizenship are found at the intersection of these processes of expansion and erosion.

These sites vary with time and place. Today, in many cities, they include the realm of the homeless, networks of migration, neighborhoods of Queer Nation, autoconstructed peripheries in which the poor build their own homes in precarious material and legal conditions, ganglands, fortified condominiums, employee-owned factories, squatter settlements, suburban migrant labor camps, sweatshops, and the zones of the so-called new racism. They are sites of insurgence because they introduce into the city new identities and practices that disturb established histories (Figures 5–7).[8] These new identities and the disturbances they provoke may be of any social group, elite or subaltern. Their study views the city as not merely the container of this process but its subject as well—a space of emergent identities and their social organization. It concentrates on practices that engage the problematic nature of belonging to society. It privileges such disturbances, emergences, and engagements because it is at the fault lines of these processes that we perceive the dynamism of society—that is, the

8. Examples of such sites of insurgent citizenship may be found throughout the essays in this volume. It is important to stress that both the elite and the subaltern mark urban space with new and insurgent forms of the social—that these forms are not, in other words, limited to the latter. For a view of this conjunction in one city, São Paulo, compare figures 5, 6, and 7; for further discussion, see Caldeira's essay in this volume on closed condominiums and Holston 1991 on autoconstructed peripheries.

"multiplicity" that van Eyck could not discern. This perception is quite different, however, from a sociological accretion of data, and its register includes the litter and not only the monuments of urban experience.

This dynamism and its perception are the theoretical objectives of a planning linked to insurgent forms of the social. It differs from the modernist objectives of planning because it aims to understand society as a continual reinvention of the social, the present, and the modern and their modes of narrative and communication. What planners need to look for are the emergent sources of citizenship—and their repression—that indicate this invention. They are not hard to find in the wake of this century's important processes of change: massive migration to the world's major cities, industrialization and deindustrialization, the sexual revolution, democratization, and so forth. The new spaces of citizenship that result are especially the product of the compaction and reterritorialization in cities of so many new residents with histories, cultures, and demands that disrupt the normative and assumed categories of social life. This disruption is the source of insurgent citizenship and the object of a planning theory that includes the ethnographic present in its constitution.

The distinction between formal and substantive citizenship is useful in identifying this object because it suggests how the forms of insurgent citizenship appear as social practice and therefore how they may be studied. Formal citizenship refers to membership in a political community—in modern history, preeminently, the nation-state. Substantive citizenship concerns the array of civil, political, and social rights available to people. In a much-quoted essay, T. H. Marshall links these two aspects: "Citizenship is a status bestowed on those who are full members of a community. All who possess the status are equal with respect to the rights and duties with which the status is endowed" ([1950] 1977: 92). As new kinds of residents occupy cities—southern blacks in Chicago, Turks in Frankfurt, Nordestinos in São Paulo, Candangos in Brasília—these formal and substantive conditions shape their urban experience. In turn, this experience becomes a principal focus of their struggle to redefine those conditions of belonging to society.

Notions of formal citizenship have become problematic especially in the context of the massive urban migrations of recent decades. As new and more complex kinds of ethnic diversity dominate cities, the very notion of shared community becomes increasingly exhausted. What now constitutes that "direct sense of community membership based on loyalty to a civilization which is a common possession" that Marshall ([1950] 1977: 101) considered essential to citizenship—essential because only direct participation secures the rights, responsibilities, and liberties of self-rule? In the past, this sense has been a supralocal, indeed, national consciousness. But both national participation and community have become difficult notions for citizenship in the context of the new urban and, often at the same time, global politics of difference, multiculturalism, and racism. One indication of this problem is that in many cases formal citizenship is neither a necessary nor a sufficient condition for substantive citizenship. In other words, although in theory full access to rights depends on membership, in practice that which constitutes citizenship substantively (rights and duties) is often independent of its formal status. Indeed, it is often inaccessible to those who are formal citizens (e.g., the native poor), yet available to those who are not (e.g., legally resident "aliens"). These kinds of problems challenge the dominant notion of citizenship as national identity and the historic role of the nation-state as the preeminent form of modern political community.

But in so doing, they indicate a new possibility that could become an important focus for urban planning: they suggest the possibility of multiple citizenships based on the local, regional, and transnational affiliations that aggregate in contemporary urban experience. Although this possibility represents a significant change in the recent history of citizenship, it is not a new arrangement. Multiple and overlapping jurisdictions predominated in Europe until the triumph of national citizenship obliterated other forms, among them the urban citizenships that organized so many regions of the ancient and the premodern world. The modern state explicitly competed with the city for the primary affiliation of its citizens. Moreover, it usurped their differences, replacing the local management of history with the national. That is, the state reorganized local diversity under the banner of national heritage. One of the most widely shared projects of modern states, this nationalization of diversity legitimates a *singular* state citizenship as the best condition for securing a society of plural cultural identities. But the recent worldwide multiplication of "rights to difference" movements profoundly challenges this claim. Their new ethnocultural politics and violence are in large part a response to the perceived failures of a singular national citizenship. In this reevaluation, the local and the urban reappear as the crucial sites for articulating not only new fanaticisms and hooliganisms but also new transnational and diasporic identities. If planning theory, as I suggest, can conceptualize this collision between state citizenship and these insurgent alternatives, planning practice can respond to this articulation first by expressing its heterogeneity—the social condition we actually live—and then by developing some of the ethnographic possibilities that are, by definition, embedded in heterogeneous conditions.

In terms of substantive issues, the insurgence of new citizenship is no less dramatic. Over the last few decades, many societies have experienced great expansions and erosions of rights. The expansions are particularly evident in the new social movements of the urban poor for "rights to the city" and of women, gays, and ethnic and racial minorities for "rights to difference." These movements are new not only because they force the state to respond to new social conditions of the working poor—in which sense they are, indeed, one important consequence of massive urban poverty on citizenship. They are also unprecedented in many cases because they create new kinds of rights, based on the exigencies of lived experience, outside the normative and institutional definitions of the state and its legal codes.

These rights generally address the social dramas of the new collective and personal spaces of the city, especially its impoverished residential neighborhoods. They focus on housing, property, sanitation, health, education, and so forth, raising basic questions about the scope of entitlements. Is adequate housing a right? Is employment? Moreover, they concern people largely excluded from the resources of the state and are based on social demands that may not be constitutionally defined but that people perceive as entitlements of general citizenship. The organization of these demands into social movements frequently results in new legislation, producing an unprecedented participation of new kinds of citizens in making law and even in administering urban reform and local government. Thus, as the social movements of the urban poor expand citizenship to new social bases, they also create new sources of citizenship rights and new forms of self-rule.

Yet if the city is in this sense an arena for a Rousseauian self-creation of new citizens, it is also a war zone for this very reason: the dominant classes meet the advances of these new citizens with new strategies of segregation, privatization, and fortification. Although the city has always been a place of such contestations, they have taken on new and especially intense forms in recent decades. Where the repressive structures of the state are especially effective, as in the United States, or especially murderous, as in Brazil, the resulting erosions of citizenship are particularly evident in the city's disintegrating public spaces and abandoned public spheres. This contemporary war zone includes not only the terror of death squads and gangs but also the terror of corporate fortresses and suburban enclaves (Figures 5 and 6). The latter too are insurgent forms of the social, subverting the proclaimed equalities and universals of national citizenship. Thus, the city-as-war-zone threatens the articulation of formal state membership as the principal universalizing norm for managing the simultaneity of modern social identities. As the war escalates, this threat ignites ever deeper anxieties about what form such coordination might take if national citizenship no longer has that primary role. As much as optimism may radiate from the city's social movements, this anxiety hovers over its war zone, structuring its possible futures.

Planning the Ethnographically Possible

In this essay, I have raised the problem of developing a new social imagination in planning and architecture. I have suggested that when citizenship expansions and erosions focus on urban experience, they constitute an insurgent urbanism that informs this development in several ways. First, they present the city as both the text and the context of new debates about fundamental social relations. In their localism and strategic particularism, these debates valorize the constitutive role of conflict and ambiguity in shaping the multiplicity of contemporary urban life. In a second sense, this heterogeneity works against the modernist absorption of citizenship into a project of state building, providing alternative, possible sources for the development of new kinds of practices and narratives about belonging to and participating in society. This "working against" defines what I called an insurgent citizenship; and its spatial mode, an insurgent urbanism (Figure 7). This insurgence is important to the project of rethinking the social in planning because it reveals a realm of the possible that is rooted in the heterogeneity of lived experience, which is to say, in the ethnographic present and not in utopian futures.

But in advocating a move to the ethnography of the present, I do not suggest that planning abandon the project of state building that modernist doctrine defined and that is basic to the notion of modernity itself. Excessive attention to the local has its own dangers. Although I argue, for example, that ethnographic investigation is the best way to establish the terms by which residents participate in the planning of their communities, such participation can be paradoxical: residents across the economic spectrum will often decide, by the most democratic of processes, to segregate their communities "from the evil outside," closing, fortifying, and privatizing their spaces in relation to those deemed outsiders. Hence, throughout the United States, it is common to find home-owner associations trying to use the powers and privileges of democratic organization to exclude and discriminate. Local enactments of democracy may thereby produce antidemocratic results.[9]

The lesson of this paradox is that planning needs to engage not only the development of insurgent forms of the social but also the resources of the

9. For examples from Los Angeles, see Davis 1990.

state to define, and occasionally impose, a more encompassing conception of right than is sometimes possible to find at the local level. An example of this transformative power of the state comes from the conflict over legal segregation in the southern United States during the 1960s, when the federal government eventually intervened in local affairs and acted against local authorities. Above all, planning needs to encourage a complementary antagonism between these two engagements. It needs to operate simultaneously in two theaters, so to speak, maintaining a productive tension between the apparatus of state-directed futures and the investigation of insurgent forms of the social embedded in the present.

In developing the latter as the counter of the former, planners and architects engage a new realm of the possible with their professional practice. But this realm requires a different kind of practice, different in both objective and method, and this difference amounts to a reconceptualization of the fields. In terms of methods, I mean to emphasize those of an urban ethnographer—or of a detective, which are similar: methods of tracing, observing, decoding, and tagging, at one moment of the investigation, and those of reconstructing, identifying, presenting, and rearticulating, at another. Both the trace and the reconstruction compose this engagement with the ethnographic present. In this proposal, I am not suggesting that planners and architects become anthropologists, for anthropology is not reducible to ethnography. Rather, I suggest that they learn the methods of ethnographic detection and also learn to work with anthropologists.

As for its objective, it is the very heterogeneity of society that baffles the architect van Eyck. To understand this multiplicity is to learn to read the social against the grain of its typical formations. The typical are the obvious, assumed, normative, and routine, and these are—as Poe illustrates so well in The Purloined Letter—hardest to detect. Rather, it is often by their deformations and counters that we learn about them. But countersites are more than just indicators of the norm. They are themselves possible alternatives to it. They contain the germ of a related but different development. Embedded in each of the facets of the multiple relations we live, such possibility accounts for the feeling we have that social life and its spaces are heterogeneous. This possibility is like a bog just beneath the surface of experience, at every step threatening to give way to something different if we let it. But generally we do not, because the technology of the normative keeps us from doubting the taken-for-granted on which we depend. Reading the social against the grain of its typical formations means showing that this surface is indeed doubly encoded with such possibility, and it means identifying the sites at which it seeps through.

To understand society's multiplicity is to learn to recognize "its counterform" at these sites—to return to van Eyck's critical mission—and "to form a more perfect union" without sacrificing this double-encoding that is the vitality of present circumstance. As I have suggested here, one path to this understanding is to hunt for situations that engage, in practice, the problematic nature of belonging to society and that embody such problems as narratives about the city. But this kind of investigation amounts to a redefinition of the practice of planning and architecture as long as these fields remain obsessed with the design of objects and with the execution of plans and policies. Even though very few architects or planners conduct their professional practice in ways that correspond to this obsession, it remains a powerfully seductive mirage. To reengage the social after the debacle of modernism's utopian attempts, however, requires expanding the idea of planning and architecture beyond this preoccupation with execution and design. It requires looking into, caring for, and teaching about lived experience as lived. To plan the possible is, in this sense, to begin from an ethnographic conception of the social and its spaces of insurgence.

References

Buck-Morss, Susan. 1977. *The Origin of Negative Dialectics: Theodor W. Adorno, Walter Benjamin, and the Frankfurt Institute.* New York: Free Press.

Caldeira, Teresa P. R. forthcoming. *City of Walls: Crime, Segregation, and Citizenship in São Paulo.* Berkeley: University of California Press.

Costa, Lúcio. [1930] 1980. "Razões da nova arquitetura." *Arte em Revista* 4: 15–23.

Davis, Mike. 1990. *City of Quartz: Excavating the Future in Los Angeles.* London: Verso.

Frampton, Kenneth. 1980. *Modern Architecture: A Critical History.* New York: Oxford University Press.

Holston, James. 1989. *The Modernist City: An Anthropological Critique of Brasília.* Chicago: University of Chicago Press.

——. 1991. "Autoconstruction in Working-Class Brazil." *Cultural Anthropology* 6(4): 447–65.

——. 1995. "Insurgent Urbanism: Interactive Architecture and a Dialogue with Craig Hodgetts." In *Technoscientific Imaginaries*, George E. Marcus, ed. Chicago: University of Chicago Press, 461–505.

Lissitzky, El. [1929] 1970. *Architecture for a World Revolution.* Cambridge: MIT Press.

Marshall, T. H. [1950] 1977. "Citizenship and Social Class." In *Class, Citizenship, and Social Development.* Chicago: University of Chicago Press, 71–134.

Olalquiaga, Celeste. 1992. *Megalopolis: Contemporary Cultural Sensibilities.* Minneapolis: University of Minnesota Press.

Sorkin, Michael. 1992. "Introduction: Variations on a Theme Park." In *Variations on a Theme Park: The New American City and the End of Public Space*, Michael Sorkin, ed. New York: Noonday, xi–xv.

Part Two · Cities and Transnational Formations

Whose City Is It? Globalization and the Formation of New Claims

The organizing theme in this essay is that place is central to many of the circuits through which economic globalization is constituted. One strategic type of place for these developments, and the one focused on here, is the city. Including cities in the analysis of economic globalization is not without conceptual consequences. Economic globalization has mostly been represented in terms of the duality national/global, where the global gains power and advantages at the expense of the national. And it has largely been conceptualized in terms of the internationalization of capital and then only the upper circuits of capital, notably finance. Introducing cities into an analysis of economic globalization allows us to reconceptualize processes of economic globalization as concrete economic complexes situated in specific places. A focus on cities decomposes the national economy into a variety of subnational components, some profoundly articulated with the global economy and others not. It also signals the declining significance of the national economy as a unitary category. To some extent it was only a unitary category in political discourse and policy; the modern nation-state has always had economic actors and practices that were transnational. Nonetheless, over the last fifteen years we can see a profoundly different phase, one where national economies are less and less a unitary category in the face of the new forms of globalization.

Why does it matter to recover place in analyses of the global economy, particularly place as constituted in major cities? Because it allows us to see the multiplicity of economies and work cultures in which the global information economy is embedded. It also allows us to recover the concrete, localized processes through which globalization exists and to argue that much of the multiculturalism in large cities is as much a part of globalization as is international finance. Finally, focusing on cities allows us to specify a geography of strategic places at the global scale, places bound to each other by the dynamics of economic globalization. I refer to this as a new geography of centrality, and one question it engenders is whether this new transnational geography also is the space for a new transnational politics.

Insofar as an economic analysis of the global city recovers the broad array of jobs and work cultures that are part of the global economy though typically not marked as such, I can examine the possibility of a new politics of traditionally disadvantaged actors operating in this new transnational economic geography—from factory workers in export-processing zones to cleaners on Wall Street. This politics lies at the intersection of actual economic participation in the global economy and can only represent and valorize corporate actors as participants, in this regard a politics of exclusion.

If place, that is, a certain type of place, is central in the global economy, we can posit a transnational economic and political opening in the formation of new claims and hence in the constitution of entitlements, notably rights to place, and more radically, in the constitution of "citizenship." The city has indeed emerged as a site for new claims: by global capital, which uses the city as an "organizational commodity," but also by disadvantaged sectors of the urban population, which in large cities are frequently as internationalized a presence as is capital. The denationalizing of urban space and the formation of new claims centered on transnational actors and involving contestation raise the question—whose city is it?

I see this as a type of political opening with unifying capacities across national boundaries and sharpening conflicts within such boundaries. Global capital and the new immigrant workforce are two major instances of transnationalized categories/actors that have unifying properties internally and find themselves in contestation with each other inside global cities. Global cities are the sites for the overvalorization of corporate capital and the further devalorization of disadvantaged economic actors, both firms and workers. The leading sectors of corporate capital are now global in their organization and operations. And many of the disadvantaged workers in global cities are women, immigrants, and people of color, whose political sense of self and identities are not necessarily embedded in the "nation" or the "national community." Both find in the global city a strategic site for their economic and political operations.

The analysis presented here grounds its interpretation of the new politics made possible by globalization in a detailed understanding of the economics of globalization, and specifically in the centrality of place given a rhetorical and policy context where place is seen as neutralized by global communications and hypermobility of capital. I assume the importance of dissecting the economics of globalization for understanding whether a new transnational politics can be centered in the new transnational economic geography. Second, I think that dissecting the economics of place in the global economy allows us to recover noncorporate components of economic globalization and to inquire about the possibility of a new type of transnational politics. Is there a transnational politics embedded in the centrality of place and in the new geography of strategic places that cuts across national borders and the old North-South divide?

Immigration, for instance, is one major process through which a new transnational political economy is being constituted, one largely embedded in major cities insofar as most immigrants, whether in the United States, Japan, or Western Europe, are concentrated in major cities. It is, in my reading, one of the constitutive processes of globalization today, even though not recognized or represented as such in mainstream accounts of the global economy.[1]

Place and Production in the Global Economy

Alongside the well-documented spatial dispersal of economic activities have appeared new forms of territorial centralization of top-level management and control operations. National and global markets as well as globally integrated operations require central places where the work of globalization gets done. Further, information industries require a vast physical infrastructure containing strategic nodes with hyperconcentrations of facilities. Finally, even the most advanced information industries have a work process—that is, a complex of workers, machines, and build-

1. The analysis presented here is grounded in a detailed study of what I think of as strategic components of today's global economy. It is impossible to include this level of detail here, and I refer the interested reader, the sceptic, and the critic to some of my other publications, which have the necessary theoretical and empirical materials and extended bibliographies. In addition to those referred to in this essay, see *The Mobility of Labor and Capital* (Cambridge: Cambridge University Press, 1988) and *Immigration Policy in a World Economy* (under preparation for the Twentieth Century Fund).

ings that are more place-bound than the imagery of the information economy suggests.

Centralized control and management over a geographically dispersed array of economic operations does not come about inevitably as part of a "world system." It requires the production of a vast range of highly specialized services, telecommunications infrastructure, and industrial services. These are crucial for the valorization of what are today leading components of capital. Rather than simply invoking the power of multinational corporations as the explanatory key of economic globalization, a focus on place and production takes us to the range of activities and organizational arrangements necessary for the implementation and maintenance of a global network of factories, service operations, and markets; these are all processes only partly encompassed by the activities of transnational corporations and banks.

One central concern in my work has been to look at cities as production sites for the leading service industries of our time, and hence to uncover the infrastructure of activities, firms, and jobs that is necessary to run the advanced corporate economy. I want to focus on the practice of global control. Global cities are centers for the *servicing* and *financing* of international trade, investment, and headquarter operations. That is to say, the multiplicity of specialized activities present in global cities are crucial for the valorization, indeed overvalorization, of leading sectors of capital today. And in this sense such cities are strategic production sites for today's leading economic sectors. This function is also reflected in the ascendance of these activities in developed economics.[2]

The extremely high densities evident in the downtown districts of these cities are one spatial expression of this logic; recentralization of many of these activities in broader metropolitan areas, rather than universal dispersal, is another. The widely accepted notion that agglomeration has become obsolete, now that global telecommunication advances are allowing for maximum dispersal, is only partly correct. It is, I argue, precisely because of the territorial dispersal facilitated by telecommunication ad-

2. Elsewhere (1991: chap. 5) I have posited that what is specific about the shift to services is not merely the growth in service jobs but, most important, the increasing importance of services in the organization of advanced economies: firms in all industries from mining to wholesaling buy more accounting, legal, advertising, financial, and economic forecasting services today than twenty years ago. Whether at the global or regional level, cities are adequate and often the best production sites for such specialized services. The rapid growth and disproportionate concentration of such services in cities signals that the latter have reemerged as significant production sites after losing this role in the period when mass manufacturing was the dominant sector of the economy.

vances that agglomeration of centralizing activities has expanded immensely. This is not a mere continuation of old patterns of agglomeration but, one could posit, a new logic for agglomeration. Information technologies are yet another factor contributing to this new logic for agglomeration. The distinct conditions under which such facilities are available have promoted centralization of the most advanced users in the most advanced telecommunications centers (Castells 1989).

A focus on the *work* behind command functions—on the actual production process in the finance and services complex, and on global marketplaces—has the effect of incorporating the material facilities underlying globalization and the whole infrastructure of jobs typically not marked as belonging to the corporate sector of the economy. An economic configuration emerges that is very different from that suggested by the concept of information economy. We recover the material conditions, production sites, and place-boundedness that are also part of globalization and the information economy (*Competition and Change* 1995).

That is to say, we recover a broad range of types of firms, types of workers, types of work cultures, types of residential milieux, never marked, recognized, or represented as being part of globalization processes. Nor are they valorized as such. In this regard, the new urban economy is highly problematic, a fact particularly evident in global cities and their regional counterparts. It sets in motion a whole series of new dynamics of inequality (Sassen 1994: chap. 5; King 1996). The new growth sectors—specialized services and finance—contain profit-making capabilities vastly superior to those of more traditional economic sectors. Although the latter are essential to the operation of the urban economy and the daily needs of residents, their survival is threatened in a situation where finance and specialized services can earn superprofits.[3]

Unequal profit-making capabilities among different economic sectors and firms have long been a basic feature of market economies. But what we see today takes place on another order of magnitude and is engendering massive distortions in the operations of various markets, from housing to labor. We can see this effect, for example, in the unusually sharp increase in the starting salaries of business and law school graduates who succeed in entering the top firms, and in the precipitous fall in the wages of low-

3. Elsewhere I have tried to show how these new inequalities in profit-making capacities of economic sectors, earnings capacities of households, and pricing in upscale and downscale markets have contributed to the formation of informal economies in major cities of highly developed countries (Sassen 1994). These informal economies can be interpreted as a negotiation between (a) these new economic trends, and (b) the existing regulatory frameworks that were engendered in response to older economic conditions.

skilled manual workers and clerical workers. We can see the same effect in the retreat of many real estate developers from the low- and medium-income housing market in the wake of the rapidly expanding housing demand by the new highly paid professionals and the possibility for vast overpricing of this housing supply.

These developments are associated with a dynamic of valorization that has sharply increased the disparity between the valorized, indeed over-valorized, sectors of the economy and devalorized sectors, even when the latter are part of leading global industries. This devalorization of growing sectors of the economy has been embedded in a massive demographic transition toward a growing presence of women, African Americans, and third world immigrants in the urban workforce, a subject I return to later.

We see here an interesting correspondence between great concentrations of corporate power and large concentrations of "others." Major cities in the highly developed world are the terrain where a multiplicity of globalization processes assume concrete, localized forms. A focus on cities allows us to capture not only the upper but also the lower circuits of globalization. These localized forms are, in good part, what globalization is about. We can then think of cities also as one of the sites for the contradictions of the internationalization of capital. If we consider, further, that large cities also concentrate a growing share of disadvantaged populations—immigrants in Europe and the United States, African Americans and Latinos in the United States—then we can see that cities have become a strategic terrain for a whole series of conflicts and contradictions.

A New Geography of Centrality and Marginality

The global economy materializes in a worldwide grid of strategic places, from export-processing zones to major international business and financial centers. We can think of this global grid as constituting a new economic geography of centrality, one that cuts across national boundaries and across the old North-South divide. It signals the emergence of a parallel political geography, a transnational space for the formation of new claims by global capital. This new economic geography of centrality partly reproduces existing inequalities but also is the outcome of a dynamic specific to current types of economic growth. It assumes many forms and operates in many terrains, from the distribution of telecommunications facilities to the structure of the economy and of employment.

The most powerful of these new geographies of centrality at the interurban level binds the major international financial and business centers: New York, London, Tokyo, Paris, Frankfurt, Zurich, Amsterdam, Los Angeles,

Sydney, and Hong Kong, among others. But this geography now also includes cities such as São Paulo, Buenos Aires, Bangkok, Taipei, and Mexico City. The intensity of transactions among these cities, particularly through the financial markets, trade in services, and investment has increased sharply, and so have the orders of magnitude involved. At the same time, there has been a sharpening inequality in the concentration of strategic resources and activities between each of these cities and others in the same country. Global cities are sites for immense concentrations of economic power and command centers in a global economy, while traditional manufacturing centers have suffered inordinate declines.

One might have expected that the growing number of financial centers now integrated into the global markets would have reduced the extent of concentration of financial activity in the top centers. But it has not.[4] One would also expect this given the immense increases in the global volume of transactions.[5] Yet the levels of concentration remain unchanged in the face of massive transformations in the financial industry and in the technological infrastructure this industry depends on.[6]

The growth of global markets for finance and specialized services, the need for transnational servicing networks because of sharp increases in

4. Furthermore, this unchanged level of concentration has happened at a time when financial services are more mobile than ever before: globalization, deregulation (an essential ingredient for globalization), and securitization have been the key to this mobility—in the context of massive advances in telecommunications and electronic networks. (Securitization is the transformation of hitherto "unliquid capital" into tradable instruments, a process that took off dramatically in the 1980s.) One result is growing competition among centers for hypermobile financial activity. In my view there has been an overemphasis on competition in general and in specialized accounts on this subject. As I have argued elsewhere (Sassen 1991: chap. 7), there is also a functional division of labor among various major financial centers. In that sense we can think of a transnational system with multiple locations.

5. For example, international bank lending grew from US$1.89 trillion in 1980 to US$6.24 trillion in 1991—a fivefold increase in a mere ten years. Three cities (New York, London, and Tokyo) accounted for 42 percent of all such international lending in 1980 and for 41 percent in 1991, according to data from the Bank of International Settlements, the leading institution worldwide in charge of overseeing banking activity. There were compositional changes: Japan's share rose from 6.2 percent to 15.1 percent and Britain's fell from 26.2 percent to 16.3 percent; the U.S. share remained constant. All increased in absolute terms. Beyond these three, Switzerland, France, Germany, and Luxembourg bring the total share of the top centers to 64 percent in 1991, which is just about the same share these countries had in 1980. One city, Chicago, dominates the world's trading in futures, accounting for 60 percent of worldwide contracts in options and futures in 1991.

6. In this context it is worth noting that the discussion around the formation of a single European market and financial system has raised the possibility, and even the need if it is to be competitive, of centralizing financial functions and capital in a limited number of cities rather than maintaining the current structure in which each country has a financial center.

international investment, the reduced role of the government in the regulation of international economic activity and the corresponding ascendance of other institutional arenas, notably global markets and corporate headquarters—all these point to the existence of a series of economic processes, each characterized by locations in more than one country and in this regard transnational. We can see here the formation, at least incipient, of a transnational urban system (Sassen 1991: chap. 7; 1994, chap. 3; Knox and Taylor 1995; Le Debat 1994).

The pronounced orientation to the world markets evident in such cities raises questions about the articulation with their nation-states, their regions, and the larger economic and social structure in such cities. Cities have typically been deeply embedded in the economies of their region, indeed often reflecting the characteristics of the latter; and generally they still do. But cities that are strategic sites in the global economy tend, in part, to become disconnected from their region and even nation. This conflicts with a key proposition in conventional scholarship about urban systems, namely, that these systems promote the territorial integration of regional and national economies.

Alongside these new global and regional hierarchies of cities lies a vast territory that has become increasingly peripheral, increasingly excluded from the major economic processes that fuel economic growth in the new global economy. A multiplicity of formerly important manufacturing centers and port cities have lost functions and are in decline, not only in the less developed countries but also in the most advanced economies. This is yet another meaning of economic globalization.

But also inside global cities we see a new geography of centrality and marginality. The downtowns of global cities and metropolitan business centers receive massive investments in real estate and telecommunications while low-income city areas are starved for resources. Highly educated workers employed in leading sectors see their incomes rise to unusually high levels while low- or medium-skilled workers in those same sectors see theirs sink. Financial services produce superprofits while industrial services barely survive. These trends are evident, with different levels of intensity, in a growing number of major cities in the developed world and increasingly in some of the developing countries that have been integrated into the global economy.

The Rights of Capital in the New Global Grid

A basic proposition in discussions about the global economy concerns the declining sovereignty of states over their economies. Economic globalization does indeed extend the economy beyond the boundaries of the nation-state. This is particularly evident in the leading economic sectors. Existing systems of governance and accountability for transnational economic activities and actors leave much ungoverned when it comes to these industries. Global markets in finance and advanced services partly operate through a "regulatory" umbrella that is not state-centered but market-centered. The new geography of centrality is transnational.

This proposition fails to underline a key component in the transformation over the last fifteen years: the formation of new claims by global capital on national states to guarantee the domestic and global rights of capital. What matters for our purposes here is that global capital has made claims and national states have responded through the production of new forms of legality. The new geography of centrality had to be produced, both in terms of the practices of corporate actors and the requisite infrastructure, and in terms of the work of the state in producing new legal regimes. Representations that characterize the national state as simply losing significance fail to capture this very important dimension and reduce what is happening to a function of the global/national duality—what one wins, the other loses.

Further, transnational economic processes inevitably interact with systems for the governance of national economies insofar as these processes materialize in concrete places. National legal regimes are becoming more internationalized in some of the major developed economies, and we are seeing the formation of transnational legal regimes (Trubek et al. 1993). Transnational legal regimes have become more important and have begun to penetrate national fields hitherto closed.

There are two distinct issues here. One is the ascendance of this new legal regime that negotiates between national sovereignty and the transnational practices of corporate economic actors. The second issue concerns the particular content of this new regime, which strengthens the advantages of certain types of economic actors and weakens those of others. The hegemony of neoliberal concepts of economic relations with its strong emphasis on markets, deregulation, and free international trade has influenced policy in the 1980s in the United States and Great Britain and now increasingly also in continental Europe. This has contributed to the formation of transnational legal regimes centered on Western economic concepts of contract and property rights.[7] Through the International Monetary Fund (IMF) and the International Bank for Reconstruction and Development (IBRD), as well as the General Agreement on Trade and Tariffs

7. An issue that is emerging as significant in view of the spread of Western legal concepts is the critical examination of the philosophical premises about authorship and property that define the legal arena in the West. See Coombe 1993.

(GATT) (the World Trade Organization after January 1995), this regime has spread to the developing world (Mittelman 1996). It is a regime associated with increased levels of concentrated wealth, poverty, and inequality world-wide. This occurs under specific modalities in the case of global cities, as discussed above.

Deregulation has been a crucial mechanism to negotiate the juxtaposition of the global and the national. Rather than simply seeing it as freeing up the markets and reducing the sovereignty of the state, we might under-line a much less noted aspect of deregulation: it has had the effect, par-ticularly in the case of the leading economic sectors, of partly denationaliz-ing national territory. For example, the International Banking Facilities in the United States, almost all located in New York City, can be seen as a free-trade zone for finance in New York City and a few other locations. In other words, it is not simply a matter of a space economy extending beyond a national realm. Globalization—as illustrated by the space economy of ad-vanced information industries—denationalizes national territory. This de-nationalization, which to a large extent materializes in global cities, has become legitimate for capital and has, indeed, been imbued with positive value by many government elites and their economic advisers. It is the opposite when it comes to people, as is perhaps most sharply illustrated in the rise of anti-immigrant feeling and various forms of nationalism.

The emphasis on the transnational and hypermobile character of capital has contributed to a sense of powerlessness among local actors, a sense of the futility of resistance. But the analysis in the preceding sections, with its emphasis on place, suggests that the new global grid of strategic sites is a terrain for politics and engagement. Further, the state, both national and political, can be engaged. Though certain agencies within the state have contributed to the formation and strengthening of global capital, the state is far from being a unitary institution. The state itself has been transformed by its role in implementing the global economic system, a transformation captured in the ascendance of certain agencies over the last decade in most governments of highly developed countries and many governments of de-veloping countries, and the loss of power and prestige of agencies associ-ated with issues of domestic equity. These different agencies are now at times in open conflict.

The focus on place helps us elaborate and specify the meaning of key concepts in the discourse about globalization, notably the loss of sov-ereignty. It brings to the fore that important components of globalization are embedded in particular locations within national territories.[8] A stra-

8. And a focus on the space economy of the leading information industries brings to the fore yet another crucial feature: significant components of globalization are located in electronic

tegic subnational unit such as the global city is emblematic of these conditions and is not well captured in the more conventional duality of national/global.

A focus on the leading industries in global cities introduces into the discussion of governance the possibility of capacities for regulation derived from the concentration of significant resources in strategic places. These resources include fixed capital and are essential for participation in the global economy. The considerable place-boundedness of many of these resources contrasts with the hypermobility of the outputs of many of these industries, particularly finance. The regulatory capacity of the state stands in a different relation to hypermobile outputs than to the infrastructure of facilities, from office buildings equipped with fiber optic cables to specialized workforces.

The specific issues raised by a focus on the place-boundedness of key components of economic globalization are quite distinct from those typically raised in the context of the national/global duality. A focus on this duality leads to rather straightforward propositions about the declining significance of the state vis-à-vis global economic actors. The overarching tendency in economic analyses of globalization and of the leading information industries has been to emphasize certain aspects: industry outputs rather than the production process involved, the capacity for instantaneous transmission around the world rather than the infrastructure necessary for this capacity, the impossibility for the state to regulate those outputs and that capacity insofar as they extend beyond the nation-state. And this is by itself quite correct; but it is a partial account of the implications of globalization for governance.

The transformation in the composition of the world economy, especially

---

spaces that escape all conventional jurisdictions or borders. Some of these are engendering what we could think of as a crisis of control that derives from key properties of the new information technologies, notably the orders of magnitude in trading volumes made possible by speed. Here it is no longer just a doubt about the capacity of the state to govern these processes, but also about the capacity of the private sector, that is, of the major actors involved in setting up these markets in electronic space. Elementary and well-known illustrations of this crisis of control are stock market crashes attributed to program trading, and globally implemented decisions to invest or disinvest in a currency or an emerging market that resemble a sort of worldwide stampede facilitated by the fact of global integration and instantaneous execution worldwide. The space economy of the leading information industries points to a reconfiguration of key parts of the governance debate: besides the matter of globalization extending the economy beyond the reach of the state, it is also a matter of control that goes beyond the issue of interorganizational coordination that is at the heart of governance theory. Insofar as speed is one of the logics of the new information technologies, it does not always correspond with the logic of the economic institutional apparatus represented by finance and advance services. See Sassen 1996.

the rise of finance and advanced services as leading industries, is contributing to a new international economic order, one dominated by financial centers, global markets, and transnational firms.[9] Cities that function as international business and financial centers are sites for direct transactions with world markets that take place without government inspection, as for instance the Euro-markets or New York City's international financial zone (International Banking Facilities). These cities and the globally oriented markets and firms they contain mediate in the relation of the world economy to nation-states and in the relations among nation-states.[10] Correspondingly, we may see a growing significance of sub- and supranational political categories and actors.

Unmooring Identities and a New Transnational Politics

The preceding section argued that the production of new forms of legality and of a new transnational legal regime privilege the reconstitution of capital as an internationalized actor and the denationalized spaces necessary for its operation. At the same time there are no new legal forms and regimes to encompass another crucial element of this transnationalization, one that some, including myself, see as the counterpart to that of capital: the transnationalization of labor. However, we are still using the language of immigration to describe this process.[11] Nor are there new forms and regimes to encompass the transnationalization in the formation of identi-

9. In the three decades after World War II, the period of the Pax Americana, economic internationalization had the effect of strengthening the inter-state system. Leading economic sectors, especially manufacturing and raw materials extraction, were subject to international trade regimes that contributed to building the inter-state system. Individual states adjusted national economic policies to further this version of the world economy. Even then certain sectors did not fit comfortably under this largely trade-dominated inter-state regime: out of their escape emerged the Euro-markets and offshore tax havens of the 1960s. The breakdown of the Bretton Woods system produced an international governance void rapidly filled by multinationals and global financial markets. Inside the state we see a further shift away from those agencies most closely tied to domestic social forces, as was the case during the Pax Americana, and toward those closest to the transnational process of consensus formation.

10. Elsewhere (1996) I have worked with the concept "regulatory fracture" rather than, say, violation, in order to name a specific dynamic, i.e., that the materialization of global processes in a place often produces a regulatory void. One result is that both "regulation" and "violation" become problematic categories and, at the limit, do not apply. We might think of it analytically as a borderland, rather than a borderline—a terrain for action/activity that remains underspecified at least from the perspective of regulation.

11. This language is increasingly constructing immigration as a devalued process insofar as it describes the entry of people from generally poorer, disadvantaged countries, in search of the better lives that the receiving country can offer; it contains an implicit valorization of the receiving country and a devalorization of the sending country. And it lacks some of the positive connotations historically associated with immigrants.

ties and loyalties among various population segments that do not regard the nation as the sole or principal source of identification, and the associated new solidarities and notions of membership. Major cities have emerged as a strategic site not only for global capital but also for the transnationalization of labor and the formation of transnational identities. In this regard they are a site for new types of political operations.

Cites are the terrain where people from many different countries are most likely to meet and a multiplicity of cultures come together. The international character of major cities lies not only in their telecommunication infrastructure and international firms, but also in the many different cultural environments they contain. One can no longer think of centers for international business and finance simply in terms of the corporate towers and corporate culture at their center. Today's global cities are in part the spaces of postcolonialism and indeed contain conditions for the formation of a postcolonialist discourse (Hall 1991; King 1996).

The large Western city of today concentrates diversity. Its spaces are inscribed with the dominant corporate culture but also with a multiplicity of other cultures and identities. The slippage is evident: the dominant culture can encompass only part of the city.[12] And while corporate power inscribes these cultures and identities with "otherness," thereby devaluing them, they are present everywhere. For instance, through immigration a proliferation of originally highly localized cultures have now become presences in many large cities, cities whose elites think of themselves as cosmopolitan, as transcending any locality. Members of these "localized" cultures can in fact come from places with great cultural diversity and be as cosmopolitan as elites. An immense array of cultures from around the world, each rooted in a particular country, town, or village, now are reterritorialized in a few single places, places such as New York, Los Angeles, Paris, London, and most recently Tokyo.[13]

12. There are many different forms such contestation and "slippage" can assume. See King 1996; Dunn 1994; *Social Justice* 1994. Global mass culture homogenizes and is capable of absorbing an immense variety of local cultural elements. But this process is never complete. I have found the opposite to be the case in my analysis of data on manufacturing electronic components, which shows that employment in lead sectors no longer inevitably constitutes membership in a labor aristocracy. Thus third world women working in export-processing zones are not empowered: capitalism can work through difference. Yet another case is that of illegal immigrants; here we see that national boundaries have the effect of creating and criminalizing difference. These kinds of differentiations are central to the formation of a world economic system (Wallerstein 1990).

13. Tokyo now has several, mostly working-class concentrations of legal and illegal immigrants coming from China, Bangladesh, Pakistan, and the Philippines. This is quite remarkable in view of Japan's legal and cultural closure to immigrants. Is this simply a function of poverty in those countries? By itself it is not enough of an explanation, since they have long

I think that there are representations of globality that have not been recognized as such or are contested representations. Such representations include immigration and its associated multiplicity of cultural environments, often subsumed under the notion of ethnicity. What we still narrate in the language of immigration and ethnicity, I would argue, is actually a series of processes having to do with the globalization of economic activity, of cultural activity, of identity formation. Too often immigration and ethnicity are constituted as otherness. Understanding them as a set of processes whereby global elements are *localized*, international labor markets are constituted, and cultures from all over the world are de- and reterritorialized, puts them right there at the center along with the internationalization of capital as a fundamental aspect of globalization.[14] This way of narrating the large migrations of the postwar era captures the ongoing weight of colonialism and postcolonial forms of empire on major processes of globalization today, and specifically those binding countries of emigration and immigration.[15] Although the specific genesis and contents

---

had poverty. I posit that the internationalization of the Japanese economy, including specific forms of investment in those countries and Japan's growing cultural influence there, has created bridges between those countries and Japan, and has reduced the subjective distance with Japan. See Sassen 1991: 307–415; Shank 1994.

14. There has been growing recognition of the formation of an international professional class of workers and of highly internationalized environments because of the presence of foreign firms and personnel, the formation of global markets in the arts, and the international circulation of high culture. What has not been recognized is the possibility that we are seeing an internationalized labor market for low-wage manual and service workers. This process continues to be couched in terms of the "immigration story," a narrative rooted in an earlier historical period.

15. The specific forms of the internationalization of capital over the last twenty years have contributed to mobilizing people into migration streams. They have done so principally through the implantation of Western development strategies, from the replacement of smallholder agriculture with export-oriented commercial agriculture and export manufacturing, to the Westernization of educational systems. At the same time the administrative, commercial, and development networks of the former European empires and the newer forms these networks assumed under the Pax Americana (international direct foreign investment, export-processing zones, wars for democracy) have created bridges not only for the flow of capital, information, and high-level personnel from the center to the periphery but, I argue, also for the flow of migrants from the periphery to the center.

The renewal of mass immigration into the United States in the 1960s, after five decades of little or no immigration, took place in a context of expanded U.S. economic and military activity in Asia and the Caribbean. Today, the United States is at the heart of an international system of investment and production that has incorporated not only Mexico but areas in the Caribbean and Southeast Asia. In the 1960s and 1970s, the United States played a crucial role in the development of a world economic system. It passed legislation aimed at opening its own and other countries' economies to the flow of capital, goods, services, and information.

of their responsibility will vary from case to case and period to period, none of the major immigration countries are passive bystanders in their immigration histories.

Making Claims on the City

These processes signal that there has been a change in the linkages that bind people and places and in the corresponding formation of claims on the city. It is true that throughout history people have moved and through these movements constituted places. But today the articulation of territory and people is being constituted in a radically different way at least in one regard, and that is the speed with which that articulation can change. One consequence of this speed is the expansion of the space within which actual and possible linkages can occur. The shrinking of distance and the speed of movement that characterize the current era find one of its most extreme forms in electronically based communities of individuals or organizations from all around the globe interacting in real time and simultaneously, as is possible through the Internet and kindred electronic networks.

I would argue that another radical form assumed today by the linkage of people to territory is the unmooring of identities from what have been traditional sources of identity, such as the nation or the village. This unmooring in the process of identity formation engenders new notions of community, of membership, and of entitlement.

The space constituted by the global grid of cities, a space with new economic and political potentialities, is perhaps one of the most strategic spaces for the formation of transnational identities and communities. This is a space that is both place-centered in that it is embedded in particular and strategic locations; and it is transterritorial because it connects sites that are not geographically proximate yet are intensely connected to each other. As I argued earlier, it is not only the transmigration of capital that takes place in this global grid, but also that of people, both rich (i.e., the new transnational professional workforce) and poor (i.e., most migrant

---

The central military, political, and economic role the United States played in the emergence of a global economy contributed, I argue, both to the creation of conditions that mobilized people into migrations, whether local or international, and to the formation of links between the United States and other countries that subsequently were to serve as bridges for international migration. Measures commonly thought to deter emigration—foreign investment and the promotion of export-oriented growth in developing countries—seem to have had precisely the opposite effect. Among the leading sources of immigrants to the United States in the 1970s and 1980s have been several of the newly industrialized countries of South and Southeast Asia whose extremely high growth rates are generally recognized to be a result of foreign direct investment in export manufacturing.

workers); and it is a space for the transmigration of cultural forms, for the reterritorialization of "local" subcultures. An important question is whether it is also a space for a new politics, one going beyond the politics of culture and identity, though at least partly likely to be embedded in it.

Yet another way of thinking about the political implications of this strategic transnational space anchored in cities is the formation of new claims on that space. As was discussed earlier, there are indeed major new actors making claims on these cities, notably foreign firms who have been increasingly entitled to do business through progressive deregulation of national economies, and the large increase over the last decade in international business people. These are among the new "city users." They have profoundly marked the urban landscape. Their claim to the city is not contested, even though the costs and benefits to cities have barely been examined.

The new city users have made an often immense claim on the city and have reconstituted strategic spaces of the city in their image: their claim is rarely examined or challenged. They contribute to changing the social morphology of the city and to constituting what Martinotti (1993) calls the metropolis of second generation, the city of late modernism. The new city of city users is a fragile one, whose survival and successes are centered on an economy of high productivity, advanced technologies, and intensified exchanges.

On the one hand, this raises a question of what the city is for international business people: it is a place whose space consists of airports, top-level business districts, top of the line hotels and restaurants, a sort of urban glamour zone. On the other hand, there is the difficult task of establishing whether a city that functions as an international business center does in fact recover the costs involved in being such a center: the costs involved in maintaining a state-of-the-art business district, and all it requires, from advanced communications facilities to top-level security and "world-class culture."

Perhaps at the other extreme of legitimacy are those who use urban political violence to make their claims on the city, claims that lack the de facto legitimacy enjoyed by the new city users. These are claims made by actors struggling for recognition and entitlement, claiming their rights to the city.[16] These claims have, of course, a long history; every new epoch

---

16. Body-Gendrot (1993) shows how the city remains a terrain for contest, characterized by the emergence of new actors, often younger and younger. It is a terrain where the constraints placed on, and the institutional limitations of, governments to address the demands for equity engenders social disorders. She argues that urban political violence should not be

brings specific conditions to the manner in which the claims are made. The growing weight of "delinquency" (e.g., smashing cars and shopwindows, robbing and burning stores) in some of these uprisings during the last decade in major cities of the developed world is perhaps an indication of the sharpened inequality. The disparities, as seen and as lived, between the urban glamour zone and the urban war zone have become enormous. The extreme visibility of the difference is likely to contribute to further brutalization of the conflict: the indifference and greed of the new elites versus the hopelessness and rage of the poor.

There are then two aspects of this formation of new claims that have implications for transnational politics. One is these sharp and perhaps intensifying differences in the representation of claims by different sectors, notably international business and the vast population of low income "others"—African Americans, immigrants, and women. The second aspect is the increasingly transnational element in both types of claims and claimants. It signals a politics of contestation embedded in specific places but transnational in character. At its most extreme, this divergence assumes the form of, on the one hand, an overvalorized corporate center occupying a small terrain and one whose edges are sharper than, for example, the one in the postwar era characterized by a large middle class; and on the other hand, marked devalorization of what is outside the center, which comes to be read as marginal.

Globalization is a process that generates contradictory spaces, characterized by contestation, internal differentiation, continuous border crossings. The global city is emblematic of this condition. Global cities concentrate a disproportionate share of global corporate power and are one of the key sites for its overvalorization. But they also concentrate a disproportionate share of the disadvantaged and are one of the key sites for their devalorization. This joint presence happens in a context where the globalization of the economy has grown sharply and cities have become increasingly strategic for global capital; and marginalized people have found their voice and are making claims on the city. This joint presence is further brought into focus by the increasing disparities between the two. The center now concentrates immense economic and political power, power that rests on the capability for global control and the capability to produce superprofits. And actors with little economic and traditional political power have become an increasingly strong presence through the new politics of culture

---

interpreted as a coherent ideology but rather as an element of temporary political tactics, which permits vulnerable actors to enter in interaction with the holders of power on terms that will be somewhat more favorable to the weak.

and identity, and an emergent transnational politics embedded in the new geography of economic globalization. Both actors, increasingly transnational and in contestation, find in the city the strategic terrain for their operations. But it is hardly the terrain of a balanced playing field.

References

Body-Gendrot, Sophie. 1993. *Ville et violence: L'Irruption de nouveaux acteurs.* Paris: Presses Universitaires de France.

Castells, Manuel. 1989. *The Informational City: Information Technology, Economic Restructuring, and the Urban-Regional Process.* Oxford: Blackwell.

Competition and Change: The Journal of Global Business and Political Economy. 1995. 1(1).

Coombe, Rosemary J. 1993. "The Properties of Culture and the Politics of Possessing Identity: Native Claims in the Cultural Appropriation Controversy." *Canadian Journal of Law and Jurisprudence* (July 1993): 249–85.

Dunn, Seamus, ed. 1994. *Managing Divided Cities.* Keele, U.K.: University of Keele Press.

Hall, Stuart. 1991. "The Local and the Global: Globalization and Ethnicity." In *Culture, Globalization and the World-System: Contemporary Conditions for the Representation of Identity,* Anthony D. King, ed. Current Debates in Art History 3. Binghamton: State University of New York.

King, Anthony D., ed. 1996. *Re-presenting the City.* London: Macmillan.

Knox, Paul, and Peter Taylor, eds. 1995. *World Cities in a World System.* Cambridge: Cambridge University Press.

Le Debat. 1994. *Le Nouveau Paris.* Special issue of *Le Debat* (summer).

Martinotti, Guido. 1993. *Metropoli: La nuova morfologia sociale della citta.* Bologna: Il Mulino.

Mittelman, James, ed. 1996. *Yearbook of International Political Economy,* vol. 9. Boulder, Colo.: Lynne Reinner Publisher.

Sassen, Saskia. 1991. *The Global City: New York, London, Tokyo.* Princeton: Princeton University Press.

——. 1994. *Cities in a World Economy.* Thousand Oaks, Calif.: Pine Forge/Sage Press.

——. 1996. *Losing Control? Sovereignty in an Age of Globalization.* The 1995 Columbia University Schoff Memorial Lectures. New York: Columbia University Press.

Shank, G., ed. 1994. *Japan Enters the Twenty-first Century. Social Justice* (special issue) 21(2).

Social Justice. 1993. *Global Crisis, Local Struggles* (special issue) 20(3–4).

Trubek, David M., Yves Dezalay, Ruth Buchanan, and John R. Davis. 1993. "Global Restructuring and the Law: The Internationalization of Legal Fields and Creation of Transnational Arenas." Working Paper Series on the Political Economy of Legal Change, no. 1. Madison: University of Wisconsin.

Wallerstein, Immanuel. 1990. "Culture as the Ideological Battleground of the Modern World-System." In *Global Culture: Nationalism, Globalization, and Modernity,* Mike Featherstone, ed. London: Sage.

Is European Citizenship Possible?

Etienne Balibar

The following reflections do not in any way claim to exhaust the question of European citizenship, but rather they address key elements of the question in order to determine its implications. This approach, while admittedly hypothetical, is dictated not only by the prospective nature of the seminars for which I developed these ideas, but also by the conviction that today these themes, "the Europe of citizens," "European citizenship," and "citizenship in Europe," cannot be the object of purely normative juridical treatment (at the legislative or regulative level), nor of deductive treatment that proceeds from a preexisting concept of citizenship and of the citizen. Above all, these themes require reflection on the stakes involved in their articulation, their tensions, and their contradictions.

This approach does not deny the importance of the juridical aspects of

This essay was originally given in French at the Ministry of Research and Technology on 12 February 1993 during the session, "Franco-European Seminar of Research and Futurology on the State: Sovereignty, Finance, and Social Issues." It has been published in French as "Une citoyenneté européene est-elle possible?" (©Etienne Balibar) in L'Etat, la finance et la social. Souveraineté nationale et construction européenne, edited by Brunot Théret (Paris: Editions, La Découverte, 1995). It has been translated by Christine Jones, Princeton University.

the problem of citizenship in general, but refuses to frame its inquiry in terms of a preconceived form or given procedure. We must avoid prescribing or in some way performing the question in terms of the existing concept of "constitution," as this concept is complicit with a given period and the very type of citizenship that is in question. If a European citizenship is to truly emerge in the future, then the very notion of constitutional order will have to change profoundly.

The particular junction at which we take up the question of European citizenship constitutes a predicted historical turning point. In fact, it was predicted at least twice: first by the settlement date in the political construction of Europe. Since the official adoption of the plans to institute free circulation (i.e., during the 1970s; see Giannoulis 1992 and Costa-Lascoux 1992), the dawn of a new era in the history of the European nations has in some ways been predetermined. The millenarian idea that circulated held that this moment of truth would soon be at hand (in 1993 or 1994), and that we would soon see its effects, or if it came to pass, would feel its tensions or crises. However, the turning point was again predicted when political changes occurred in Eastern Europe between 1988 and 1990, a change that several journalists and politicians, particularly Ralph Dahrendorf (1992), called the "Revolution of 1989." The fall of communism was interpreted as both producing a supplementary degree of historical necessity and calling for a more precise realization of European citizenship, including as a corollary a new balance of forces in the world and the emergence of a new, more "continental" level of the crystallization of power.

However, the amazing fact that has emerged over the past three years is that the path of historical evolution systematically diverges from what had been predicted. This is not to say that a new era is not dawning, but precisely that it will not follow the path that was envisioned. Consider the sudden awareness of contradictions—between European nations, between social groups within each nation, between European "political classes" and the "peuple,"[1] or "popular classes"—which resulted from the Treaty of Maastricht. The vicissitudes of the treaty's ratification are precisely at the origin of the proliferation of debates on democracy and citizenship at the European level. Despite their very different forms from one country to the next, these debates explicitly addressed the question of sovereignty to arrive at clear-cut oppositions on the political and monetary unification of Europe. Judged by some to be confused and savage, by others to be a saving grace, the reaffirmation of this sovereignty constituted the implicit tenor of

1. All French words in the essay are from the original. Original French terms are also footnoted by the translator in cases of equivocal or problematic translations.

the demonstrations of the independence of public opinion against the decisions made by governments and experts. But what is more, the external boundaries (with the fall of the "Wall") of the new European entity were again being questioned. The very real possibility of this entity giving rise to constitutional crises and a questioning of national unity in certain of the member states (United Kingdom, Italy, et al.) also cannot be dismissed today.

The conjunction of the institution of "European citizenship" and the status of extra-European Community immigration also presents itself in unforeseen terms: it is no longer simply a postcolonial question of inter-penetration of the "North" and the "South," but also a general problema-tization of the notion of border in the world. Without warning, Europeans have emerged from a bipolar world of "two camps" in which antagonism overdetermined all of the borders. But what are the geopolitical borders of today, and what exactly is a border?

Such a situation allows for several interpretative possibilities. One might think that the debate on European citizenship is the result of a process begun long ago that finally has found its political and reflexive moment (see, for example, Rosanvallon 1992). One might also decide that this debate is symptomatic of the "catastrophic" turn that history is taking in Europe today. Each perspective has its merit, so that the paradigms gener-ate the expectation of a predicted turning point and then react to the unforeseen catastrophe. Perhaps the most interesting aspect of this is the discrepancy between the paradigms and the objects that confront them.

Thus, the situation demands a radical historicization of both the present and the past. Nothing could be more demanding precisely because of the rapid transformation of the terms of the debate. The causes of this rapid transformation are not reducible to European construction, this being, in many ways, nothing more than an attempt to respond to the profoundly altered conditions of the existence of the state. Rather, they are revelatory of a larger category of political questions, notably those concerning collec-tive identity, the role of popular participation and representation in the economy of power, and the weaving of the *communal* and the *social* into the fabric of concrete politics. Before debating the new relational mode be-tween collective behaviors and the organization of public services required by supranational construction, one must understand why the turning point in European history coincides with a crisis of the very notion of the citizen, precipitated to some degree by its entire history. The current debates are haunted by the search for a paradigm in which cultural pluralism will no longer be residual or subordinate, but constitutive. They are only partially aware of the need to reexamine each implication, each justification of the equation, "citizenship equals nationality." Even if this equation is no longer considered by everyone to be sacrosanct, it nonetheless operates at the basis of the organization of civic rights and dominates even the prospect of an evolution. Very often the idea of supranational citizenship has no meaning other than the displacement to a "higher" echelon of the very characteristics of national citizenship.

Models of Citizenship

There are, to be sure, several historical models of citizenship. According to the historical and sociological tradition of the nineteenth and twentieth centuries, of which Marxism from this point of view is no exception, these models were divided into two main categories: ancient citizenship and modern citizenship. The citizen of antiquity, inscribed in a network of community *affiliations* that constituted the very structure of the city, was characterized by *his* objective personal status, be it hereditary or quasi-hereditary. Modern citizenship, founded on both subjective and universalist principals (universalism of individual rights, in particular, the right to political participation; universal suffrage; universalism of access to the elite; generalized education; universalism of proclaimed democratic ideals, whatever the real degree of their institution), must nevertheless be inaugurated by a positive institution. This institution corresponds historically to the European nation-state, later exported throughout the world through colonization and decolonization.

The shift from the ancient model to the modern model of citizenship would thus constitute a reversal of primacy between the community pole and the individual pole. However, this reversal would only further demonstrate the formal continuity, that is, the permanence of a rule of closure, associated with citizenship. By definition, citizenship can only exist where we understand a notion of city to exist—where fellow citizens and foreigners are clearly distinguished in terms of rights and obligations in a given space. This formal distinction is in no way threatened by the existence of intermediary categories such as *metoikoi* (foreigners living permanently in Athens and enjoying special rights) and residents, provided that those belonging to these subcategories do not enjoy those rights of sovereignty reserved for full citizens. In this respect, the modern nation is still, and must still consider itself, a city. The move from ancient to modern citizenship is thus marked by a continuity, that of the principle of exclusion, without which there would be no community and thus no politics, with the community constituting both the defining interest and the legitimating principle in either model.

However, historical reality is more complicated than these models. The global antithesis of the ancient city and the modern city is invoked either in terms of a return to antiquity, a reconsecration of the civic community, or, on the contrary, as proof of the irreversible trend toward individualization of social relations. This antithesis conceals many unresolved problems.

We might begin by accounting for the tendentious oppositions at the very heart of the ancient conception of citizenship. Nicolet (1976, 1982) astutely demonstrated what distinguishes the Roman Republican city, even more the Imperial city, from the Greek polis: Rome tended to unify under a single authority the ensemble of those who share the same "culture." Yet Rome was led to conceptualize and practice this participation or affiliation as if it were infinitely capable of extension—not to all human individuals, but to some individuals from all walks of life who, having acquired and hereditarily maintained the status of citizen, would form the ruling class of the empire. Hence the possibility of tracing analogies with either the modern nation or the empires to come, especially empires that have as their center colonialist nation-states such as Holland, Britain, and France, which will also be states conferring rights.[2]

> The fact that the Roman state could have unified and directed several hundred thousands of citizens over several centuries without exploding . . . is a unique phenomenon in ancient history. Well before the France of the declining monarchy and the Revolution, or the England of 1688, Rome was able to transform Italy into a nation, the first of its kind in history—a nation which responded, two thousand years before its articulation, to the famous definitions elaborated by French nationalism: a "consent to live together."[3] It is altogether indicative of the Roman political system that the last war and the only war fought by Rome against the Italians, a civil war, was fought against a people who were knocking harder and harder on the door of the city and who, in doing so, finally got it open. (Nicolet 1976: 514)

We must, however, also consider the history of "citizenship" and the "bourgeoisie" (Bürgertum) of the medieval town and of the confederations, the principalities, and the monarchies of the Old Regime, which tends precisely to problematize a global comparison between the ancient city and the modern city. It is easy to understand why: such a citizenship always represents an equilibrium between autonomy and submission. In other words, as opposed to at least the theoretical implications of national citizenship, citizenship construed as such corresponds for the collectivity

2. Etats de droit.
3. Vouloir vivre ensemble.

(*le peuple*) to a limited sovereignty (see, for example, Ullmann 1966 and Dilcher 1980). And conversely, it is even easier to understand why in the case of France and elsewhere, the identification of the rights of man with the rights of citizens and the conquest of the popular sovereignty under the name of nation have caused the strong association in the collective imaginary of citizenship (the universal right to government)[4] and nationality, even if the signification of the latter term has profoundly changed over time. This has not prevented different analysts (among them, recently, Barret-Kriegel 1988) from trying to inscribe the republican form in the continuity of this model, in a profoundly Tocquevillian manner.

These considerations are essential to this discussion for at least two reasons. On the one hand, it is only through a study of the traces left over time by the Roman Empire and by the medieval monarchies that we can understand the formation of the modern ideal of cosmopolitanism (of which the internationalism of workers and socialist intellectuals will have only been a variant in the end). Positive or legal citizenship in modern bourgeois nations, which is national, is ideally referred to a cosmopolitan concept of the unity of humankind. Modern cosmopolitanism is to real politics what the rights of man are to the rights of citizens: a utopian future, nourished by the memory of a lost unity. Yet, for such a community of citizens, the idea and practice of a limited sovereignty within the framework of a world order that imposes constraints on the community, even as it confers representation and rights, certainly does not belong purely and simply to the past. It seems, on the contrary, that whatever the form—neo-imperialist or democratic or transnational—that the reorganization of relations between the states takes after the Cold War (during which limited sovereignty was practiced but not admitted within each camp), this reorganization is surely the political and juridical horizon of globalization.

Which Rule of Exclusion for Europe?

Significantly though, all prospects of supranational or transnational citizenship immediately create a fearsome difficulty. Clearly, it is not enough simply to define the new "community of citizens" as an addition to the preexisting national communities, one that would add nothing to the already established concepts of citizenship, or that would signify that the various national citizenships were henceforth combined, absorbed one into the other or into one citizenship that had become dominant. Must we then proceed in reverse to the normative definition of a community of

---

4. *Droit universel à la politique.*

citizens[5] that history did not produce as such, even if it conferred on the concept a certain number of justifications? This is what seems to happen. We look for this definition in a purely artificial[6] perspective (the conclusion of a new "contract" between Europeans), or rather by supporting it with naturalist elements, that is, the community of culture and of common history rather than lineage in the strict sense.

Nevertheless, the stumbling block is always the same: it is the need to formulate a rule of exclusion founded on rights and principles. Despite the definition proposed in 1991 by the European Commission and employed in the drafting of the Treaty of Maastricht ("S/He is a citizen of the union who possesses the nationality of a member state" [Heymann-Doat 1993]),[7] we cannot be satisfied with simply reinstating the exclusions that already exist (something to this effect: "European citizens" will be those who were not excluded from their respective national citizenships). What is implicitly required, in reference to a whole series of contemporary experiences (some truly traumatic) and of moral principles, and under the pressure of exacerbated interests, real or imaginary, is a supplementary rule of exclusion that properly belongs to the new citizenship of the postnational era.

This difficulty manifests itself acutely in terms of the citizenship of immigrants. Included in this category and beyond the different denominations in use today are all the extra-Community workers and their families who have taken up residence for one or more generations in European countries, as well as at least some of the refugees requesting asylum. It is difficult to decide if this is a cause or an effect of the current resurgence of xenophobic sentiments in the European Community. Despite the naturalization procedures (facilitated very unequally from country to country) and the restrictions on immigration officially imposed by most of the countries in the mid-1970s, it is estimated that immigrants make up 8 percent of the population in Europe (Schnapper 1992; Noiriel 1992). Preexisting distinct national citizenships can, at least without apparent inconsistency, keep in an extraneous statute on their own territory foreign individuals who entered their territory at a given moment provided first, that these individuals are neither too numerous nor too stable, and second, that they do not integrate themselves either into a large number of institutions—such as academic, medical, or those related to local government—or into economic, as well as athletic and cultural enterprises. But the dilemma[8] is

5. *Concitoyenneté.*
6. *Artificialiste.*
7. *"Est citoyen de l'union toute personne ayant la nationalité d'un Etat membre."*
8. *L'aporie.*

obvious as soon as entire groups of "foreigners" appear tendentiously,[9] owing to anticipation or adaptation, to be typical of a new sociability and citizenship concurrent with national sociability and citizenship. From that point on, the "immigrants" of extra-Community origin risk appearing as quintessential *Europeans*. This is not without analogy to the way that Germany and France during the last century assimilated Jews, who, although not ascribed regional affiliation (rootedness), passed as quintessential *national* citizens. If a new citizenship created on European soil does not succeed in conceiving itself and putting itself into practice collectively as though open by design, then it is likely to be constrained to decide, and theoretically posit that citizenship does not extend to some of the individuals who nonetheless occupy this soil, and that in this sense, it "separates them from the others" according to a certain *generic* criterion similarly applicable in all countries. This poses grave problems of definition if we do not want to consider explicitly the criteria of lineage or geographic origin. This would lead to forging the purely fabricated category of "noncitizen residents in Europe," implicating citizenship in the constitution of apartheid, at the very moment when it proclaims progress in universalism.

What then is the alternative? It can only be the coupling of a definition of civic community with a principle of openness, even possibly a regulated openness. Such a coupling would acknowledge not only that the European entity and identity are the result of a convergence of groups originating from all parts of the world on European soil, but also specifically that citizenship defines itself in principle as a nonexclusive membership.

This idea is logically enigmatic and unprecedented even if it seems to resemble certain personal statutes of multinationality or the principles of naturalization in nations with traditions of immigration like France and especially Australia or nations in North and South America. Nations of emigration have, on the contrary, rejected the idea, traumatized as they were by the loss of their "substance." There is much to say about all of this. Modern statutes of multinationalism are always strictly individual and do not confer much power. In this sense they confirm rather, in virtue of individual exceptions, the ideology of the affiliation of individuals to their nation-state, and the practice of their administrative appropriation. For their part, nations of immigration have most often used their ethnic quotas to regulate procedures for accepting new citizens, and symbolically overdetermined their citizens' surrender of their nationality or culture of origin. In this way, they redraw their borders precisely where they risk becoming relativized. The paradoxes in France are quite profound, because in one

9. *Tendanciellement*.

sense modern communities of citizens owe their historic permanence solely to diverse processes of assimilation, that is to say, to the sum of the means used to practically transgress the principle of exclusion, to which these means theoretically object. Here in France it would entail a reevaluation of this principle itself, with the ultimate purpose being to institutionally inscribe a historically and sociologically extant phenomenon.

Rights and Statutes

There is more. The alternatives mentioned above, at least as the outline of the problem—the constitution of a type of *apartheid* or the transition to a largely open, transnational citizenship—is accompanied by another problem that concerns the contractual founding of democratic citizenship and its relationship to the notion of statute. Statute or contract: this old dilemma takes on new meaning today. One could argue that the question will inevitably resurface in the two hypotheses envisioned. Simply stated, in the European apartheid hypothesis, the statute will be a pseudohereditary privilege that operates according to the law of all or nothing. This would permit restricting the extension of citizenship and of all juridical and political recognition of the sociological reality of immigration. In the hypothesis of open European citizenship, however, the statute will be the expression of a regulation, of a political and administrative control exercised over the stages and modalities of the openness and thereby susceptible to variations in degree.

For all that has been said, I do not think that we can simply follow the jurists and politicians (e.g., Leca 1992) who define citizenship primarily as a statute, which is tantamount[10] to nationality. What allows for relative continuity between the various modes of institution of citizenship and permits us to understand the theoretical and always problematic links that they maintain with concepts such as democracy and popular sovereignty is never merely the reference to a *communauté*. It is rather the reference to a *commune* (in English, commonwealth rather than community; in German, *Gemeinde* rather than *Gemeinschaft*). It is the fact that the notion of citizen, derived from an initial reference to insurrection as in the case of France, or to the right to resist as in the case of the United States, in short, to "constitutive power" (Negri 1992), is the expression of a collective political capacity to constitute the state or the public space. Hence, it is this notion that provides the link between the idea of citizenship and that of equality, which constitutes the main theme of its historical dialectic. I do not mean to reduce this dialectic to a progression in the sense of universalization, but

10. À l'égal.

it seems to me incontestable that the telos, or the ideal of the free community of equals, permanently constitutes one of the dialectic.

One would agree, however, that if citizenship never defines itself according to a simple statutory position—thus in an inegalitarian or hierarchical manner—this position is nevertheless immediately reintroduced; not only externally through the distinction between citizens and foreigners, but also internally. Citizenship corresponds to the constitution of a differentiated society and to the functioning of a state. Thus, at the very least, citizenship implies a distinction between those who govern and those who are governed, and a separation of public service and civic society. The importance assumed by the immigrant worker in modern capitalist societies leads in effect to this: that statutory inequality simultaneously projects itself from two sides into the national political space—through nationality and the social division of labor; and that the egalitarian demand or request is recast in terms of a set of movements and social rights that have been more or less acquired, more or less incorporated in the concept of citizenship, independently of the ethnic-national origin.

This historical tension between the egalitarian pole and the statutory (or hierarchical) pole effectively generates the multiple resonances of the concept of citizenship, which is impossible to confine a priori to a single form or to declare conclusively perfected. However, the history of the struggles and the compromises that this multiplicity masks have never adequately been documented. This is due primarily to the myth of continuous progress toward civic participation, typical of the philosophy of the Enlightenment and its legacy in this respect of the Romantic philosophy of history. It is also due to the correlative illusion, sustained by the political science and sociology of twentieth-century institutions, of an irreversible decadence that would lead to apathy, individualism, and collective consumerism.

I would like here to put forth the hypothesis that two movements are occurring simultaneously. The first leads from a conceptualization of citizenship as a statute to the conceptualization of citizenship as a producer of statutes. From an initial situation in which institutions specify the more or less restrictive conditions of a full exercise of civic rights, or of participation in the political sphere (a situation that persists in the modern city in the case of "passive citizens," and especially of the citizenship of women), we move to a situation in which, the universality of civic rights being presupposed, the capacity of citizen brings about the recognition of specific rights, and notably of social rights. The primary interest of the now classic definition of citizenship put forth by T. H. Marshall ([1950] 1965) is to present citizenship as a historical movement whose modus operandi does not reside so much in the realization of a self-same formal concept of the citizen in historically successive spaces or frames, as in the incorporation into this concept of new functions and exercise fields, which then transform it. This is the ideal type of passage from civil citizenship, first to political citizenship, and then to social citizenship. However, the greatest difficulty with this schema, which the current conditions of European political construction and, more generally, the state of politics in the world make apparent, is its profoundly teleological nature. It immediately presupposes a linear and irreversible progress—beyond the delays or the inequalities of development—as well as a compatibility of principles between the different aspects of citizenship successively put into place. Consequently, not only is it out of the question here that social citizenship should go hand in hand with the limitation and regression of civil rights and political rights, but there can be no question of contradictions, even virtual, between the conditions that permit the realization of different aspects of citizenship at any given moment.

The second movement is one theorized notably by Hegel as constitution of the state and by Weber as rationalization. It leads from the right to government,[11] exercised in an undifferentiated manner, but by a socially or territorially limited collectivity, to participation in the activities of the state and civil society that becomes larger and larger, but also more and more differentiated. Such participation then takes the form of an equilibrium between multiple administrative posts and multiple nonexclusive groups (in contemporary parliamentary regimes those of the electorate, politickers,[12] experts, militants, national or multinational lobbyists).

At least in theory, the moment of insurrection during the French Revolution, symbolized by the work of the Convention, constituted a conciliation between the two opposing exigencies of, on the one hand, the lack of differentiation of political functions (which gives its absolute power to the sovereignty of the people), and on the other, the virtually limitless extension of the civic collectivity. It is certainly not by chance that the Marxist tradition, while critiquing the juridical-political ideology dominating this popular form of representation, never stopped trying to find it in practice and in the movement of the historical emancipation of the masses themselves. Nor is it by chance that the most radical contemporary theoreticians of the decline of classical sovereignty, for example, Foucault in France, have continued to take the opposite point of view.

From this perspective, does the question of European citizenship take an unprecedented form? Perhaps. In light of the discussions for and against

11. *Droit à la politique.*
12. *Hommes politiques.*

supranationality, we should not pass too quickly over necessary comparisons with the preceding processes of which it inevitably bears the traces. Consider, for example, the construction of the U.S. federal government and its various repercussions in the world, or, more important, the construction and deconstruction of the "citizenships of empire" on a global scale in the British Commonwealth and in the French Empire with their more or less lasting successors. Another process comes to mind—the construction and regression of Soviet citizenship—since in theory it combined universal openness with the recognition of individual and collective social rights, and made these principles the basis of the existence of civil rights and political participation, thus inverting in a certain sense Marshall's ideal-typical order. Nevertheless, the fact remains that today we are faced with an extreme form of the tension between the egalitarian and the statutory aspects of citizenship, a situation from which it seems difficult to emerge without a profound redefinition of both aspects.

The State and Counterpowers

Why this critical situation? One could give strategic reasons that bear witness to the transformations brought about by economic globalization. The new phase of centralization of the movements of capital, of hierarchization of the laborer, and of distribution of territorial resources makes the most of the revolution in communication and engages in a competitive relationship with the Nation-States. The fall of historical communism has profoundly modified this situation. After this event, the Western European Union found itself in a quasi-imperial situation, as it was the only supranational construction in Europe. However, as a result, the question of the margins or the markets of this quasi empire, in terms of business and of potential integration, becomes crucial. With this question come others concerning the stages, modalities, and degrees of integration of Eastern Europeans into European citizenship, or at least into the field of equality relative to civic rights in Europe. Is the Yugoslavian civil war not, in many respects, a "social war" in the Roman sense of the term—one in which the "allies" fight among themselves? In this new situation, a triple constraint exists: colonial heritage, the importation of cheap labor, reunification of the "two halves" of Europe. Under terms such as associates, refugees, or migrants, it tends to define others who are not perfectly "foreign" as being in a position neither outside nor inside in relation to the economy and to the ideal type of affiliation to the community and sometimes even to its institutions.

From this perspective, European citizenship always risks returning to a statutory definition. This will not be due so much to an essential equation with nationality as to the way in which, as a criterion for access to civil and political rights and to social rights that have historically become their counterpart in the social-national state, European citizenship will find itself at the intersection of multiple processes of differentiation. Locally, national citizenship is complemented at the bottom by diverse "partial" or "approximate" citizenships, whereas on a global scale—along with U.S., and perhaps tomorrow Japanese, citizenship—the passport of the European Community citizen tends to function as a guarantee of privileged personal status in the open space that corresponds to the global economy. This is the modern equivalent of the *civis romanus sum* that Saint Paul invoked before the praetor of Judea.

However, by a symmetry inscribed throughout the history of the concept of citizen, the emphasis on the statutory and hierarchical aspect of citizenship allows us to reformulate the question in reference to its egalitarian aspect. This question never comes up in the abstract, but always in terms of the characteristics of an existing state, in a dialectic of representation and conflict. Experience teaches us in this way that democratic citizenship is not so much the type of citizenship that elides the state in the name of a hypothetically autonomous civil society (that is to say, which would exist completely outside the game of state institutions), as it is the type that manifests itself in the constitution of strong *counterpowers*: in the face of the autonomization[13] of the apparatuses of the state (removed as they are from the average citizen), they exercise on these apparatuses a power of constraint, repression, or supervision. Inasmuch as the construction of counterpowers is not purely defensive or reactive, it tends also toward a collective control exercised by individuals on the social powers on which they depend for their very existence. Is not one of the main reasons for the "preference" in democracies for the organization of public powers the fact that these powers (at least in principle and in contrast to private powers) are less likely to escape the control of those whom they control? It is fairly clear, however, that in the recent operation of most administrations and governments, privatization prospers under the guise of the public.

How, then, can we broach the question of controlling the controllers, or of publicizing[14] the exercise of powers at a European level? The paradox is, in this respect, once again obvious. As we have seen, the European state is a phantom. Officially denied sovereignty, it continues nevertheless to develop its domains of intervention and its skill at negotiating with the centers of economic decision. These are the ensemble of practices of the state

13. *Autonomisation.*
14. *Publicisation.*

of which the exact center of legitimacy, authority, and public nature is a mystery to the very individuals who theoretically occupy it. As far as the current insidious crisis of European institutions has pushed the evolution of this situation, it manifests itself rather as a regression to the extent that it reactivates the competition between the apparatuses of the national states and the embryo of a supranational apparatus, in which each pole attempts to present itself as the preeminent site of sovereignty.

One reason for this is obviously that nationalist discourse considers equally unacceptable both the idea of limited sovereignty of the states (even when it corresponds closely to practice) and that of a politics of the masses, using different means of representation and pressure to limit the autonomy of the apparatuses of the state and of the ruling classes or castes. Note that such a discourse is liable to include hegemonic interests as well as defensive reactions to the erosion of the social-national state. Unfavorable economic conditions simply do not explain the incapacity of trade unions, and more generally of the labor and socialist movements, to break through their barriers in order to organize their political thought and action on the same scale as those of the ruling classes.

The collective control of powers in the European context is currently all the more unreal in that the constitutional postulate of collective identity masks an administrative proliferation that does not present itself as a state. In fact, the displacement of decisions to the European level is accompanied by an extreme disequilibrium between the possibilities for the different social categories to use the political and administrative apparatus in the service of their respective interests. The sentiment of neutrality of the state—real or fictitious—in general is thus quickly losing speed. This must obviously be read in conjunction with the fact that the construction of European citizenship intervenes at the same time as an extraordinarily brutal rupture of continuity in the history of social movements—and especially the labor movement, whose relationship with the state, characterized by both irreconcilable and reconcilable conflict for more than a century, constituted one of the basic principles behind the emergence of counterpowers.

This situation, which may appear to be a vicious circle, is not without import since again, in Western as in Eastern Europe, the signification of the terms *peuple*, *Volk*, or *narod* as community, affiliation, or identity (which I have called *fictive ethnicity* in Balibar and Wallerstein 1988 and Balibar 1992a) prevails over their signification as will and egalitarian collective power. The problem has no obvious solution, but this must not prevent us from asking if the counterpart of a limited sovereignty—including the limitation of exclusive appropriation by the states of their own nationals— would not reside precisely in the growing publicity and the recognized exercise of counterpowers at different levels where decisions are henceforth focused. In this way one would constitute transnational political subjects according to national as well as transnational procedures and not merely create citizens out of national subjects.

Civic Pride, Patriotism, and Nationalism

There is one final dimension of the problem to investigate: the role of the nation, constructed by the history of institutions, social struggles, and collective ordeals (transformed by the imaginary into founding events), in the civic and political formation of individuals. We could base our discussion here on a remarkable text by Rusconi (1993) on the Italian situation, in which the questions almost always have general import and find their analogues in the French context or are relevant to the problems we have in common in the new European context. Such an analysis has no real French equivalent, although it would be just as necessary in France as in Italy. Thus, we risk finding ourselves unarmed before the critical economic situations and political movements that have begun to bombard us. Do we see in nationalism the past or the future? This reexamination of a notion whose meaning seemed fixed has become the very condition of an understanding of politics. The risk of speculation is lower in this respect than the risk of remaining the prisoner of a lazy confrontation between the dogmatisms of national defense and those of supranationality.

The history of national formation and its interaction with the construction of the state and the phases of economic development must lead to a veritable historicization of the nation form, the correlative of the discussion of citizenship above. This leads us in turn to question—without an already formulated response—which alternative formations have been suppressed by the dominant formation in the past, and why such alternatives are reemerging with more or less violence under the conditions of recent globalization. In this respect, Italy is an extreme example, but it also attests to the fact that political crisis is not limited to the phenomena of the corruption and the privatization of the state, or the mutation of the modes of communication and collective representation. It is a crisis of the social-national state itself, better known as the welfare state, and of the concrete form of the institution of citizenship over the last fifty years. Whatever the very unequal, and sometimes seemingly false degrees of its realization, the social-national state is an irreversible stage of nationality in the world. Under its old form, the social-national state has also become literally impossible in developed countries (to say nothing of elsewhere), generating a crisis in the nation form whose outcome remains undetermined. Obviously, European construction, even if it becomes social, only represents one factor among others, one that generates its own alternatives. Here, we have reached the point at which the problems raised by the state's loss of legitimacy and credibility, which can give rise throughout Europe to the phenomena of violence, nihilism, and authoritarianism, intersect the fundamental questions of political philosophy and the philosophy of history. What relationship does a political democracy have with the existence of a community consciousness of its own citizens?

Rusconi (1993) is fairly close in this respect to a kind of leftist Gaulism. From a philosophical point of view, he situates himself well within the Hegelian tradition, focusing on the need for democracy to actualize a new synthesis of civic universalism and historical rootedness, so as to reconstitute its sense of solidarity and responsibility. Fortunately, his polemical argument is against ahistorical conceptions of citizenship, yet it seems to me insufficiently historicized.

If democracy as a system of living traditions finds its expression in both the representation of the governed and the control of those who govern—by a sufficient appropriateness of the representation of the population's interests and ideas and by a sufficient degree of popular control over the controllers themselves—it is never more than a fragile equilibrium between the functions of consensus and the functions of conflict. Ultimately, democracy lives on the inverse excesses of these functions. In this way, democracy depends at least as much on *fortuna* as on *virtù*, as much on favorable circumstances as on the initiative of the ruling class, the parties, and the citizens. It is essential, if we want to understand history, that we not exaggerate the importance of consensus to the detriment of conflict.

In saying this, I do not mean to resuscitate a reductive conception of politics as the expression of class struggle. I want rather to ask that politics be conceived in terms of its real conditions, ideological as well as social. In France, as in Italy, during about a thirty-year period, a certain degree of democracy was achieved, notably because the forces capable of mobilizing the masses—workers who considered themselves or were considered outside the system, or who aimed at its suppression,[15] filled within it the *tribunician function* of keeper[16] of social conflict (Lavau 1981). It is true that this exteriority had a double meaning, loaded with a fearsome equivocalness: social exteriority with respect to free-market capitalism and strategic exteriority in terms of an "occidental camp," the repercussions of which were felt throughout the history of the labor movement, even in cases where it did not acknowledge an allegiance with communism.

15. *Dépassement.*
16. *Entretien.*

To the vitality of democracy we must then apply Machiavelli's theorem rather than Hegel's theory, or we must at least correct one with the other. Again, the object is to understand the stakes and possible consequences of the crisis of the social-national state. One may well be astonished by the fact that the decline of the labor movement and of class ideologies, which has both moral and economic sources, soon leads not to a triumph but to a crisis of their historical "opposite"—unitary national feeling and the idea of civic community, to which attest the phenomena of disinterest in politics as well as outbursts of identity nationalism, or ethnicization[17] of national consciousness. But these two phenomena probably constitute a single phenomenon. And from now on, the most important task at hand is to rediscover for democracy more collective ideals and closer connections with libertarian and egalitarian movements that protest against the status quo.

These conditions have contributed to the topical resurgence of discussions on patriotism. For his part, Rusconi approaches the question through a critical analysis of "constitutional patriotism" (*Verfassungspatriotismus*), defended by Habermas (1992a) in the debates on the revision of the German historical past (*Historikerstreit* 1987), and again in the recent confrontations concerning the reform of the Federal Constitution and of the right of asylum. Idealist though Habermas's perspective may appear, the question that he raised by publicly attacking stereotypes of political and historical normality, which regard it as normal for a nation to have its own unitary state, is destined to remain topical for a long time (1992b). Patriotism is an affair of ideals. And it is precisely ideals capable of linking generations that are required for democratic politics today, materialist though it may want to consider itself. But there are no ideals without their share of repression, without latent contradictions that find themselves sublimated.

Significantly though, contrary to what we might hope, there are also ideals in nationalism and even in imperialist nationalism. The idea of the French nation, like that of the German nation, fed on an orgy of spiritualism in 1914. This fact is occulted by all histories of European nationalism, which consider their historical association with Republican institutions an essential truth, or believe themselves able to distinguish between good (democratic, political) and bad (ethnic, exclusive, cultural) nationalisms. Precisely in order to deny any political equivalence between democratic nationalism and a nationalism of aggression and ethnic purification, it becomes indispensable to conduct a thorough analysis of their common ideological bases.

Just as we must agree to question the ambiguity of the references to the

17. *Ethnicisation.*

"pact of the Resistance," we must agree to examine what affinities there might be between the "heroic" activism of fascist *engagement* (at least at a certain point in time) and the "moral" activism of *engagement* in the French or Italian Resistance. Such symmetries do not lead to the conceptual amalgamation of these ideologies, but rather to a better understanding of why political stereotypes have never sufficed in determining behaviors and why at certain times choices, even risky ones, were necessary. The choices are no simpler today than they were in the past, because the signifiers and the imaginary of nationalism float between multiple usages and multiple levels: "old" nation-states searching for a new role on the world stage; infranational entities with their fictive ethnicity attached to their name—Flanders, Corsica, or Scotland; and supranational entities. Indeed, a European nationalism exists and is more or less influential according to the historical conjuncture; it is a component of each of our political spaces and has definitively displaced the old federalism.

All of this concerns the definition of citizenship and the ways in which citizenship is affected by immigration as well as by the conflicts, or even the manipulations caused by immigration. Recent debates, notably in France, have begun to generate reflection both on the effects of European construction and on the new character of immigration in Western Europe. What is important here, and this bears repeating, is not so much to propose a recasting of the equation, citizenship equals nationality, or to transpose it onto the supranational level, or conversely, to proclaim it obsolete, but rather to shatter the veneer of the obvious, to expose it as a problem rather than accept it as a given or a norm.

This equation, involving the nationalization of citizenship by the state and the evolution of the nation into a nation of citizens, could not become essential and reconstitute itself periodically without a strong element of internal democracy, a productive tension between the idea of *peuple* as a community (*Ein volk*) and the idea of *peuple* as a principle of equality and social justice (*das Volk*). In short, this equation could not have lasted through the trauma of "European civil wars" and the ordeal of class struggles without an element of intensive universalism (that which the nondiscrimination of individuals requires) and not simply extensive universalism (that which seeks the uniformity of individuals). The crucial factor here is how this dynamic of universalism works in politics today. For the past ten years in France, the "left of the left" have been suggesting that the stable presence of immigrants and their children, while socially necessary, will inevitably pose the problem of their nondiscrimination, thus of their citizenship. It appears, however, that if this prediction were right, then the imagined evolution concealed a certain number of illusions: in particular, the illusion that consists in imagining that the idea of an expanded and nonexclusive citizenship would advance more easily at the two extreme positions of the institutional chain, just short of and beyond the nation-state. These two positions are, to put it plainly, local collectivities (citizenship of residence) and European citizenship. In the present situation regional nationalisms have tendentiously become not less but more exclusive than the nationalisms of the state, and here the example of the Italian Leagues sounds a warning. Furthermore, the organization of European citizenship begins through the presence of law enforcement and the restrictions on obtaining the right to asylum (Schengen, Dublin), rather than through an expanded democratic participation. Consequently, it is precisely to the center of the equation, "citizenship equals nationality" (in the analysis and the critique of the concept of "community" that it defines) that the reflection and the research on the dynamics of transformation must lead.

The debate on European citizenship may well seem academic today, at least as seen from France, as if it had never been more than a utopia destined to sooner or later give up its seat to the "real" questions of politics. And yet in 1994 the Treaty of Maastricht went into effect. This marked an irreversible stage in the emergence of a new political entity. Beyond juridical formulae—sometimes deliberately equivocal—the definition of this new political entity still conceals no unanimity, neither among national components, nor within each one of them. But, de facto, it cannot leave unaltered the civil relations between the residents of the European space, nor by consequence, their personal and collective status. In this respect, it is only ostensibly paradoxical to maintain that the convergence of constitutional revisions (in Germany and Holland) and measures to control the influx of individuals across the "community border" could, in the long run, have greater consequences than the persistent divergence of commercial and monetary politics and the acceptance of a construction "at multiple speeds." For until all traces of the "rule of law" have formally disappeared from our political space, the *anti-citizenship* represented by regulating exclusion or enhancing the power of apparatuses of repression without increasing the possibility of democratic control implies a latent redefinition of citizenship itself. And the framework and presupposition of this redefinition, whether we like it or not, is the European space, which, little by little, is taking on the characteristics of a territory.

It is thus even more urgent to keep open the dialectic of the different ideas suggested here, which, although necessarily related, are by no means synonymous: community and exclusion; citizenship of Europeans, that is, identity of "origin," and the prior national membership with which the

French, Germans, Greeks and others enter into the sphere of community rights and obligations; European citizenship; citizenship in Europe, that is, the "Europe of citizens," meaning above all else, a space of civic rights and their progression, which Europe would see advance; and finally, open transnational citizenship of which European construction would at least partly be the support.

References

Balibar, Etienne. 1992a. *Les frontières de la démocratie*. Paris: La Découverte.

———. 1992b. "Internationalisme ou barbarie." *Lignes* 17 (October): 21–42.

Balibar, Etienne, and Immanuel Wallerstein. 1988. *Race, nation, classe: Les identité ambiguës*. Paris: La Découverte.

Barret-Kriegel, Blandine. 1988. *L'Etat et les esclaves*. 2d ed. Paris: Calmann-Lévy.

Costa-Lascoux, Jacqueline. 1992. "Vers une Europe des citoyens." In *Logiques d'états et immigrations*, J. Costa-Lascoux and P. Weil, eds. Paris: Editions Kimé.

Dahrendorf, Ralph. 1992. *Betrachtungen über die Revolution in Europa*. Bergisch Gladbach.

Dilcher, Gerhard. 1980. "Zum Bürgerbegriff im späteren Mittelalter: Versuch einer Typologie am Beispiel von Frankfurt am Main." In *Uber Bürger, Stadt und staädtische Literatur im Spätmittelalter*, J. Fleckenstein and K. Stackmann, eds. Göttingen: Abhandlungen der Akademie der Wissenchaften.

Giannoulis, Christina. 1992. *Die Idee des "Europa der Bürger" und ihre Bedeutung für den Grundrechtsschutz*. Ph.D. diss. Universität des Saarlandes: EuropaInstitut, Sektion Rechtswissenschaft.

Habermas, Jürgen. 1992a. "Cittadinanze e identità nazionale." In *Morale, Diritto, Politica*. Torino: Einaudi.

———. 1992b. "Die zweite Lebenslüge der Bundesrepublik: Wir sind wieder 'normal' geworden." *Die Zeit*, 11 December.

Heymann-Doat, Arlette. 1993. "Les institutions européenes et al citoyenneté." In *Les Étrangers dans la cité: Expériences européennes*, O. Le Cour Grandmaison and C. Wihtol de Wenden, eds. Paris: Editions La Découverte/Ligue des Droits de l'Homme.

"Historikerstreit": *Die Dokumentation der Kontroverse um die Einzigartigkeit der nationalsozialistischen Judenvernichtung*. 1987. München: Piper Verlag.

Lavau, Georges. 1981. *A quoi sert le parti communiste français?* Paris: Librairie Arthème Fayard.

Leca, Jean. 1992. "Nationalité et citoyenneté dans l'Europe des immigrations." In *Logiques d'états et immigrations*, J. Costa-Lascoux and P. Weil, eds. Paris: Editions Kime.

Marshall, T. H. [1950] 1965. "Citizenship and Social Class." In *Class, Citizenship, and Social Development*. New York: Anchor.

Negri, Antonio. 1992. *Il Potere Costituente: Saggio sulle alternative del moderno*. Carnago (Varese): Sugarco Edizioni.

Nicolet, Claude. 1976. 2d rev. ed. *Le Métier de citoyen dans la Rome républicaine*. Paris: Gallimard.

———. 1982. "Citoyenneté française et citoyenneté romaine: Essai de mise en perspective." In *La nozione di "romano" tra cittadinanza e universalità: Da Roma alla Terza Roma*. Roma: Documenti e Studi, Edizioni Scientifiche Italiane.

Noiriel, Gérard. 1992. *Population, immigration et identité nationale en France. XIXe–XXe siècle*. Paris: Hachette.

Rosanvallon, Pierre. 1992. "Préface." In *Discussion sur l'Europe*, Jean-Marc Ferry and Paul Thibaud, eds. Paris: Calmann-Lévy/Fondation Saint-Simon.

Rusconi, Gian Enrico. 1993. *Se cessiamo di essere una nazione: Tra etnodemocrazie regionali e cittadinanza europea*. Bologna: Il Mulino.

Schnapper, Dominique. 1992. *L'Europe des immigrés*. Paris: Edition François Bourin.

Ullmann, Walter. 1966. *The Individual and Society in the Middle Ages*. Baltimore: Johns Hopkins University Press.

Violence, Culture, and Democracy: A European Perspective

Michel Wieviorka

Urban terrorism, perpetrated by sects or people from the extreme right, riots, religious fundamentalisms including Islamism, racial harassment, racist and xenophobic attacks: in the contemporary world, violence seems to find new, or renewed spaces, and to signify, in its own way, considerable changes. At the same time, the ways it is perceived, interpreted, and often fantasized bear witness to a gap between the phenomena of violence in their objectivity and their representation, which is broadly linked to a feeling of insecurity, which has no necessary bearing on its empirically verified manifestations. The question would be secondary if the reality and perception of violence were in direct and constant correspondence. But this is not the case.

Collective Violence

In some cases, there is scarcely any correlation between the feeling of insecurity and the direct experience of violence, as the work of Hugues Lagrange (1984), Pascal Perrineau (1989), or Renaud Dulong and Patricia Paperman (1992) demonstrates for France; in other cases there is a direct relation, as in the case of the cities in Brazil studied by Angelina Peralva (1994). This is why it is necessary to make a clear distinction between two analytical objects: on the one hand, violence in its concrete expressions; and on the other, the representations of violence, which we shall not consider here, adding, simply, that the problem is further complicated by the fact that some consideration should be given in the analysis to the mass media that produce information about violence, playing a part in its representations, and perhaps also influencing its genesis and transformation.

A sociological object. For some considerable time, social science proposed two contradictory paradigms of collective violence. On the one hand, an evolutionist argument formed the main school of thought and postulated a direction for history that led societies from tradition to modernity, or from Gemeinschaft to Gesellschaft, and this movement could be thought of in terms of continual progress in which violence, apart from the state's legitimate monopoly of it, could only diminish. Political and economic modernization in this perspective seemed to imply a decrease in violence, an idea developed in the 1940s, 1950s, and even still in the 1960s, for example in Daniel Lerner's *The Passing of Traditional Society* (1964).[1] But, at the same time, even evolutionist social thought has usually been dominated by the preoccupation, at times even the obsession, of seeing violence developing specifically in times of change and modernization, or by the idea that was simply the reverse of the same coin, that historical change could only be convulsive and revolutionary.

In reality neither the idea of progress, of the advance of mankind toward less violent societies, nor that of the inevitable character of violence as the consequence or cause of change are acceptable. The former idea is no longer credible, given the Nazi experience, which definitively demonstrated that one of the foremost societies on the path of progress could invent the worst barbarism using thoroughly modern forms of violence. And who today would dare to invoke Lerner's optimism in a reinterpretation of the last twenty years of history in the Middle East—in Lebanon, for example? Certain statistical data, themselves of a questionable nature, demonstrate that in a century violence has declined in the West;[2] but this in no way enables us to postulate a law of history. Similarly, we must admit that there is nothing inevitable about violence, and that civil war, chaos, and ethnic or religious "cleansing" are not necessarily the fruits of change, spectacular as they may be: after all, the destructuring of the Soviet Empire

1. Michel Seurat, in the collected manuscripts entitled *L'Etat de barbarie* (1989), published after his death, is extremely critical of this type of thinking.
2. See, for example, Chesnais 1989.

was accompanied by violence in some regions, but not in others where there have been considerable transformations. In the last resort, change may take place without violence, and this suggestion enables the reversal of the order of the terms: change does not inevitably involve violence, and the latter is not necessary for change to take place. This formulation may seem banal, but it moves away from what was at the heart of revolutionary projects, and, further, of many social, national, racial, or other liberation aims, and which we find theorized either in the various transformations of Marxist-Leninist thought sketched by terrorism or in authors like Franz Fanon or Georges Sorel.[3]

If violence is neither condemned to decline, nor inevitable or necessary, we can begin to study it as a special type of action. It is not a question here of discovering it, for example, along the lines of commission set up in the United States at the request of President Lyndon Johnson in 1968 with the task of "going as far as knowledge could in the search for the causes of the violence and the means of preventing it." Indeed, various studies demonstrate its important role in American history and society, at a time when the integrated and harmonious image of a society conforming to the Parsonian functionalist model was beginning to disintegrate under the pressure of the anti–Vietnam War movement, student demonstrations, race riots, and campaigns for civil rights.[4] The question is not of reintroducing violence into the collective conscience, in discussions, intellectual and political life, or history. Instead, it is a question of lucidly examining its contemporary expressions, of attempting to understand its sources and the meanings that it conveys as well as constructing violence as a sociological object, and not of seeing therein the nonsociological figure of evil or of historical necessity.

Violence and history. Although the permanence, if not of the reality of violence, at least of its possibility, must be recognized, this analysis also demands the introduction of two complementary principles that enable us to situate violence in its sociohistorical context. The first principle consists of distinguishing between the meanings of collective violence depending on whether the challenge is to the social structure or its functioning, or whether it is linked to social change. In practice, these two registers may coexist. However, this first principle enables us to distinguish and analyze the diachronic and synchronic dimensions of violence, for example, a workers' strike that becomes violent and turns into a riot is part of the functioning of industrial society, whereas a revolution is part of social

3. See Wieviorka 1993a.
4. On this episode, and for a stimulating discussion of political violence, see Michaud, 1979.

change. The second principle, while bearing in mind the first of which it is an extension, consists of considering that each historical period, whether it be defined in terms of structure and function, or instead, in terms of change, is characterized by a set of expressions of violence that form a specific whole. Charles Tilly (1986) has brilliantly demonstrated and illustrated this second principle, by speaking of a "repertoire" and by examining the concrete expression that violence and collective mobilization assumes in industrializing societies, like France, as from the nineteenth century. But we would like to formulate this principle in a way that enables us to go beyond the simple description of forms of violent mobilization, period by period: each type of society, but also each transition from one type of society to another, produce specific expressions of violence, which refer not only to special forms but also, and primarily, to meanings.

The Crucial Change

Now, precisely, our societies—and here we shall restrict our remarks to Western Europe—are undergoing a far-reaching change, which can in no way be reduced to the idea of a crisis, that is to say to a lack of regulation of the social systems. This change does indeed take the form of a total historical transformation, a change of societal type in which everything is radically modified—social relationships, the political system, the state, cultural practices and demands, and the forms of knowledge. This phenomenon is widely recognized today and is most frequently interpreted by using an analytical model based on two main ideas.[5]

The first is that the societies in question formed relatively integrated units in the recent past, which we can describe as national societies, articulating social relationships characteristic of the industrial era: a state acting as the guarantor of individual rights, of citizenship and of solidarity by means of the welfare state, and a nation affording the symbolic and cultural framework within which economic and political modernization took place, even if the idea of nation might also include elements of opposition to modernity—which is what, rightly speaking, we refer to as nationalism.

The second idea at the center of most analyses of change, and the one that interests us here, is that this type of integration is no longer efficacious and in this instance for reasons related to the globalization of the economy. From the point at which international economic exchanges are intensified, states and political systems are weakened, becoming subject to actors and a logic that are beyond them and that deprive them of at least a part of their previous domination. At the same time, the nation can no longer constitute

---

5. See Wieviorka 1993b, and in particular, the introduction.

the privileged framework for economic modernization. On the contrary, it is threatened by change, which it does not control and which destabilizes it. The globalization of the economy has a multiplier effect because it also involves the internationalization of mass culture and of information, which further challenges many national identities. Economic rationality at a global level thus seems to be opposed to identities and to nations, which renews the old theme of the separation between reason and culture, universal and specific values, and in fact denotes a profound crisis in contemporary modernity.[6]

The change in Western European societies—which in many respects resembles that in the United States as Robert Reich (1991) analyses it—cannot be simply reduced to external factors but is also due to a major internal factor, common to all societies: the destructuring of the social relationships specific to the industrial era. Until the 1960s, and even into the 1970s, these societies were in fact industrial, that is to say that they were structured by a social conflict between the working-class movement and employers. The political system was to a large extent conditioned by this structural conflict, to the point that the idea of the left was linked to that of representation of the working-class movement. Social life outside the factory, in local and rural areas, in schools and universities, in administrations, and in all sorts of organizations was also widely influenced by anti-capitalist action and the working-class movement, and the same was true for cultural life, as can be seen by the considerable number of associations which, in one way or another, claimed to be part of the same struggle as that of the working class.

The theme of postindustrial society began to circulate in the late 1960s, and was introduced into sociological thinking by authors as different as Daniel Bell (1976) and Alain Touraine (1969). Today it is no longer possible to conceive of our societies on the basis of relationships of production, the working-class movement, and action aimed at liberating the industrial proletariat to liberate mankind as a whole. This form of class conflict is no longer dominant; this, as we have shown with Alain Touraine and François Dubet (1987), obviously does not mean the end of trade unions nor of a certain amount of conflict at the level of the working-class, but the end of an era in which the working-class struggle challenged the more general orientations of collective life. And whereas it was legitimate, until the 1960s, to consider that our societies were organized on the basis of a social conflict, it now seems preferable—at least provisionally—to think of them on the basis of a lack of social conflict, of a rupture, a fracture in which two subgroups, instead of opposing each other, are increasingly parting com-

6. See Touraine 1992

pany: a considerable part of the population is in society, participates in modern life, in employment, in consumption, has good access to education and to health care, while another is subject to exclusion.

The theme of social cleavage and of exclusion developed, particularly in France, in the late 1980s. It had the merit of ridding the intellectual scene of the vestiges of a mode of thinking that continued, in an increasingly artificial manner, to make the working-class movement the center of social life. But its limits were obvious. It reduced the "excluded" to an abstract image, to what they do not have, the things they are deprived of—housing, employment, and the access to consumption—without realizing that "exclusion" may be only partial, that its victims may also be involved in social relationships, and that they often participate in culture. The discourse on exclusion can be criticized from Marx to Proudhon: there is a tendency to see only poverty or deprivation in places where the mark of social relationships can also be found.

In other countries, the theme of the underclass tends to dominate. This refers to a population that is not entirely excluded but does have access, if only in part and in an impoverished fashion, to employment or to housing—conveying perhaps an Anglo-Saxon model that differs from the French one in the sphere of employment, that is, in France the underclass is associated with part-time workers and others with limited access to employment.

These transformations referred to above vary from one country to another in their concrete expression and can, for example, be spectacular at the political level, or on the contrary, tend to express themselves in infrapolitical forms. Thus, in a comparative study dealing with the rise of racism and xenophobia in Europe,[7] we have shown that there are significant differences in particular between Great Britain, where this phenomenon is widespread in the form of violence on a day-to-day basis, but nonexistent at the political level, and France, where it is primarily the object of a political campaign of the national-populist type, carried out by the Front National. In Germany the phenomenon combines infrapolitical grassroots violence and political racism that are conveyed by extreme right-wing parties with varying degrees of nostalgia for Nazism; we shall come back to this later. But for now, we would like to emphasize that these differences must not conceal the profound unity of contemporary change, since everywhere the challenge is the destructuring of entities in which industrial society, a political system, and a state in a modern nation were formerly integrated.

In this type of situation, the sociologist must avoid at least three dan-

7. See Wieviorka 1993b.

gers. The first is that of decadence, which operates with a somewhat mythical image of an overall decline, and with a vision restricted to disintegration, degradation, and in the last resort, regression. We must avoid this approach, which often teaches us more about those who promote it than about the realities with which it claims to deal. Instead, we should formulate the minimum hypothesis that there are various tendencies in present developments, which are much more complex and ambivalent, in which there is a combination of destructuring of old societies and emergence of new forms of collective living. This is why we cannot restrict ourselves to what has just been said about the end of the industrial era and the decline of the working-class movement. We must also examine the instances in which discussions and social conflicts are being reconstituted, as well as think about the issues that are emerging to replace those provided by work and forms of domination and alienation specific to industrial societies. Furthermore, we must increasingly learn to formulate these issues in terms of culture, whether it be a question of religion, memory, ethnicity, sexuality or, more generally, in terms of subjectivity and personality.

A second danger involves framing our analysis by a category that in itself contains all the others, and in fact weakens the analysis. In the present set of circumstances, the city often constitutes this category and too frequently enables the presentation of a change that is visible or legible in urban space as an urban crisis. However, this should not be reduced to a pathology of the city, or even to the idea of its transformation. The city, said the Marxist sociologists of the 1960s and 1970s, shows us the spatial representation of the social relationships that are projected therein;[8] similarly, today, declining suburbs or inner cities that have become ghettos and even, in the words of William Julius Wilson describing American cities, hyper-ghettos,[9] are the spatial and physical expressions of the ruptured social relationships associated with the socioeconomic dualisation of our societies. But the occurrence of socioeconomic problems in the city does not eliminate an analysis in terms of urban sociology that constantly, of necessity, oscillates between two impasses: either the town becomes a metaphor, the pretext for reading social and political problems that are not intrinsically in any way urban; or it is perceived as conditioning the existence and the expressions of these problems that, in this perspective, present a high degree of urban specificity, an analysis leading to utopias or technocratic projects in the belief that they can change the town and thereby change life. It is necessary to resist this type of urban sociology. But this does not mean that

8. See in particular Castells 1972.
9. See Wacquant and Wilson 1989.

the reference to the town should be totally abandoned; it is a sphere of collective life where citizenship and democracy could perhaps be considered, or reconsidered.

Finally, a third danger arises from the fact that given the present destructuration of social life, the tasks of sociology become more urgent, while at the same time sociology itself is increasingly less able to propose an integrated way of reasoning about these social changes. On the one hand, new forms of domination, exclusion, and alienation variously challenge what is most personal and most subjective in each individual, they also influence one's identity, dignity, and capacity for both personal choice and control of one's experiences; they seem to demand that questions of identity and personality be addressed in contexts in which the classical modes of socialization have become inoperative for many, in which the concept of role seems totally inadequate, and in which the actors, in fact to a large extent deprived of action, seem to have nothing at all in common with the system. And on the other hand, despite references to the end of history (Fukuyama 1992), our societies are constantly changing historically, which leads us to study macrohistorical processes, strategies of collective actors, political mechanisms, or again the functioning and transformation of systems.

We can now link this proposed fact of total societal change in Western Europe with the previously outlined and analytical principles of violence to consider the transformations of collective violence in this part of the world since the 1970s.

A Change in Paradigm

The end of industrial society. The collective violence associated with the conflicts that structured industrial societies until the beginning of the 1970s—when these conflicts were at their height—was in the 1950s and 1960s primarily a restricted social phenomenon, a feature of struggles and strikes, usually without rising to the political level, or only sporadically. This violence was more often defensive than counteroffensive, activated by threats to employment, by instances of organizational blockages that prevented any negotiation of workers' demands, or by severe repression.

At the end of this period, we enter a phase in which the same references to a working-class and anticapitalist struggle are the moving force behind a violence that becomes political and then terrorist. Violence may at the outset arise in a context of agitation and workers' struggles, as was the case in Italy at the end of the 1970s. But fairly rapidly, it distanced itself from its social interpretations of the workers' experience and demands and became solely an ideological-political phenomenon of the extreme left diverted toward radical forms of behavior. Extreme left terrorism was in the first instance the outcome of the disintegration of the working-class movement, as well as the senile dementia of Marxism-Leninism.

This form of terrorism combines these two phenomena in the *inversion* mode,[10] transcribing into action a mistaken and artificial identification with the working-class movement, and a theoretical approach claiming to be that of Marx and Lenin in terms that would only be likely to make the two turn in their graves. In this sense, terrorist violence is an indication of the end of one type of society. On the whole, the experiments of the extreme left, which became violent, therefore, can be understood as an endeavor to artificially maintain the foundations of a society in decline. Sometimes, but in a very restricted and confused manner, they also included cultural themes that foretold entry into a new type of society, as can be seen in the analysis of the Italian experience and in certain aspects of "autonomy," which ended in blind violence. This confirms the image of a phenomenon linked to a transition, to the passage from one societal type to another.

Extreme left terrorism, to which one can add its extensions or links with international terrorism, is not the only expression of political violence that we meet in the 1960s and 1970s. The extreme right also practices terrorism, in particular in Italy, attempting to destabilize the state. Since the late 1960s, we see elsewhere the appearance of movements that speak in the name of the nations oppressed by the big nation-states and denounce the internal colonialism of which they are victims in terms that mix specifically national demands with social and political demands influenced to varying degrees by Marxism-Leninism. When violence occurs in Northern Ireland, Spanish Basque country, Brittany, Corsica, and elsewhere, it challenges the nation-state and appears to be linked to change and not to the structure and functioning of society.

More precisely, it would be necessary to examine the experiences of collective violence country by country, to consider those which involve the ongoing effects of colonialism, decolonization, and neocolonization, taking into consideration the existence of authoritarian regimes, for example in Spain, in Portugal and, more briefly, in Greece. The fundamental aspect, however, is in the most substantial meanings that collective violence implements, expressing them instrumentally, or to some extent maintaining them artificially; violence constantly refers to the social question, it finds its meaning, absurd and blind as it may be, in a representation that the actors have of social life in which the predominant image is of a central conflict that opposes the workers' movement to the employers or to cap-

10. On the concept of inversion, see Wieviorka 1993a.

italism. Even violence with cultural and nonsocial inspiration, as is the case with nationalist movements, requires this representation and endeavors to capture it, accompanying its acts by speeches often including an anti-capitalist theme. The Basque ETA in Spain, for example, developed by breaking with the classic nationalism of the Basque National Party (PNV), first moving closer to workers' struggles, then to the new social movements of women, then to antinuclear campaigns, as well as by assuming a Marxist-Leninist political line.[11]

The new meanings of violence. Twenty years later, there have been significant changes, and the new meanings of violence are in fact part of a general evolution. The working-class movement is no longer the actor capable of challenging the directions of collective life. Its historical decline, while accompanied by sporadic, defensive, and increasingly limited violence, has reached a point of nonreturn such that the terrorist projects that spoke in its name, and at times hoped to arouse or awaken the working class, have lost their momentum and are themselves totally exhausted.

This is not to say that the social sources of violence have disappeared, they have changed. The former central conflict is now expressed in social cleavages and socioeconomic dualization, both of which are often inscribed in urban space. Being socially marginalized also entails being deprived of the capacity to act effectively, and being excluded from participating in a conflictual social relationship, which may result in apathy and withdrawal into oneself or into primary groups. The effects of social marginalization, however, may also be transcribed into forms of violence.

Thus in Great Britain and in France, much more frequently than in other European countries, riots have taken place throughout the 1980s and 1990s in declining inner-city areas or suburbs.[12] These riots, in which young people attack the police and destroy property, beginning with shopping centers, are more social than ethnic, contrary to their portrayal by the media. Angry young people, who say they "hate," are indeed, to a large extent, immigrants and children of immigrants. But their violence is not of a communal type, impelled by a minority culture or religion. On the contrary, its main source is social and economic: it originates in unemployment, failure at school, and difficult living conditions, as well as from a feeling of being despised and victims of discrimination, in particular by the police, whose racism has been documented, if only in the reports following

---

11. On the Basque ETA, see Wieviorka 1993a.
12. For a useful perspective on the two countries, as regards these riots and other topics, see Lapeyronnie 1993.

the British riots.[13] Rioters are characteristically young men; and their social violence expresses a rupture, an exasperation. Heavy with real rage, this violence translates the anger of those who see before them a society that rejects them, when it doesn't insult or abuse them. To recall the classical distinction, as well as being a form of expression, riots may also be instrumental; for example, by assuming a deliberately spectacular aspect, the actors intend to attract media attention and draw politicians to the scene with announcements of social and economic measures directed to the locality of the riot.

When communist and leftist revolutionary ideologies were capable of inspiring the dream of conquest of state power, political violence could itself be the backdrop to this dream, with representations of the state insisting on its supposed all-powerfulness and, to use Gramsci's terminology, its capacity to impose an "armed hegemony of coercion" to legitimate itself. From the time when neoliberal ideologies were popular and when, everywhere, it was a question of reducing the role of the state and its intervention, the criticism was reversed: the state was denounced as being powerless, increasingly incapable of developing the "welfare state," and tending to withdraw. On the left, political violence, deprived of its Marxist-Leninist references, ceased to tend toward the taking of state power. When political violence is expressed on the right, it is principally in an instrumental manner, in a very limited fashion, to maintain or obtain a particular balance of power vis-à-vis the state, for example in Italy with the mafia.

In fact, what is really new, over and above the French and British outbreaks of rioting, and already in the last resort contained therein, are the links between violence and cultural demands and statements. The nation, religion, community, and behind them often race, have become the central meanings of violence, which, in a few years, have therefore changed from being a social phenomenon linked to problems of industrial labor, to an identity-related phenomenon, linked to cultural belonging. The phenomenon of violence associated with identity or culture is not in itself new, and for centuries Europe has paid heavy tolls to religious wars, to confrontations between nations, and to anti-Semitism. But it is clear that contemporary violence brings us back to this type of signification, which in many respects was less prominent from the 1940s through the 1960s.

In the most significant cases, violence is in the first instance a nationalist statement tending to racism and xenophobia aimed at the expulsion or exclusion of a particular group or groups. In Germany, since September 1991 in Hoyerswerda (ex–East Germany), there has been a sharp increase

13. See Monet 1993.

in attacks against immigrants from Central Europe, as well as against Turkish or Moroccan immigrant workers: according to the *Verfassungsschutz* (state security police), there were 270 racist actions in 1990 and 1,483 racist actions in 1991. The 2,286 officially recorded acts of racist violence in 1992 included 696 acts of violent destruction of property, 598 attacks on people, 701 criminal fires and bomb attacks, and 17 murders.[14] Similarly, in Great Britain the official statistics on "racial harassment" record thousands of cases each year, and the Home Office notes that there is a racist attack every half hour.[15]

Racist violence comes in the first instance from the majority group, which perceives its national identity to be threatened. In most instances, the reference to identity is itself the outcome of real social difficulties and fears which are anticipated or acknowledged by the racist group. The most serious incidents in Germany are inseparable from a general deterioration of the system of professional relations and its capacity to ensure the maintaining and overall progress of purchasing power. The most active protagonists of violence are not the unemployed, or the victims of downward social mobility, but it is effectively the widespread climate of increasing economic difficulties that creates conditions that incite the rejection of otherness and a differentialism full of hatred. Here, violence means a combination of these difficulties, as well as resentment between the two formerly separate parts of Germany.

In some cases, the same phenomenon of violence conveys fairly directly the move from a social definition of the actor to an identity-based definition. This can be clearly seen in the evolution of the skinhead movement, which started in Great Britain, as one indication among others of the disintegration of the working-class movement and the expression of a working-class subculture. After a period of withdrawal, it later became an extreme right movement spreading to Germany and Belgium, more than other European countries, and was based on a racial definition of the actor and his enemies, with strong nationalist effects and a distinctive aesthetic.[16] And even when there is not visibly or directly a move by the actor from a social reference to a cultural reference, it is clear that everywhere, including in the most widespread expressions of identity, violence thrives on the economic crisis and the accompanying loss of the points of reference that industrial society provide.

But sometimes also, and in a minor key, identity-linked violence is initi-

14. See Peralva 1993.
15. See Couper and Martuccelli 1993.
16. On skinheads, see Brake 1974; and Knight chapter 10, "Les skinheads," in Wieviorka et al. 1992: 307–37.

ated by actors from minority groups. The fantasies here, and in particular those promoted in the media, are disproportionate to the reality; threats of violence by minority communities or Islamic terrorists are periodically brandished and inflated. It is true that in France or Great Britain gangs that could be described as ethnic exist, but on a very small scale. The larger ones may seem like their counterparts in the big American cities, but they are not comparable in number or influence, nor is the comparison between the black ghettos of the American inner cities and the suburbs or declining inner-city areas in Europe one that is really tenable.[17]

Yet it must also be noted that Islamic terrorism did find an echo in Germany, Belgium, and France; and the *fatwa* pronounced in Tehran, condemning Salman Rushdie to death for blasphemy, aroused some favorable support in Great Britain. It is also the case that as a result of social exclusion and racism, populations in the process of integration may feel, at least in part, rejected and this in turn leads them to processes of ethnicization that may ultimately include violence. Thus in France, the Harkis (the Muslim irregulars in the French army during the Algerian war) have been so despised, ignored, and segregated for over thirty years that some of their children and grandchildren have become partly ethnicized and have mobilized violently—in particular in 1992 and 1993, putting up road blocks and throwing stones at the police. At times tensions between different minority groups are noted, particularly in Great Britain. But on the whole, to date these phenomena are insignificant. The main expressions of collective violence in Western Europe in the 1990s are related to either the social anger of the excluded or the anxiety of the majority cultural group about identity that is expressed in a differentialist nationalism inherently racist and xenophobic.

This general evolution has increased steadily since the 1970s, first in Great Britain, then in France, Belgium, and Germany, appearing more recently in Southern Europe, Italy, and Spain. We have analyzed it in its most spectacular collective expressions; the examination of diffuse violence— thieving, rape, rackets for school students, drug trafficking and its attendant violence, the climate of insecurity in schools, delinquency, and criminality—in no way invalidates our affirmation of a renewal of the meaning of violence throughout Western Europe.

Violence and politics. On the whole, the collective violence described above is barely perceptible at the political level, at least for the time being. But here we should be more specific and distinguish at least three different situations.

17. See, for example, Wacquant 1993.

The first situation is that in which the new meanings of violence are neither directly associated with the political or ideological-political practices of parties and organizations, nor influenced by them. Thus, in Great Britain, racist violence has not really found a political outlet. Instead, it is forcibly restricted to an infrapolitical space for reasons that are related not only to the failure at the beginning of the 1970s of National Front leaders, who were incapable of imbuing their nationalism with a social theme that would have afforded them wider popular support, but also to the politics of Margaret Thatcher and the Conservative Party, who, on the contrary, adeptly referred to the nation while flattering the electorate without being unacceptably racist or nationalist.

The second example is that of France, where collective violence remains very low-key as far as racism and nationalism are concerned, probably because of the Front National's increasing power since 1983. This party, unlike the British National Front, succeeded in finding a populist tone, playing on references to the nation and other emotive themes; its racism and xenophobia have never drawn it into violence, nor even to demonstrations of support or encouragement for violent practices. The Front National's populism is conditioned by a strategy to attain power through electoral successes. Thus, any violence that would be carried out in its name would threaten its respectability and hence its electoral prospects. However, the party has everything to gain from capitalizing on nationalist, anti-Semitic, racist, or xenophobic attitudes that originate in society, and even by informing them, channeling such fears, frustrations, and anger without allowing them to be transformed into violence. What is specific to the French experience is that with this party, nationalist or racist violence has neither a political space nor any great infrapolitical space.[18] In this respect the Italian experience is in some ways similar to the French. Indeed, since the end of the 1980s, Italy has experienced an expansion of the expressions of racism and xenophobia. But since the Leagues in Northern Italy—which up to then had been tempted by a populist and vaguely racist tone—and the neofascists who came to power under the umbrella of Berlusconi in March 1994, not only was there no radicalization toward nationalism, populism, or escalation of racism, but preoccupation with these themes decreased in the Italian press, which has always been extremely sensitive to them.[19]

The situation in Germany is different: neo-Nazi organizations are a fact of life; skinheads are a widespread reality; and the Republican party itself

18. On the Front National, see Mayer and Perrineau 1989; and Tristan 1987.
19. See Martuccelli 1993.

encourages a differentialist and bitter nationalism. In this situation, it would be excessive to say that nationalist, xenophobic, and racist violence rises directly to the political level. But it is clear that unlike France, Germany experiences a degree of coordination between the discourse of its radical right wing and the practice of grassroots violence, which has no difficulty in being legitimated in neo-Nazi propaganda or in the xenophobia manifest on the political level.[20] We should add, but with caution, that the very low electoral support for the German extreme right in the June 1994 elections to the European Parliament do permit the hypothesis that there is a change, with Germany turning away from the dangerous direction it has been headed since reunification.

Whatever the case, we must therefore distinguish among different situations: those in which violence based on identity has no political space because its meanings have no political space in which to express themselves, even nonviolently; those in which it has none because a party occupies this space entirely and cannot adapt its practices for strategic reasons; and finally, those which give the most cause for concern, where a continuum ensures communication between the ideological-political level and the practices of grassroots violence.

Culture and Identities

The production of culture. Collective violence today in Western Europe therefore reveals a variety of meanings that assume various forms and a variety of social and cultural themes that have at least two fundamental characteristics. The first is that the social demands that are not met and that lead to violence tend to indicate deprivation rather than domination, exclusion rather than conflict, and a lack of social relationships rather than a position of inferiorization. This first characteristic constitutes a favorable condition for the transformation of social demands into cultural statements: those who are thus deprived of action, and excluded from the space within which opposition and negotiation take place, may consider themselves as people apart, and feel they are being treated as different, and, should the case arise, tend to assume an identity that ensures them of the collective reference points that they do not have. These references can no longer be provided by the working-class movement, its hopes, promises, and capacity to fight for the control of historicity, and since no referents are to be found in other social movements, the excluded produce them or adapt them in the cultural field, in the broad meaning of the term. When they can afford it, some rush into wholesale individualism and its associ-

20. See Moreau 1994; and Peralva 1993.

ated consumer behavior; others turn to religion, nationalism, ethnicity, and all sorts of artistic expression in which they oscillate between consumption and production; still others succumb to or choose destructive forms of behavior—those to which we have already referred in relation to violence—and self-destructive forms, especially drug abuse and suicide. The deficit in social relationships, for the moment linked to the disintegration of the various concrete expressions of the working-class movement, has the effect of burdening the cultural field with demands that are not met socially. These demands either originate in what remains of the working-class movement, particularly when it was transmitted by strong communities as in Great Britain, or convey the loss of meaning that this movement contributed and the disappearance of the landmarks that it could offer to all sorts of social or cultural actors at the local level, in the sphere of consumption and elsewhere. This defines the first mode of cultural production: based on exclusion, downward social mobility, social and economic difficulties, often intensified by indifference, contempt, ostracism, discrimination in employment, housing, education, and health, and disparaging treatment by the media. From this point of view, statements of identity, for example religious or ethnic, are regarded as ensuing from social change and even appear to be distinctly socially conditioned.

However, the second fundamental characteristic of the present period—the increased importance of culture—cannot be reduced to these social sources alone, for the cultural field has its own specific dynamics. It is not necessarily exclusion or discrimination that encourage the actors to produce their cultural references, or to live them with increased intensity. For example, if one considers the history of European societies over the last thirty years, it is evident that cultural renewal and identity movements originate to a large extent in the middle classes. Let us examine the French situation since the late 1960s where, as in other countries, ethnic revival and the production of the Occitan, Breton, and later the Corsican movements are not dependent on phenomena of crisis or downward social mobility. Almost simultaneously, the Jewish community in France began an impressive process of affirmation, becoming more visible than beforehand, breaking with the model inherited from the Enlightenment and the French Revolution, according to which one was Jewish in the private sphere, and a full citizen in the public sphere. This considerable transformation is not due to processes in which social demands have not been met; but rather, it demonstrates the greater capacity of the Jews in France to act against anti-Semitism. During this same period, women's movements, along with the ecology and antinuclear movements, advocated other relationships between the sexes (the term gender, *genre* in French, has not become widespread in France, despite the efforts of some feminists), pleaded for other modes of development, and therefore had an effect on culture once again without a situation of downward social mobility or social exclusion. It must therefore be recognized that to the first logic of cultural production we must add a second, which is the outcome of the work of the actors on themselves, more than of stigmatization or social exclusion. These two sorts of logic are not incompatible, they often even combine with one another, interacting in ways that make it rapidly impossible to distinguish between what is due to the work of the actor on herself or himself and what is due to the work of society and its effects on the actor.

But the idea that our societies produce their cultural expressions and identities has to be tempered by the reminder that these same societies are also hosts to foreign populations, who bring cultural specificities that are often highly visible and very different from those of the host society. Is it the case that immigrants came to Western Europe with their cultures of origin, which are reproduced all the more easily as the capacity of the host societies for integration has decreased? This point of view is too superficial to be acceptable. It must be borne in mind, in the first instance, that the presumed cultures of origin are often themselves recent and linked to the transformations that have taken place in the phase preceding departure. Above all, it must be recognized that what seems to translate into an imported ethnicity is often a "kit," to use Lévi-Strauss's expression, in which elements borrowed from the culture of origin are mixed with others, found in situ or imported from elsewhere, in a process of syncretism of which Great Britain definitely offers the most outstanding examples in Europe.

We would like to add one last remark: cultural production, whether or not it is directly linked to social processes, does not in itself create situations inherently prone to conflictuality, that is to say, social relations of domination. It outlines collectivities, it defines values, but on this basis only three main types of behavior are evident: the attempt to make possible within a single societal whole the coexistence of differences, and therefore their democratic articulation; forms of behavior in which the actor endeavors to put herself or himself at a distance, to confirm a distance, or to live one's culture as one wishes to, at the risk of being communitarian or sectarian; and forms of behavior involving war or violence, in which the differences are experienced as being incompatible with each other and irreducible, and can only assume the form of a radical confrontation. It is more difficult for the growth of cultural identities to be a source for enriching democracy and easier for it to be a factor, or expression of the fragmentation and breakup of our societies, of which it forecasts or signals the disintegration. In this sense, it is imperative to develop ways of thinking about the capacity of democracy for generating new modes of integration of cultural differences.

Getting uptight about national identity. Making the problem even more serious is the fact that national identities are themselves also a part of the profound cultural upheaval that Western European countries are experiencing, all of which are subject to similar developments.[21] There is indeed a decline in the image of the nation as the symbolic and cultural framework within which modernization takes place, whether it be a question of industrial development, or of the means of exchange and communication, or of science; and those who identify with it, do so increasingly in terms that are differentialist and, above all, hostile to the globalization of the economy and the internationalization of culture. The nationalization of the radical right is the most spectacular expression of this retraction. At one and the same time it includes appeals to economic closure and exacerbated protectionism; a rejection of the political construction of Europe; possibly an anti-Americanism exalting the refusal of a culture that is rapidly described as cosmopolitan; and marked tendencies to racism, anti-Semitism, and xenophobia. But we should note that the categories of the radical right very often tend to give it a quasi monopoly in defining the nation, and in informing the political discourse well beyond its electoral or even political sphere of influence.

This leads to discussions that are still confused, but whose contours can be discerned by specifying the four main positions that mark out the political and intellectual space confronted with the growth of the less acceptable forms of nationalism. Some, like the British historian Eric Hobsbawn (1990), consider that this nationalism is a residual or archaic phenomenon and that the idea of the nation is historically past its peak—perhaps a correct prognosis. The major difficulty with this view is that it leaves the nation to the nationalists.

Others, such as the German philosopher Jürgen Habermas (1988: 57–58) plead for a "constitutional patriotism," which also sees itself as being postnational, but which in reality maintains an attachment to the idea of the nation. Habermas requested, at the time of the *Historikerstreit*, and in relation to the German nation, that the latter be defined primarily in terms of democratic and political space, rather than historically in terms that encourage the demand for the country's past to be in its totality, including

21. See Wieviorka 1993c.

the Nazi period.[22] In our opinion, this is a weak proposal: what is a nation deprived of a part of its culture or its history?

Yet others consider that the contemporary nation-states in Western Europe are undergoing a crisis that does not challenge their classical formula. In this perspective it is primarily a question of resisting an overly rapid construction of a politically unified Europe, of resisting the potential for reducing the sovereignty of member nations, and of maintaining confidence in institutions that ensure familiar forms for integration of the nation, even if they are exhausted or outdated as Dominique Schnapper (1990) clearly demonstrates for France, for example, in the state school system, the trade unions, the Catholic Church, and the Communist Party. This point of view is respectable and exerts considerable influence over all political actors and most intellectuals. It is met both in countries with pluriculturalist traditions such as Great Britain and the Netherlands, where it is a question of maintaining a mode of functioning that recognizes cultural differences in public space, as in countries in which, on the contrary, like in France, only individuals and citizens are accepted in public space. Its main weakness is that it is based on the unproven idea that it is possible to create new institutions ensuring socialization and national integration, or to relaunch in their present form or with minor changes, some of the institutions at present in decline despite the fact that these same institutions are increasingly ineffective or in crisis. Moreover, we note the beginning of a European trend of convergence, the most pluriculturalist countries endeavoring to come closer to universalist French-like models, with France itself discussing the need for a degree of flexibility concerning cultural difference in public space.

Finally, a fourth point of view, with which we ourselves identify, insists that the idea of nation be re-anchored to fresh projects for modernity. In Europe, this position implies an argument that integrates three levels: the level of the nation itself, which should then preferably constitute the framework for the process of political rather than economic modernization, and for a cultural dynamic with history and language acting as decisive vectors; the infranational level, where all sorts of cultural specificities intervene that the nation must tolerate and even valorize and not despise, or attempt to crush or marginalize; finally, the European level where political, economic, and cultural unity must also be articulated with national and infranational specificities, instead of being their negation. Obviously it is far easier to outline this position than to translate it into practice.

22. *Historikerstreit* refers to a very important debate in the German press in the late 1980s among historians, philosophers, and social scientists, starting with the question of the relationship between Nazism and Bolshevism.

Cultural diversification. Contrary to widespread belief, globalization of the economy and internationalization of culture and communication do not entail making culture uniform and transforming the planet into a gigantic consumer society. This tendency does indeed exist, but it is much less widespread than the opposite tendency to cultural diversity. This is already the case in economics, and directors of firms or those in charge of marketing are well aware of it, as they are constantly called on to diversify the range of products which they market. Furthermore, the spread of consumer capitalism does not mean by itself uniformity, and moreover, creates reactions where cultural identities are defending themselves against it, rather than being dissolved by it. And much more profoundly, it is noted that everywhere the identities and loyalties that individuals manifest and demand are on the rise and that all sorts of cultural groups are being formed, of which we are still insufficiently aware when we consider the main historical identities, the emergence of nationalism, and the return of the religious factor. Indeed, contemporary cultural production assumes forms that are not all as stable or related to deeply rooted historical trends nor, on the scale of territories, as vast as those associated with world religions or modern nations.

Even more striking in some cases is the instability of identity and its contradictory character. This is particularly so for forms of ethnicity that can signify not the calm certainty of belonging to a group but a heterogeneous space associated with three demands: conformity, which implies subordinating the individual to the community; individuality, which involves participating in modern economic and political life; and subjectivity, that is, functioning as a subject, creating one's own existence, outlining one's basic chores.[23]

In other cases, identity is restricted to a limited territory, possibly to the area controlled by a gang, or it may have only the fleeting life of a fad. And much more often than is realized, identities are themselves constantly on the move. This can be seen in religious matters, for example with European Islam, which is highly varied within a single country, or with Christianity, where we witness the development of a number of variants of Protestantism, as well as of Catholic integralism, which ended in a split in the 1980s. This can be even more directly observed if we consider artistic or literary forms of expression and the movements in which they are created and popularized. For example, who can fail to recognize that Great Britain is a cultural laboratory, with its specific black cultures in which music, dance, and the relationship to the body play an important rule, with its skinheads whom Kobena Mercer has described as being examples of "white eth-

23. See the chapter devoted to ethnicity in Wieviorka 1993c.

nicity," its Indo-British literature of which Salman Rushdie is the best known example, and its numerous ethnic associations acting as political lobbies at the local level?[24]

Continuous cultural production, however, does not exclude the opposite phenomenon: the formation of sects, in which everything is fixed, under the aegis of a totalitarian type of power and where the community forbids individuals to be anything other than what it commands. And, more generally, the work of actors on themselves—when they innovate, create, and produce new forms and cultural values, or when they resort to their collective memory, and endeavor thereby to influence history—requires spaces of liberty and autonomy. Yet such spaces are constantly threatened by the closure of the community, integralism, fundamentalism, and the assorted, possibly sectarian variants of withdrawal into identity. Whether it is a question of the main macrohistoric, religious, or national identities disseminated at the international level, as in the black diaspora which Paul Gilroy (1993) studies, straddling North America, the Caribbean, and Great Britain, or a question of identities that are more limited in time and space, the processes through which culture lives, is composed and recomposed, are in constant tension, where death can threaten life. The threatening face of identity, tempted by withdrawal or violence, is always capable of eclipsing its positive aspects, where the actor is the subject.[25]

A Challenge to Democracy

Western Europe has not yet been swept into the torrent of the worst form of violence threatening it, that based on identity, and it assuredly has a fairly considerable capacity to resist it. But "ethnic cleansing" in ex-Yugoslavia, or the vicious circle of Islamic terrorism and military counterterrorism in Algeria, are proximate realities that have escalated so rapidly that it is impossible to consider oneself protected from or immune to such threats.

However, Western Europe today has the immense good fortune to be still able to make certain choices. Cultural diversification includes the elements of innovation and of opening up to the world that we have outlined; it does not always or necessarily imply communalism or totalitarian closure. The question that arises is in fact whether or not European societies are going to accept the growing separation between the market and culture. This acceptance would in turn ratify the separation which juxtaposes the following groups: the array of middle classes participating in

24. See Mercer 1987: 50; more generally on these problems, see Lapeyronnie 1993.
25. The consideration of the subject is particularly developed by Alain Touraine (1992, 1994). See also Dubet and Wieviorka 1995.

employment, consumption, and cultural innovation; the communities or identities functioning in a tribal mode; and finally, those who are possibly ready to return to the tribal world or who tend to copy the individualism of the better off, that is, marginalized individuals and groups, the underclass, the excluded who have nothing whatsoever to unite them.

The hypothesis is not unreasonable, and there is nothing new in well-meaning people insisting on the rise of individualism and market consumerism, while others stress the tribalism that in their opinion has filled the social vacuum, while others recall the suffering or the difficulties of the excluded.[26] But is it not possible to envisage societies in which there is room for alterity, where differences can rub shoulders without being telescoped, and in which cultural minorities are neither ignored nor marginalized by the majority?

The realization of this vision depends on a single condition: dealing with the exhaustion or decline of the political systems inherited from previous periods and solving the crisis of the political formulas for representative democracy. If we consider contemporary populism—a particularly significant expression of this crisis—we can see that there is still hope.

Populism is a feature of periods of change; it proclaims and promises that it will abolish the distance between the people and power. It gains momentum particularly easily when the political system is nonexistent, or deficient in the processing of social demands, deaf or impotent when confronted with the expectations of the population or certain groups. It primarily functions as a myth, offering people the possibility of changing while at the same time remaining themselves, stating that cultural continuity is the guarantor of change, that the nation and reason are one and the same thing, and that the past and the future belong to the same trajectory. In short, populism constitutes a mythical synthesis, a discourse that reconciles the irreconcilable in a total fusion. In Western Europe, therefore, populism spreads today by linking appeals to cultural and usually national identity—possibly with Catholic connotations, sometimes also with regional ones, as in the case of the Northern Leagues in Italy—with demands for economic participation emanating from those segments of the population who are experiencing rejection, exclusion, downward social mobility, and threats to their status, or from elites who are anxious about their capacity to remain ahead in the economic race. Whether it be a question of the Leagues, or more generally, in Italy, of the Forza Italia governmental coalition, the Front National in France, the right-wing version of a populism of which a left-wing version can be found in Bernard

26. See, for example, Lipovetsky 1983; Maffesoli 1988; and Bourdieu 1993.

Tapie, or less open political tendencies in other countries, populist experiences are a necessarily provisional reply both to the separation of culture and the instrumentality of the market. Indeed, they promise to reunite them, whereas they have no means of effecting this reunification, apart from a discourse that requires mediation by a charismatic leader. Populism is not in itself a portent of fascism or an authoritarian regime, it appeals to direct democracy, nonparliamentarian and even antiparliamentarian. The major question that it poses concerns what will follow it. History suggests that the disintegration of populist movements, for example of the People's Party in the United States at the end of last century, may end in the recomposition of the traditional political system, but at a considerable cost (in this case, for the United States, the exacerbation of the racism of Jim Crow laws).[27]

Contemporary populism in Western Europe must be considered as a sort of warning, the answer of those who suffer or who are the most alarmed at the separation of reason from culture, or who are frightened of being excluded from modernity, but who do not opt, or not yet, for radical forms of behavior, nationalist and racist violence, or the appeal to fascist rule. This answer can only last for a limited length of time, for the populist myth cannot stand up to the ordeal of power, nor even the delays and hazards of electoral politics. Indeed, populism, even weighted with forms of racism, xenophobia, and anti-Semitism, is less threatening than what is to be expected in what follows populism, in what appears when there is no longer the cloak of the myth to contain the extremist tendencies and the violence.

Populism is not a satisfactory reply to the question of how to define the conditions enabling us to envisage the rearticulation of universal values and cultural specificities. On the contrary, populism is symptomatic of the very issue confronting European democracies: the reinstating of forms of political and institutional mediation required for this rearticulation. The absence or inadequacy of these forms leads either to widespread cultural fragmentation and violence far worse than described here, or to processes of fusion with the populist amalgam as the least alarming example, while awaiting the establishment of an authoritarian state.

Would it not be possible to find alternatives to the populist, or worst still, the post-populist theses in a new approach to citizenship? The idea is attractive, particularly as one consequence of the crisis of national societies in Europe has been the ending of the close link between citizenship and nationality. Indeed citizenship can and must be considered in terms over

27. See Woodward 1955.

and above the framework of the nation with which it must nevertheless continue to be associated. It might now be considered as an articulated whole that would function at the supranational level of Europe, the national level, and the local level, thus allowing for the principle of subsidiarity according to which all problems would be dealt with at the lowest possible organizational level. In this respect, should an appeal not be made to strengthen and enlarge citizenship, and particularly to increase citizens' political involvement in decision making at local levels? The limits of this approach are demonstrated by considering the following two observations. The first is that mobilization of actors cannot be decreed by regulation or by law; it is not because citizenship is strengthened at the local level that it becomes a living reality. Today in Europe there is only a weak demand for more citizenship at the local level, and the plans that aim at enlarging it may be perceived as being an order to participate instead of a form of political progress. The second observation is that the sphere of identity does not necessarily coincide with an administrative area, whether it be the nation or the town. In fact, the idea of a reinforced form of citizenship refers to legal and political reforms that postulate increased rights for all citizens. The present rise in identities is more an appeal to collective recognition and therefore to rights that are not exactly those provided by citizenship. There is a demand for minorities to be recognized and possibly supported or helped; there is a greater concern for an increase in democracy than for an extension of citizenship. For this reason, while encouraging progress in the sphere of citizenship, particularly at local levels, the most urgent need is to plead for an extension of democracy, in keeping not only with the expectations of the majority, but also, and primarily, with the expectations emanating from minorities.

The fall of communism, by ridding us of the totalitarian contrast, at least in its Soviet version, gives us an opportunity to rethink democracy. Now more than ever, it is insufficient to describe democracy as the opposite of either totalitarianism or authoritarianism. We must consider the capacity of democracy to meet the social, political, and cultural demands that it not only tolerates but also permits and encourages—demands, which if ignored and unmet, can always very rapidly transform into violence.

Expansion of citizenship, from my point of view, always contributes to democracy, but this is not the issue for cultural minorities. They need not only more citizenship—more political and juridical individual rights. They also need more democracy, that is, a democratic system better able to address cultural, collective demands, even if these demands are unstable and divisive. Given the city's limited scale and its capacity to generate concrete social and political relationships, the city may be the best arena for such an expansion of democracy. But this approach also requires vigilance so that the needs of larger cities do not supersede those of smaller cities, and so that differences among cities do not reinforce or generate principles of discrimination and inequality.

References

Bauman, Zygmunt. 1991. *Modernity and the Holocaust*. London: Routledge.

Bell, Daniel. 1976. *The Cultural Contradictions of Capitalism*. New York: Basic Books.

Bourdieu, Pierre. *La Misère du monde*. Paris: Seuil.

Brake, Mike. 1974. "The Skinheads: An English Working Class Subculture." *Youth and Society* 6(2).

Castells, Manuel. 1972. *La Question urbaine*. Paris: Maspéro.

Chesnais, Jean-Claude. 1989. *Histoire de la violence en occident*. Paris: Hachette.

Couper, Kristen, and Danilo Martuccelli. 1993. "L'Expérience britannique." In *Racisme et xénophobie en Europe: Une comparaison internationale*, Michel Wieviorka, ed. Paris: La Découverte, 29–102.

Dubet, François, and Michel Wieviorka, eds. 1995. *Penser le sujet: Autour d'Alain Touraine*. Paris: Fayard.

Dulong, Renaud, and Patricia Paperman. 1992. *Le Reputation des cités HLM*. Paris: L'Harmattan.

Fukuyama, Francis. 1992. *The End of History and the Last Man*. New York: Free Press.

Gilroy, Paul. 1993. *The Black Atlantic: Modernity and Double Consciousness*. London: Verso.

Habermas, Jürgen. "Une manière de liquider les dommages." In *Devant l'histoire: Les Documents de la controverse sur la singularité de l'extermination des Juifs par le régime nazi*. Paris: Cerf.

Hobsbawm, Eric. 1990. *Nations and Nationalism since 1780*. Cambridge: Cambridge University Press.

Knight, Nick. 1982. *Skinhead*. London: Omnibus Press.

Lagrange, Hugues. 1984. "La Perception de la violence par l'opinion publique." *Revue Française de Sociologie* 15: 635–57.

Lapeyronnie, Didier. 1993. *L'Individu et les minorités: La France et la Grande Bretagne face à leurs immigrés*. Paris: Presses Universitaires Français.

Lerner, Daniel. 1964. *The Passing of Traditional Society: Modernizing the Middle East*. New York: Free Press Glencoe.

Lipovetsky, Gilles. 1983. *L'Ere du vide: Essais sur l'individualisme contemporain*. Paris: Gallimard.

Maffesoli, Michel. 1988. *Le Temps des tribus*. Paris: Klincksieck.

Martuccelli, Danilo. 1993. "L'Expérience italienne." In *Racisme et xénophobie en Europe: Une comparaison internationale*, Michel Wieviorka, ed. Paris: La Découverte, 215–83.

Mayer, Nonna, and Pascal Perrineau. 1989. *Le Front national à découvert*. Paris: FNSP.

Mercer, Kobena. 1987. "Black Hair-Style Politics." *New Formations* 3 (winter).

Michaud, Yves. 1979. *Violence et politique*. Paris: Gallimard.

Monet, Jean-Claude. 1993. "Police et racisme." In *Racisme et xénophobie en Europe: Une comparaison internationale*, Michel Wieviorka, ed. Paris: La Découverte, 307–17.

Moreau, Patrick. 1994. *Les Héritiers du IIIème Reich*. Paris: Seuil.

Peralva, Angelina. 1993. "L'Expérience allemande." In *Racisme et xénophobie en Europe: Une comparaison internationale*, Michel Wieviorka, ed. Paris: La Découverte, 159–212.

——. 1994. "Violence à Rio: Faits et mythes." Report, CADIS/EHESS and University of São Paulo, May.

Perrineau, Pascal. 1989. "Les Etapes d'une implantation électorale (1972–1988)." In *Le Front national à découvert*. Nonna Mayer and Pascal Perrineau. Paris: FNSP, 37–62.

Reich, Robert. 1991. "The Work of Nations: Preparing Ourselves for the Twenty-first Century Capitalism." New York: Knopf.

Schnapper, Dominique. 1990. *La France de l'intégration: Sociologie de la nation en 1990*. Paris: Gallimard.

Seurat, Michel. 1989. *L'Etat barbarie*. Paris: Seuil.

Tilly, Charles. 1986. *The Contentious French*. Cambridge: Harvard University Press.

Touraine, Alain. 1969. *La Société post-industrielle*. Paris: Denoël.

——. 1992. *Critique de la modernité*. Paris: Fayard.

——. 1994. *Qu'est-ce que la démocratie?* Paris: Fayard.

Touraine, Alain, Michel Wieviorka, and François Dubet. 1987. *The Workers' Movement*. Cambridge: Cambridge University Press.

Tristan, Anne. 1987. *Au front*. Paris: Gallimard.

Wacquant, Loïc. 1993. "Banlieues françaises et ghetto noir américain: Eléments de comparaison sociologique." In *Racisme et xénophobie en Europe: Une comparaison internationale*, Michel Wieviorka, ed. Paris: La Découverte, 263–77.

Wacquant, Loïc, and William J. Wilson. 1989. "The Cost of Racial and Class Exclusion in the Inner City." *Annals of the American Academy of Political and Social Science* (January): 8–25.

Wieviorka, Michel. 1993a. *The Making of Terrorism*, David Gordon, trans. Chicago: University of Chicago Press.

Wieviorka, Michel, ed. 1993b. *Racisme et xénophobie en Europe: Une comparaison internationale*. Paris: La Découverte.

——. 1993c. *La Démocratie à l'épreuve: Nationalisme, populisme, ethnicité*. Paris: La Découverte.

Wieviorka, Michel, et al. 1992. *La France raciste*. Paris: Seuil.

Woodward, C. Vann. 1955. *The Strange Career of Jim Crow*. New York: Oxford University Press.

From the Atlas to the Alps:
Chronicle of a Moroccan Migration

Marco Jacquemet

You can live one hundred years but if you do not travel,
you only have a half life.—Beni Meskines proverb

Beni Mellal. Two days after the end of Ramadan.

Beni Mellal is on the road linking Marrakesh to Fez, in the foothills of the Atlas, bordering the great plain of phosphates. From this town every Wednesday and Saturday two buses leave for Italy. They are top-of-the-line buses, with wide windows, forty-eight reclining seats, video and sound systems, fast and powerful engines. They run a nonstop itinerary from Beni Mellal to Milan, three days and two nights, crossing all of Morocco, Spain, and France. The average convoy has two buses, but in the summer the demand for seats is so high that they fill three, sometimes even four buses,

The article is based on three months of research (two in Beni Mellal and Rabat, Morocco, and one in Milan, Italy). The fieldwork was supported by a grant from the Institut de Recherche sur le Maghreb Contemporain, Rabat. This final write-up was accomplished while in residence at the International and Area Studies Department, University of California, Berkeley. I would like to thank these institutions, especially the Dean of International and Area Studies, Richard Buxbaum, and the director of IRMC-Rabat, Susan Ossman. I would also like to thank Dawn Cunningham and Mia Fuller for their comments.

and reservations of one week in advance are usually mandatory. But this is the low season, and I manage to secure a seat for this Wednesday's departure just by showing up one day in advance to buy a one-way ticket costing around $150.

The buses leave in the afternoon, but even the night before people start gathering around the café tables near the travel agency that issues the tickets. Some people come from far away, from the Berber villages high up in the Atlas mountains reached only by criss-crossed mule tracks. A few come from the *dir* around Beni Mellal, an area of intensive agriculture with rich soil, patchworked fields, and a sophisticated irrigation system. The majority come from the plain of phosphates, a dry and bare land spreading from the Atlas foothills to the coastal area 300 kilometers away. They are Beni Meskines, not long ago a people of shepherds, today a people of migrants. In the 1940s and 1950s the local economy was strong, the flocks fat and numerous, the land rich enough to attract new residents from the overpopulated cities. Then the demographic explosion of the 1960s and two long droughts in the 1970s and 1980s caused a long-term downturn in the economy. When dry, the phosphate-rich earth ("a blessing for Moroccans but a curse for the Beni Meskines") became poisonous, entire flocks were destroyed, and the men had to leave to feed their families. Since that time, this has been a land of destitute emigration toward the northern cities of Casablanca, Rabat, Tangier, and Europe. Opportunity, chance, and timing made Italy the migrants' first choice for relocation. The earliest images of immigrants to Italy—traditionally a country of emigration—are linked to these people, rambling in the streets or on the beaches with the carpets and blankets woven by their women on their shoulders, selling local artifacts door-to-door, sleeping in the hallways of railroad stations.

Talking with the young men seated at the café the night before the trip, I was struck by the mythical character they attributed to Italy. Their social imaginary pictures Italy as the land of fabulous adventures. While they migrate to France to find a safe job, secure a clean apartment in the suburbs to relocate the family, and share in the social values of French petite bourgeoisie, they go to Italy to search for easy money, make a fortune, build up capital, have incredible adventures. Italy for them has the seductive halo of a mythical and golden elsewhere.

People see Italy as a land of plenty, a new America where wealth comes easy: "A lot of people here have never heard of New York, but everybody knows Loreto" [a hub subway station in Milan] says Khaleb, one veteran of this migration. "I am just doing what Italians did in America one hundred years ago. Italy is the place you go to get rich." Zaki, a teenager who has just started the procedure to get a valid passport, enthusiastically supports this view. He is eager to leave and join a friend living somewhere in Naples: "In southern Italy life is easy. Nobody bothers you. You can do whatever you like. You can even steal. Let's say you are in a restaurant when a fight breaks out. You can seize this chance and grab wallets, jackets and everything else handy, and split unscathed. There nobody knows you, see?" Others around him seem to share this image of a free land with few social interdictions: "A couple of months ago we had an Italian guest," Larbi tells me. "He asked how much I made in one month and I told him 1,000 dirhams. Then he said that in Italy I could have made the same money in one day. So I decided to leave for Italy to raise some capital. There I could take up jobs that here I'd be ashamed to do, like street cleaning or garbage collection. Nobody knows me there." Larbi has a ticket for the next day's departure on the bus with me.

Around us, those who cannot leave talk with a mixture of envy, admiration, regret, but also scorn for the veterans who show off work permits, an apartment lease, or a letter from an Italian girlfriend. Not everybody participates in the general enthusiasm for Europe. Hamid speaks of Europe as a "trap" that has lured the best people away: "In Europe you have more freedom and life is easier, and Europeans aren't mired in complexities and problems like we are." After looking over his shoulder he continues: "Here we are in a prison and we cannot speak the truth, but the migrants have run away instead of fighting to change our ancestral structures." The other people around us seem unable, or do not care to see this connection between politics and economics. The pull of Italian wealth shown off by the return migrants is just too strong.

The veterans have come back for Ramadan driving luxury cars, bought used to be resold at home after the long journey and maybe weeks of parading the entire family around. Many of the cars in the streets still have the license plates of northern Italian cities (Milan, Verona, Pavia, Torino); Rome and some areas of the South are also well represented. These automobiles enter the local economy as taxis, utility vehicles, or family cars, and will be around for many years thanks to the local ability to fix most mechanical problems through a progressive cannibalization of nonfunctioning cars. Local garages and body shops have an ample supply of these cars, which they dismantle part by part as the need arises. When these old cars have been stripped of their parts, the bare frame is then abandoned in some barren field, like camel skeletons in the desert.

Moroccans even find a use for foreign license plates, which are transformed into semiotic mementos of the outside world. These license plates find their way into the local system of shop signs, where shop owners signal their cosmoplitanism by incorporating the plates into the sign-

Figure 1. Beni Mellal, Morocco. Sign for international travel agency. Destinations include Milan, Genova, Turin, Paris, Brussels, and Libya.

boards for their shops. In Beni Mellal's streets, the presence of the West is visible everywhere, from the clothes young people wear to these shop signs. The sandwich board outside the town's only international travel agency advertises destinations—Milan, Genova, Bordeaux, Libya—in a mixture of local forms and Western images. Decorative motifs inspired by both local artifacts—such as the ornamental pins, or fibulas, used by local women—and Arabic calligraphy blend in with images of fast and powerful buses (see Figure 1).

Beni Mellal and the surrounding cities of Fqih Ben Salah, El Bourouj, and Qalaat Sraghina display the cosmopolitan style the migrants have brought back with them. Building construction is in full boom, but the houses now being built no longer retain the traditional Arab style, with its focus on the inside and surrounding high walls to make them barely visible from the outside, thus protecting inhabitants from the "evil eye" of jealous neighbors. Nowadays, houses are built in a potpourri style, which mixes Italian suburban design with ostentatious displays of new wealth. Mercedes and Fiat Regatas have arrived loaded with sliding glass doors, French doors, skylights, washing machines, bathtubs, and bidets. These expensive commodities and signs of Western luxury deeply affect local perceptions and expectations, causing breakdowns in the communal mechanisms of social solidarity and equality.

The migrant brings home economic wealth and social change, but his transformation from the young man who took off in search of adventure into the skilled migrant sending home a steady and reliable income is neither easy nor fast. "When one of my young kin leaves for Italy, we strongly fear losing him forever," says Abdelrhammane, an old and well-spoken man who has joined our conversation. "Thus we must tie him to the family for good. The best way is to find a wife for him and marry him off at the first opportunity. But this is not enough: there must be children, even better if they are males, who will be raised by the family with the money sent home by their father." Only when the young adventurer is married and has children is he considered a migrant worker in all aspects, a somewhat steady source of income to rely on.

The wedding of a migrant is an important rite of passage, a ceremony that must be planned months, sometimes years, in advance. Now, with the globalization of techniques of video reproduction, sophisticated video cameras record the event down to the most minuscule detail. The videotapes will then be viewed by whole groups of migrants in the long nights of life away from home, allowing them to keep in touch with their communities, to be informed of the latest news. The video system on our bus will provide previews of the new crop of wedding videos, which passengers will greet noisily with gossip, jokes, laughter, and applause.

The Departure

On the morning of our departure we still have to purchase enough food and beverages to last three days. The provisions will be stored in a special section of the trunk, the only one that can be opened during the journey. People load roasted chickens, fresh bread, juicy oranges, dates, and tomatoes. The baggage is sealed in another, more ample section of the trunk, to be opened only by the drivers for custom's inspections.

Mohammed and Hassam, the two drivers, will be solely responsible for the safety of the baggage and the passengers. They are in control of every detail of the journey. As soon as we board, they collect our passports and will keep them until we reach the Italian border, at Ventimiglia. Between them they speak Spanish, French, and Italian. Hassam spent some years in Spain and knows by heart the roads of the Iberian peninsula, while Mohammed worked for some time in Toulouse and speaks excellent French. Their knowledge of southern Europe, of its borders, social rules, and codes of behavior, will be more than once extremely useful in negotiating the migrants' clash with the unfamiliar social topography of the land we cross. More than simply drivers, they are full-fledged guides, not just Charons ferrying the migrants' souls but Virgils as well.

My bus leaves first, only half full, after a long explanation of the off-limits status of the baggage. The passengers travel alone, or at the most with a friend. Only three are women, all on their way to join their husbands: two travel together and one is barely a teenager, escorted by an uncle who will "give" her to her promised spouse. They are seated in the first row, under the drivers' protection. After a half hour, we are in Fqih Ben Salah. My neighbor points out the numerous cars with Italian license plates. "Milano Two," he comments sarcastically. Even before the bus stops, it is already stormed by new passengers. People with and without reservations scramble to enter. A man with a reservation on the second bus has to be carried out. He cannot read and does not trust the driver's assurance that the other bus is on its way. It takes him half an hour to renounce his conquered seat, all the time showering the drivers and other passengers with insults, prayers, and curses. In the melee, the only woman boarding the bus in Fqih Ben Salah has been forced to sit in the back, foreboding trouble in the long nights ahead.

The bus is now full, except for four or five seats reserved in Casablanca and Rabat. We finally leave. The excitement of the struggle for the seats dies out and is replaced by an eerie silence. People stare out of the windows, letting their eyes wander across the landscape of fields brilliant green after winter's heavy rains. The Beni Meskines say, "going to green one's eyes," to refer to the relaxing, almost meditative custom of spring outings in the countryside. The green fields, which here do not last more than a few weeks, bring joy to the entire community. "They look like a carpet," whispers my neighbor, and I can read his sorrow for this abandonment. The bus speeds along, passing or pushing aside old Renaults, trucks burning oil, mule riders. Wanna-be passengers throw themselves in the middle of the road, their hand peremptorily held high. They cannot read the bus's destination, they just know that it is going in the right direction. The driver ignores them, forging ahead, and they scatter to the shoulders.

Almost all of the passengers belong to the new migrant generation. They are young, between twenty and thirty-five years old, have a valid residential and work permit and a job waiting for them, generally in northern Italy. At this time of year, their composition is quite homogenous: employed in hotels and restaurants, they took advantage of the slow winter months to visit family and observe Ramadan in a congenial environment. Ramadan's prescriptions are some of the greatest factors of discomfort for Moroccans in Italy. In a land of cured ham, wine, the Vatican, and relatively long working days, it can be very difficult to comply with injunctions for Ramadan—fasting during the day, avoiding drinking alcohol, praying seven times each day. On top of this, one has to deal with the resistance of Italian society against needs perceived as frivolous or not completely understood. The contempt of the bulk of the Italian population for foreign practices causes Muslims to feel unwelcome, uneasy, and unable to express their beliefs. Therefore, when they can, they spend Ramadan at home.

Many of my fellow passengers have only recently obtained a residence permit, after long years underground as illegal aliens, through the Legge Martelli. This regulatory program, set up by then Minister of Justice Claudio Martelli in 1990, gave overdue residence and work permits to more than 200,000 migrants. The migrants still remember the years previous to 1990 as a time of duress, abuse, and endurance.

Migrants' Stories

As the sun sets on the Moroccan plains, people relax, and start sharing with me tales of clandestine migrations and their past experiences entering Italy.

Hammed tells me how in 1988 he decided to "burn" (leave home) after having met an old friend who had just returned from Italy in a flashy Mercedes. "When I realized how much money could be made in Italy, I went to Tangier, got rid of my identity card, and hooked up with some fishermen to cross the straits. One night we left in a small fishing boat, overweight with people. The ocean was rough and we kept bailing water out the entire night. For me and others that was the first time ever on a boat, and I was seasick for the entire time. Finally we landed on a small beach near Bilbao, in Portugal. There I bought a train ticket for the furthest destination I could afford. It turned out to be Barcelona. But I did not want to stay in Spain, so once in Barcelona I slipped onto a freight train leaving for Marseilles. Italy was still my goal, so I inched (hitchhiking, walking, and jumping on local buses without ticket inspectors) toward the Italian border at Ventimiglia. In Nice I met a street vendor from Argentina and we became friends. He had a station wagon, and we decided to enter Italy at night with me completely buried under his merchandise. The custom's police knew him and we got into Italy without problems. He dropped me off in Genova where I contacted Caritas, a Catholic relief organization, and they helped me find a room. But Genova is too racist, people were beaten up in the streets at night, so I moved to Milan, then to Parma. The police stopped me many times, but they always let me go. I think they pitied me. I worked as a dishwasher, handyman, farmworker. Then I took advantage of the Martelli amnesty. Now I work as a waiter on Lake Como."

Others tell stories of disappointment and humiliation. "My cousin," Mustafa tells me, "did not have good luck at all. Married with two children, two years ago he decided to enter Europe without a visa. He sold four sheep and went to Tangier with a friend who put him in touch with a *passeur* (the Moroccan equivalent of a Mexican 'coyote') to cross the Gibraltar strait. Two days later he was on a rowboat facing the sea, which he had never encountered before. One mile off the Spanish shore he had to take a lifejacket and drift to shore. After getting there more dead than alive, he spent one day hiding on the beach, drying out, and resting. Then he started hitchhiking north, but a border patrol caught him and sent him back to Tangier where the local police beat him up, threw him into jail, and stole all his money. The total of the adventure: a financial hole of 20,000 dirhams ($10,000), a police record, and a shameful return." But the temptation of the Italian El Dorado is always there, and the desperation of a hopeless life is too strong. "Now," continues Mustafa, "my cousin swears he'll try again as soon as possible. Just last night he told me: 'Here there is only dust, wind, raging desire, boundless boredom, and the certitude of an endless agony. I must leave at all costs.'"

The bus continues its run through the night. We sleep a restless sleep. The huge sprawl of Casablanca's slums accompanies us for a long stretch before we stop for a brief pick-up. Just time enough for a restroom stop, and we continue north toward Rabat's rational and clean streets, then to Kenitra and finally to Tangier.

Europe

In a milky dawn we embark on a ferryboat to Cadiz, Spain. The line for passport control is long and chaotic, but the checks are quick and efficient. Frankly, I expected that there would be greater difficulty for my fellow travelers, since Spain has been officially entrusted by the European community to "stop the Africans." Evidently the effort and resources are directed against illegal migrants, against the thousands of desperadoes like Mustafa's cousin who try to sneak in on dangerous boats, without knowing how to swim or where to go. Many illegal migrants die during the crossing, and in many cases their families never know of their fate.

The Spanish border patrol in recent years has stepped up its efforts, and now many illegal migrants look for alternate itineraries. On the ferryboat Ali tells me of his last journey to Europe as an illegal migrant: "For 30,000 dirhams ($15,000) in the early nineties you could take a completely different, although longer, route. You toured almost the whole Mediterranean Sea, but it was no vacation. You could carry only the clothes you wore and a pair of shoes, no baggage or merchandise, nothing. From Beni Mellal we headed east, crossed Algeria and Tunisia. In Tunis we took a boat to Athens. From Athens's port, Pyreus, people with vans took you to Belgrade, where other cars took small groups of us to the Italian border. From there we had to walk. During the day we hid, at night we trekked. Four days later, tired, without papers, our shoes destroyed, we arrived in Trieste. There we split. I was hungry and did not know where to go. My first act in Italy was to stretch out my hand and beg. Thus I was able to buy myself some food and a train ticket to join a cousin in Milan. Now however, the war in the Balkans has stopped the flow, but they told me that in Greece, or maybe Albania, you can find boats to cross into southern Italy." The porous state of the European southern border is all too evident in these words, and increasing numbers of unemployed young North Africans will keep knocking at the door.

Crossing Spain takes us a full day. We never stop for more than half an hour. The drivers take turns at the wheel, sleeping in a makeshift niche in the food storage area in the back of the bus, next to the exhaust pipe, shut and locked from the outside. When we stop, the driver goes to free his partner. I do not want to think what kind of air they breathe there, or about the consequences of a rear-end accident.

The bus's continuous motion makes us slip into a state of restless sleepiness, careful not to miss a stop. We quickly learn to seize every occasion to eat, drink, and use the restroom, since we never know when we will have another opportunity. Spanish rest areas are equipped with the migrants in mind. There are Spanish and Arab signs for the restrooms, and some have a small area set aside for morning prayers.

We eat alone or in small groups, around the bus or on the lawn, away from Spanish cars and eyes. There is very little group solidarity, as if we do not trust each other. Everybody keeps to himself or his buddy. We fear being exploited by the other migrants. Mustapha, the driver, even warns me not to get too close to the other passengers, "otherwise you end up with your living room full." He tells me stories of people exploited by veteran migrants, of promised hospitality turned into exorbitant requests for rent. He heard of ten people forced to share two rooms in Bergamo, each paying another migrant 300,000 lire ($200) just to have a roof over their heads. Just because he had a lease, the older migrant pocketed 6 million lire ($4,000) a month for the sublet of two rooms.

When we stop for gas, we storm the café shop. Some of the youngsters buy beer, smiling broadly at me as they violate Koranic law. Then the bus becomes livelier. We trade impossible sex stories. They show me how to hiss at Moroccan women to get their attention, and if acknowledged how to follow them into secluded areas of the Medina for a secret meeting. We listen to music. They share with me the music of Raïs Bihti, a migrant worker for the French car maker Citroën, and his song of migration and sorrow:

> When the bus driver came to look for me:
> "Come Raïs, your vacation is over."
> My throat went dry,
> And I know this happened to you too,
> My fellow migrants.

They translate another song for me, this one by Raïs Mohammed Damciri, "I Won't Forget You Paris," in which a woman cries over the departure of her man:

> I won't forget you Paris
> I won't forget you North
> I won't forget you Belgium
> you have taken my man away
> I won't forget you Telephone
> for never ringing my beloved's voice
> I won't forget you Airplane
> boxy as a coffin
> you take away and don't give back.

The music sparks an atmosphere of conviviality and camaraderie. It is now time to view videotapes of recent weddings. The viewings offer a great opportunity to express solidarity and knowledge of the local community— mostly through comments on the behavior and social standing of the families involved. The clothes of the spouses, the food, music, carpets, and decor are carefully scrutinized. The good songs are accompanied by rhythmic claps and youyous, the piercing guttural shrieks used by the women to signal a happy occasion, here ambiguously imitated by the passengers, already resigned to a long period among other men with only occasional contact with prostitutes or the rare visit of a female relative.

The younger passengers are particularly eager to comment bitterly on the more "traditional" elements of the wedding ceremony, such as the exposure, the morning after, of the sheet bloodied by the rupture of the hymen—promptly recorded on film. They express their will to break with traditions they view as backward from their mutated perspective, in which local customs blend with European lifestyles and attitudes. They almost feel ashamed for this traditional image of Moroccan society, and they blame it for many of the problems the migrants encounter in the host country. Abdeslam, one of these youngsters, confides to me that he is convinced that much of Italian racism is due to the social behavior of the first wave of migrants, the dispossessed shepherds of the 1970s: "Those who arrived first have soiled our reputation with their lifestyles and behavior. They came to Italy with one single purpose: to build capital. They refused to spend a single penny to improve their life, and kept whining to the Italians that they did not have any money and their family was hungry in Morocco. They begged when they did not really need to. I want to save too, but I don't want to live in misery." The ideology of consumer society has penetrated the generation that grew up with satellite television sets bought in Europe by their fathers, and these young Moroccan migrants are part of a cosmopolitan community unbounded by national limits.

This new migrant context is putting a heavy burden on traditional values and is creating a rift between the younger generation and the older adults. During the second night, while traversing southern France, a group of these young men spark the only noteworthy incident of the entire trip. From the dark seats in the back, the woman who boarded at a later stop and could not find a front seat screams angrily. The driver stops the bus immediately and charges toward the back seats, swinging a heavy chain. Waking with a start, I cannot understand the angry shouts, and my neighbor's only comment is, "Punks—they are really punks!" After five minutes trading insults in the back, the driver makes one man in the front give up his seat to the woman, and the bus resumes its run. The morning after, the driver tells me that one of the young guys in the back had sexually harassed the unescorted woman and that he had to intervene to avoid more serious problems. After further probing, he finally acknowledges that the man had brushed his foot "three times!" against the arm of the woman, who was seated in front of the offender. "These youngsters don't have any sense of honor, they are shameful (hshuma)," are the driver's last words on the incident.

The Arrival

Around noon on the third day we finally reach Ventimiglia. My Italian passport is the only document to provoke surprise for the border police, and only my baggage is duly searched for one of the few Moroccan goods Italians really like, hashish.

One hour later we reach the railroad station of Genova Principe, where almost a third of the passengers disembarks and quickly disappears, some into the narrow streets descending toward the port, some to the railroad platforms to catch a southbound train. After a quick coffee, we leave again, headed to Milan. The mood on the bus is somber, people are tired, and the reality of another season of work away from home is settling in. They seem resentful that I am "going home" and that here in Italy our social asymmetry is now evident. Their job opportunities are in fact scarce and precarious; Italian entrepreneurs exploit their minority status. "I want to have a stable job," Rachid tells me—he works as a seasonal shepherd in the high Alpine pastures—"and be paid a fair salary. I'd be happy to be paid as much as two of Maradona's hairs" [the Argentinean who used to play for the Naples soccer team and is now a millionaire].

Milan in the evening is dark gray, dirty, and cold. The first-timers are surprised how Milan's spring is a copy of Beni Mellal's winter. In the parking lot of Central Station the group disperses quickly. Nobody stops to chat, say farewell, or exchange addresses. They leave one by one or in pairs, under the weight of huge suitcases, merging with the crowd. My last image is not of a group of workers heading toward the place where they are needed, but of a group of clandestines seeking to be unnoticed, to fend off the intolerance of a local population suddenly feeling that there are too many "others."

Contributors

Arjun Appadurai teaches anthropology and directs the Globalization Project at the University of Chicago. He is the author of *Worship and Conflict under Colonial Rule* (1981) and *Modernity at Large* (1996), editor of *The Social Life of Things* (1986), and coeditor of *Gender, Genre, and Power in South Asian Expressive Traditions* (1991, with Margaret Mills and Frank Korom). He is currently studying ethnic violence in Bombay.

Etienne Balibar is a professor of political philosophy at the Université de Paris I, Nanterre. His many books include *Reading Capital* (1970, with Louis Althusser), *Race, Nation, Class* (1991, with Immanuel Wallerstein), *Les Frontières de la Democratie* (1992), and *Masses, Classes, and Ideas* (1994). His recent research is on extreme violence and the problem of civility.

Thomas Bender teaches American intellectual and urban history at New York University. His books include *Toward an Urban Vision* (1975), *Community and Social Change in America* (1978), *New York Intellect* (1987), and *Intellect and Public Life* (1993). He has also edited *The University and the City* (1988) and coedited (with Carl E. Schorske) *Budapest and New York* (1994) and *American Academic Culture in Transformation: Fifty Years, Four Disciplines* (1998). He is the director of the Project on Cities and Urban Knowledges in NYU's International Center for Advanced Studies.

Teresa P. R. Caldeira teaches anthropology at the University of California, Irvine, and is also a research associate at CEBRAP (Centro Brasileiro de Análise e Planejamento) in São Paulo. She is the author of *A Política dos Outros* (1984), and her book *City of Walls: Crime, Segregation, and Citizenship in São Paulo*, is forthcoming from the University of California Press.

Mamadou Diouf is a historian who is on leave from Cheikh Anta Diop University and currently Research Program Officer with CODESRIA (Council for the Development of Social Sciences Research in Africa) in Dakar. He is the author of *Le Kajoor au Dix-Neuvième Siècle* (1990) and *Le Senegal sous Abdou Diouf* (1990, with M. C. Diop) and coeditor of *Academic Freedom in Africa* (1994, with Mahmood Mamdani). His current research is concerned with urban and popular culture in Senegal.

Dilip Parameshwar Gaonkar is a professor of rhetoric and cultural studies at Northwestern University and is codirector of the Chicago-based Center for Transcultural Studies. His work is the subject of a collection of commentaries, *Rhetorical Hermeneutics* (1996), edited by Alan Gross and William Keith. He has coedited (with Cary Nelson) *Disciplinarity and Dissent in Cultural Studies* (1996). His recent interests concern the rhetoric of globalization and alternative modernities.

James Holston teaches anthropology at the University of California, San Diego. His research focuses on citizenship and democratic change in the Americas, especially Brazil, and transformations in the social and spatial organization of cities. He is the author of *The Modernist City* (1989) and is currently working on a book about citizenship in uncivil democracies.

Marco Jacquemet teaches anthropology at Barnard College, Columbia University. His previous publications include *Credibility in Court: Communicative Practices in the Camorra Trials* (1996) and *Il Galateo del Cibernauta* (1995). His current research is on conflict talk, Albanian migrants, and media politics.

Christopher Kamrath is a Ph.D. candidate in the Department of Communication Studies at Northwestern University.

Cristiano Mascaro is a professional photographer in São Paulo, Brazil. Trained as an architect, he has been a professor of photojournalism and visual communication. His photography focuses on the everyday life of cities and is exhibited internationally.

Saskia Sassen teaches sociology and urbanism at the University of Chicago. Her books include *The Global City* (1991), *Losing Control? Sovereignty in an Age of Globalization* (1996), and *Globalization and Its Discontents* (1998). She is currently completing a study of immigration policy in the global economy.

Michael Watts is a professor of geography and directs the Institute of International Studies at the University of California, Berkeley. He is the coauthor of *Reworking Modernity* (1992, with Allan R. Pred) and coeditor of *Liberation Ecologies* (1996, with Richard Peet) and *Globalising Food* (1997, with David Goodman). He is currently working on a book on photography.

Michel Wieviorka is a professor of sociology at the Ecole des Hautes Etudes en Sciences Sociales in Paris and directs the Centre d'Analyse et d'Intervention Sociologiques. He is the author and editor of many books, including *La France Raciste* (1992), *La Democratie a l'Epreuve* (1993), *Une Société Fragmentée* (1996, an edited volume) and *Commenter la France* (1997). In English, he has published *The Making of Terrorism* (1993) and *The Arena of Racism* (1995).

Index